BREAD AND BIBLES

D. L. Moody's Evangelism *and* Social Action

GREGG QUIGGLE

MOODY PUBLISHERS
CHICAGO

Portions of this book have been revised from the author's previous work: "An Analysis of Dwight Moody's Urban Social Vision," PhD thesis, The Open University, 2010.

Portions of chapter 3 were previously published as "The History of the MBI Doctrinal Statement" in *Standing Firm: The Doctrinal Commitments of Moody Bible Institute* (Chicago: Moody Publishers, 2019), 24–25. Another portion of chapter 3 was previously published as "2020 and the Chicago Fire of 1871," moodycenter.org, September 25, 2020. Used by permission.

All Scripture quotations are taken from the Holy Bible, New International Version®, NIV®. Copyright ©1973, 1978, 1984, 2011 by Biblica, Inc.™ Used by permission of Zondervan. All rights reserved worldwide. www.zondervan.com. The "NIV" and "New International Version" are trademarks registered in the United States Patent and Trademark Office by Biblica, Inc.™

Some historical documents quote from the King James Version.

Interior design: Brandi Davis
Cover design: Erik M. Peterson
Cover photo of D. L. Moody (public domain)
Author photo: Emily Quiggle

Library of Congress Cataloging-in-Publication Data

Names: Quiggle, Gregg, author.
Title: Bread and bibles : D.I. Moody's Evangelism and social action / Gregg Quiggle.
Description: Chicago : Moody Publishers, [2023] | Includes bibliographical references and index. | Summary: "D. L. Moody was a servant to poor and immigrant communities, an evangelist who traveled the globe, and a champion of Christian education. Quiggle focuses on Moody's social vision and missionary work-triumphs and failures-and tells the story of a man whose impact continues to this day"-- Provided by publisher.
Identifiers: LCCN 2023038176 (print) | LCCN 2023038177 (ebook) | ISBN 9780802424914 (paperback) | ISBN 9780802475442 (ebook)
Subjects: LCSH: Moody, Dwight Lyman, 1837-1899. | Evangelists--United States--Biography. | BISAC: RELIGION / Christian Ministry / Evangelism | RELIGION / Christian Ministry / Missions
Classification: LCC BV3785.M7 Q54 2023 (print) | LCC BV3785.M7 (ebook) | DDC 269/.2092--dc23/eng/20231122
LC record available at https://lccn.loc.gov/2023038176
LC ebook record available at https://lccn.loc.gov/2023038177

Originally delivered by fleets of horse-drawn wagons, the affordable paperbacks from D. L. Moody's publishing house resourced the church and served everyday people. Now, after more than 125 years of publishing and ministry, Moody Publishers' mission remains the same—even if our delivery systems have changed a bit. For more information on other books (and resources) created from a biblical perspective, go to www.moodypublishers.com or write to:

Moody Publishers
820 N. LaSalle Boulevard
Chicago, IL 60610

1 3 5 7 9 10 8 6 4 2

Printed in the United States of America

BREAD AND BIBLES

CONTENTS

INTRODUCTION

When I was at work in the City Relief Society, before the fire, I used to go to a poor sinner with the Bible in one hand and a loaf of bread in the other. . . . My idea was that I could open a poor man's heart by giving him a load of wood or a ton of coal when the winter was coming on, but I soon found out that he wasn't any more interested in the Gospel on that account. Instead of thinking how he could come to Christ, he was thinking how long it would be before he got another load of wood. If I had the Bible in one hand and a loaf in the other the people always looked first at the loaf; and that was just contrary to the order laid down in the Gospel.[1]

—DWIGHT MOODY

Do all the good you can, to all the people you can, in all the ways you can, and as long as ever you can.

—MOTTO IN MOODY'S BIBLE

Reading the Bible and remembering the poor—a combination of faith and works—will always bring joy.[2]

—DWIGHT MOODY

Although Mr. Moody labored on behalf of the individual, he was also interested in society. His conception of the Gospel was comprehensive and was not indifferent to man's intellectual and physical needs. He placed first emphasis on spiritual values because he insisted that the most efficacious means of reformation was through the individual.[3]

—WILLIAM MOODY

I taught my first class at Moody Bible Institute in 1985. My sister had attended Moody, so I had a vague understanding of the school. I had done graduate work in church history, but I really did not have a grasp on Mr. Moody. Over time, I found myself increasingly fascinated by the man and began to read about him more deeply. D. L. Moody soon captured my imagination. As soon as I thought I knew him, I would come across another event or relationship that surprised and fascinated me. His life was remarkable, his sphere of influence incredible, and he lived in one of the most exciting and tumultuous times in the history of the United States.

For me, one of the most interesting pieces of Moody's work was his understanding of the relationship between evangelism and social ills. As I read others, I was often troubled by the lack of understanding of Moody's efforts in each area. Too often interpreters saw Moody as two-dimensional, emphasizing solely his evangelistic activities. Others even went so far as to claim he discouraged addressing the struggles of the poor. Over my years of study, I have come to see this is simply not true. The purpose of this book is to right that misreading of Moody.

In his day, Moody was one of the most well-known figures in the English-speaking world. His legacy is profound and foundational for evangelicalism. For those readers who were raised in or currently identify with evangelicalism, this is not merely the study of a man and a movement; it is a family story. For those who have no connection to evangelicalism, Moody provides a glimpse into a movement that may seem confusing or even perplexing. He can also serve as a measuring stick to see how the movement has evolved. Perhaps the best way to think about this is in terms of the country I call home, the United States. For the United States, we often talk about two presidents who shaped this country, George Washington and Abraham Lincoln. It may be helpful to see Moody as kind of an Abraham Lincoln figure for evangelicalism. Indeed, after his death a Boston newspaper exclaimed: "American boys in the next century should study the lives of a model patriot and its preacher of righteousness."[4]

In many ways, the span of Moody's life, 1837 to 1899, was a defining period for evangelicalism in America. While it is true the giants of the previous century, Jonathan Edwards, George Whitefield, and John Wesley, cast a long shadow, most of what we today call evangelicalism was shaped in the 1800s. During this century the foundational figures were Moody and his friend Charles Spurgeon, the English pastor. In the academic world, one indication of their impact comes from a series published on the history of evangelicalism. The title of the volume about their time is, *The Dominance of Evangelicalism: The Age of Spurgeon and Moody.*[5]

That interpretation of Moody is shared broadly throughout the academic world. Other prominent American church historians described his influence. For example, Martin Marty wrote, "The Chicago-based evangelist could plausibly have been called Mr. Revivalist and perhaps even Mr. Protestant."[6] Lyle Dorsett concurred, stating, "Dwight L. Moody's name is synonymous with evangelism and revivalism."[7] Timothy George saw Moody as "the founder of contemporary interdenominational evangelicalism."[8] George Marsden presented Moody as the head of a broad evangelical empire that towered over the American religious landscape: "Scarcely a leader in American Protestantism in the next generation, it seemed, had not at some time been influenced by Moody."[9]

The same could almost be said of his impact on the United Kingdom. He traveled to Britain on six different occasions, and his stays were always lengthy, ranging from a few months up to several years. In his great campaign of 1873–1875, the London portion single-handedly drew over 2.5 million attendees.[10] During the campaign, figurines of Moody and Ira D. Sankey were hawked on the streets along with copies of Moody's

American cap. Even some popular poetry of the day reflected their influence. One line read, "The rich the poor, the good the bad, have gone mad over Moody and Sankey."[11] In the summer of 1875, British royalties on the Sankey hymnal totaled $35,000, or seven thousand pounds sterling. Although the records are sketchy, estimates are that British publishers had single-handedly sold between fifty and eighty million copies of the hymnals by the end of World War II.[12] Consequently, by his death in 1899, "Moody" was a household name throughout the English-speaking world. His work cast a long shadow over the evangelical world for decades after his death.[13] Perhaps the late Billy Graham summed it up best in a letter he wrote to Moody's daughter: "I am wondering if you all are really aware of the many movements that now exist throughout the world that flowed from the ministry of Dwight Moody."[14]

Given his importance and lingering influence, Dwight Moody helps us understand how evangelicals think about important issues. While surveying the broad story of Moody, this book centers on a simple question: How did Moody understand the relationship between evangelism and social problems? It is a question with which evangelicals currently struggle. Although the issues are somewhat different, the question is the same. Specifically, how should Christians think about the relationship between evangelism and addressing social issues?

Like all of us, Moody was at least partially shaped by the time in which he lived. In his case, they were tumultuous times of rapid change in almost all spheres of life in the United States. Throughout the book, we will seek to provide context for Moody's life and work. In the meantime, what follows is a brief sketch of Moody's day and age.

After the Revolutionary War, no event has shaped the United States more than the Civil War. It even changed the way the country is described. Before the war, the United States were referred to as plural—the

United States "are." Afterward it become singular—the United States "is." Moody lived through this conflict. The war ripped the United States apart, killing hundreds of thousands, leaving in its wake throngs of maimed soldiers and a country heavily populated by widows and orphans. What happened to the country was predated by schisms in its Protestant churches. Before the war, the Baptists, Methodists, and Presbyterians were all divided into Northern and Southern branches.[15]

In addition to the Civil War, Moody lived when both the United States and the United Kingdom were going through the throes of a significant change. Urbanization, industrialization, and immigration changed both societies and created a new set of issues for Christianity. These changes included a collection of social ills that developed as urbanization gripped both countries. Immigrants poured into cities seeking jobs offered in the new industries. Overcrowding led to waves of epidemics. Sewage buildup, contaminated drinking water, lack of health care, poor or no education, and a host of other issues flourished in the cities. Substandard houses with no housing codes created fire hazards leading to the most significant urban fire in history, the Chicago Fire of 1871. On top of these, racial and ethnic strife ran rampant. Churches on both sides of the Atlantic struggled in dealing with these urban migrations and the resultant social problems.[16]

The period after the Civil War is often called the Gilded Age in America. It covered the period from roughly 1870 until 1900. The era was marked by the industrialization, immigration, and urbanization mentioned above. However, while wages among workers grew, it was also marked by abject poverty and massive inequality in wealth.[17] These years were dominated by a group of men sometimes referred to as "robber barons" or "captains of industry." These men amassed enormous wealth in stark contrast to the millions of immigrants populating newly formed cities. In some ways, Moody lived with one foot in each situation. On the one hand, Moody maintained cordial relationships with many great captains in American industry, especially in Chicago. Names like McCormick, Field, Armour, Scott, and Farwell bankrolled much of Moody's work. But, on the other hand, Moody would focus his work on the poor, especially targeting cities.

Moody also lived during the so-called Victorian age. He embraced the middle-class values of that era. This is hardly surprising as the middle-class values of the Victorian era found their origin in the evangelical revivals in the early eighteenth century, making middle-class sensibilities a function of evangelical theology. These middle-class evangelical values played an important role in society. First, evangelicalism allowed the middle class to differentiate itself from the lower class and the aristocracy. Second, it fueled social concerns like temperance and abolition. Third, evangelicalism defined gender roles, providing structure for men and women of the middle class. Thus, it shaped family life, especially the family altar and the man's role in the religion of the home. It also circumscribed public roles for men and women. While tightly prescribing the role of women in the public arena, it also provided outlets for women in the religious sphere. Finally, evangelicalism informed the middle class's personal ethics by emphasizing work, selflessness, order, and charity.[18]

The challenges extended into the theological world as well. Liberal or modern theology migrated from Germany into the United States and the United Kingdom. What ensued were decades of theological wrangling, heresy trials, and the dissolution of coalitions. These would continue into the twentieth century, eventually leading to new denominations, mission agencies, seminaries, Bible colleges, and parachurch organizations.[19] The so-called *social gospel* (or *social Christianity*) movement also developed during Moody's life. Led by men like Walter Rauschenbusch and Washington Gladden, it attempted to address the social problems that emerged during the Gilded Age. Most of its leaders were liberal Protestants. However, some were more evangelical in their theological leanings. The movement also expanded into the Roman Catholic Church. Moody was well known and admired by most of the major players in these various movements. In fact, Moody partnered with many of these people during his years of ministry.

This was the world of Dwight Moody, a world of massive social and theological changes. It was in this world Moody lived out his faith. It is a world that in many ways mirrors our own. Both our times are marked by significant technological advances, increasing disparity of wealth, accelerating urban problems, and increasing disagreement among Christians about responding to these problems. Given his influence and the similarity of our times, Moody is the perfect person to study.

The four quotes at the beginning of the introduction provide an insight into Moody's approach. They also are the impetus for this book. They point out that Moody valued both evangelism and caring for the poor. Some have claimed Moody turned his back on social problems in favor of solely focusing on evangelism. This book is an attempt to set the record straight.

Since at least 1972, with the publication of David Moberg's *The Great Reversal*, Moody has been sometimes portrayed as unconcerned about the poor. Moberg described Moody as championing a point of view that saw the destruction of society as inevitable and therefore emphasized personal conversion rather than stressing personal and social salvation. This change was a "great reversal" from evangelicalism's social activism during the nineteenth century. The claim was that evangelicals turned from causes like child labor laws, prison reform, and women's suffrage and focused solely on evangelism. From Moberg's perspective, Moody was critical in ushering in this change.

On the contrary, we will see how Moody's life and ministry embraced both evangelism and care for the poor. Specifically, we'll explore how Moody understood the relationship between addressing social ills and evangelism. The book will examine the importance he placed on charity and attempts to formulate social change. In the end, I will argue that although Moody is often accused of denigrating social work in favor of evangelism, a closer look at his work reveals a commitment to both evangelism and practically addressing the needs of the poor. It must be granted that Moody turned from structural and legislative reforms to alleviate urban ills in favor of mass conversions. While he did occasionally speak to structural and legislative issues, he never engaged in a sustained dialogue or functioned as an advocate for these types of causes. Yet, at the same time, Moody created educational institutions to educate the poor and improve their lives. Moody was concerned about the moral state of the country and the lot of the poor. However, in the end, he maintained the only way to improve public morality and the suffering of the poor was through transformed lives.[20]

Consequently while Moody expressed concern for society and alleviating poverty, they remained secondary to personal conversion. To be clear, while conversion was primary, as some of the quotes at the beginning of the chapter illustrate, Moody insisted true Christianity was committed to addressing the needs of the poor and outcast.

This book focuses on Moody's urban social vision. It is not an attempt to evaluate the effectiveness of Moody's social work; instead, it will seek to present a summary of his work addressing social ills. It will also look at Moody's motives and how Moody came to his conclusions. Finally, while it will explore what Moody did, it will focus on his rationale and methods.

Moody was a gregarious, larger-than-life person. However, most notably for this study, Moody was in many ways stereotypically American. He was a practical person who was far more interested in doing things than in understanding why things worked. He was a concrete thinker, not given to speculation—especially theological speculation. In many ways, Moody's ultimate doctrinal test was its practicality and usefulness for evangelism. He was also innovative and entrepreneurial, like a salesperson who was always open to trying new things.

Pulling together these various elements, Moody forged a response to urban ills. Therefore, in a sense, his own life became a template for his social vision. He practiced things with others that had worked in his life. In the end, Moody believed that large numbers of individual conversions linked with charitable endeavors were the answer to urban centers' social problems.

While this study is primarily historical, I think it can be instructive. Moody was profoundly practical. I believe there is much to be learned from Moody, both positively and negatively. Because of the breadth of his experience, much can be gleaned from examining his life and work. I hope we can learn from his triumphs and avoid repeating his mistakes as we seek to live out the gospel in our time.

1

THE JOURNEY TO CHRIST

His Boyhood and Adolescence

THE BOY IN NORTHFIELD

I think Northfield is just about as near Paradise as we can get on earth.[1]

—DWIGHT MOODY

Nothing in Dwight Lyman Moody's origins foreshadowed his later prominence.[2] The son of Edwin Moody and Betsy Holton, Dwight was the sixth of nine children, seven boys and two girls. He was born on his mother's birthday, February 5, 1837, in the western Massachusetts town of Northfield. The town straddles the Connecticut River close to the New Hampshire and Vermont borders.[3] Northfield was and remains small. In some ways, it is the stereotypical New England town. The Moodys lived in a small white clapboard-sided house on a hill on the north side of town. Its location provides a commanding view of the river and mountain ridges of nearby Vermont and New Hampshire. If you visit, you will quickly understand Moody's affection for this place.

Moody's father was hardworking but allegedly a drinker and financially irresponsible. Tragically, in 1841, he died suddenly, leaving Betsy with seven children, eight months pregnant with twins, and saddled with debt. The amount of debt Edwin left must have been staggering. By the evening of his death, much of the house had been stripped by debt collectors. Edwin was a brick mason by trade, and the only way the family could retain his tools was by hiding them from the collectors. Unfortunately, while the tools survived, little else did; they even took the family's supply of kindling wood.

However, Betsy was of sturdy stock. Given the lack of firewood, she simply instructed the children to remain in bed to stay warm until they needed to leave for chores or school. She also received help from relatives. Moody later describes the joy the family felt when Uncle Cyrus showed up with a whole load of firewood for their home. "I remember, just as vividly as if it were yesterday, how I heard the sound of chips flying, and I knew someone was chopping wood in our wood-shed, and that we should soon have a fire. I shall never forget Uncle Cyrus coming with what seemed to me the biggest pile of wood I ever saw in my life."[4]

Faced with severe financial straits, Betsy often sent the boys away to live with other families during the winter months. In Dwight's case, this was his lot for seven years after his father's death; he spent many of these years thirteen miles away in Greenfield, Massachusetts. Moody complained to his mother during these years, saying he only received cornmeal porridge and milk. When his mother learned he was fed as much as he could eat three times a day, she sent him back to his hosts.[5]

Betsy was a loving but strict parent. She did not suffer a fool gladly; indeed, Moody talks of running afoul of his mother and facing spankings with a switch. While he eschewed delivering this kind of punishment to his children, he understood and respected his mother's efforts to keep him on the straight and narrow.

In Dwight's case, that was a tall order. It appears Dwight was rambunctious and mischievous by nature. Hearkening back to the spanking incidents, Moody's account of these episodes reveals this part of his character. "Mother would send me out for a stick, and I thought I could fool her and get a dead one. But she would snap the stick and then tell me to get another." Another story involves his playing a prank on the whole town. As a schoolchild prank, Moody posted a notice on the schoolhouse door of an upcoming lecture from an out-of-town temperance speaker. Of course, the lecturer never appeared, but the meeting drew a large crowd, much to the delight of young Dwight.

But discipline was not the only way Betsy sought to bring Dwight to heel. She also looked to her faith. We know little about Betsy's religious convictions in the years following her husband's death. But we know she prayed and prayed in a manner that marked her children. For Dwight, this seems to be his first exposure to consistent prayer. It is clear it impressed him. Before his death, Edwin had given a Bible to Betsy. One of Dwight's siblings described how prayer and this Bible came to play a role in her life. She describes hearing Betsy weeping and praying over the Bible. Later the child would look at the Bible and found her mother had marked Jeremiah 49:11, "Leave thy fatherless children, I will preserve them alive, and let thy widows trust in me." Betsy anchored her soul on this text and taught her children to pray to God, believing He would care for the orphan and widow. Dwight recalled moments when Betsy became overwhelmed with managing the children. He said she would head off to her room to pray for wisdom and patience, pleading with God to help her keep order in the family. Speaking at her funeral, Moody recalled often awakening and hearing his mother pouring out her burdens to God in prayer.

RELIGIOUS LIFE

Betsy Moody also sought to steer the children through religious instruction. William Moody states that the family library consisted of three books: a Bible, a catechism, and a collection of devotional thoughts and prayers. Every morning she read the devotion and prayed with them before they embarked on the day. She also insisted they keep the Sabbath together.

Mrs. Moody required her entire family to attend church. On Saturday night, the older boys who had been out working would return home. On Sunday, they would all head off together for services. Preparations for Sunday included making a lunch to take along, as church was an all-day affair. First, there was a sermon, followed by Sunday school and a second sermon. Moody found these days excruciating. Later in life, he admitted, "On one occasion, the preacher had to send someone into the gallery to wake me up. I thought it was hard to have to work in the field all the week and then be obliged to go to church and hear a sermon I didn't understand."

Moody's church was the local Unitarian church. As a result of their plight, the family had been brought into contact with the local Unitarian church and its pastor, Rev. Oliver Everett. William Moody's biography of his father describes Everett as visiting "the destitute family and [helping] them both by counsel and material assistance." Indeed, after the death of Moody's father, Everett became actively involved in the family's life.[6] He encouraged Betsy "not to part with the children but keep them together as best she could, to trust God and to bring them up for him."[7] He helped Betsy keep the family together by giving them food. He also intervened by taking the young Dwight Moody into his home until his transfer to another parish in 1848. Everett introduced the family to a kind, compassionate God who loved people. The death of Edwin Moody made a strong impression on Dwight.[8] It makes sense that he was equally impressed by the Christian charity of the young minister, who undoubtedly taught the young Moody repeatedly that God loved him. It is hardly coincidental that this early lesson became a dominant theme in Moody's later preaching.[9] Rev. Everett and the First Parish of Northfield, Unitarian, would have a lingering effect on the life of Dwight Moody.[10]

The church traced its religious roots back to early Puritan days. In the early eighteenth century, the town was affected by the revival work of Jonathan Edwards at nearby Northampton, Massachusetts. However, by the early nineteenth century, Congregationalism, the state's established religion, had splintered, and a fledgling Unitarian movement emerged. Northfield's First Parish Church was identified with the Unitarians in 1827.[11]

Oliver Capon Everett came to Northfield at the age of twenty-five, relatively fresh from seminary.[12] He was descended from a prominent Massachusetts family. Everett's uncle Edward served as president of Harvard University, congressman and senator, and governor of Massachusetts. Edward Everett also delivered the less famous of the two speeches at the Gettysburg cemetery's dedication in 1863. Although not nearly as prominent as Edward, Oliver's father, Otis, had made a name for himself by amassing a fortune as a merchant in Boston.[13]

Everett's theological convictions are a bit uncertain. One source described him as "liberal in doctrine and imbued with the teaching of Christ."[14] Later in life, Moody is purported to have called him "*the true shepherd of God.*"[15] What is clear is that Northfield had two different congregations—Unitarian and Trinitarian—indicating Everett's commitment to Unitarianism. Nevertheless, this Unitarianism seems a bit dubious. William Moody's biography asserts that the whole family was baptized "in the name of the Father and of the Son and of the Holy Ghost."[16] Dorsett also points out that Moody's friend W. H. Daniels corroborates the story and supports William Moody's claim that Everett was, in fact, an orthodox Christian. Daniels maintains that at that time, Unitarianism was fluid and not as consistently non-Trinitarian as it was later in the nineteenth century.[17] Daniels's assertion is correct. From 1800 to 1835, Unitarianism was in a formative stage. Mainly influenced by English philosophy, it was semi-supernatural, imperfectly rationalistic, and devoted to philanthropy and practical Christianity.

It is true that later Moody distanced himself from Unitarianism. However, some of this resulted from later developments within the denomination. Further, Moody did not derive his doctrine primarily from theological texts; he got it from the Bible and his life experience. Primarily because of Everett, his mother remained Unitarian after Dwight left Northfield. Moody admired his mother. His wife, Emma, acknowledged this in a letter she wrote to Mrs. Moody in the early 1860s.

> I thought also that you might have thought that because Mr. Moody was of a different denomination to what I had been trained in youth that his love and respect for his mother had abated, but I know such is not the case. Besides some of Mr. Moody's warmest friends are Unitarian.[18]

As Moody matured in his faith and distanced himself from the family's Unitarian roots, there would be times of tension, as the above letter implies. Nevertheless, while Moody came to reject much later Unitarian doctrine, it seems difficult to believe the practical example of Everett was so quickly jettisoned.[19] By taking Moody into his own home and securing what education he could for the lad, Everett functioned as more than merely a minister to young Dwight. In fact, Everett and the First Church became defining religious influences for the boy and the family. Again, Moody's son William's biography reinforces this point. He writes,

Shortly after the father's death, this good man visited the destitute family and helped them. . . . No sooner had the attendance of the Moody children been secured than they were commissioned to bring in other scholars. In a sense, therefore, Mr. Moody's Sunday-school mission work began at an earlier date than is commonly supposed, for as a child, he and his brother George frequently acted as aggressive home missionaries in securing recruits for the village Sunday school. . . . It was not till after he left home that his actual personal conversion occurred, but it was to a tender conscience and an open heart that the gospel invitation was given, and a soul already trained to love and honor God readily accepted His offer of salvation. The Christian training of his mother and the faithfulness of her good pastor were a sacred remembrance in all his after experiences, and he ever spoke appreciatively of the debt he owed to the ministry of Mr. Everett.[20]

Given the family's financial situation, education was a luxury.[21] Dwight Moody is known to have received four years of education from the local school between ages six and ten. In addition, the 1853 Northfield Institute catalog lists Dwight Moody as a student (he would have been sixteen). The same catalog lists Oliver Everett as a "reference," indicating he likely paid the tuition.[22]

These early years provided a lesson on God's love. They illustrated to Moody a response to poverty that linked the notion of a loving God with a charitable response to the needs of others. This made a powerful impact on the young Dwight Moody, and it was influential in his family's case. While Moody may not have fully processed the theological import of these acts of charity, the fact that he recalled and referenced them indicates their critical role in his life.

THE CONVERT AND THE BOSTON DAYS

I was born of the flesh in 1837. I was born of the Spirit in 1856. That which is born of the flesh may die. That which is born of the Spirit will live forever.[23]

—DWIGHT MOODY

The early years at Northfield served as Moody's introduction to organized religion and as a demonstration of Christian charity. Boston, New England's urban center, would be the place of his continued theological formation. Northfield could not hold the fancy of the energetic young Moody; he reportedly remarked, "I am tired of this! I am not going to stay around here any longer. I am going to the city."[24] So, as a seventeen-year-old, he migrated to Boston, seeking new opportunities and financial gain.[25] Although Moody's time in Boston was relatively brief, it would provide two critical pieces in the formation of his theology. First, Boston provided Moody's first look at the new urban face of America. Second, Moody was converted to evangelical Christianity during his time there.

By 1854, when Moody arrived, Boston was a growing, bustling, diverse city of about 150,000. Before arriving in Boston, Moody probably had never even seen anyone who was not Anglo-American. Upon arriving he would have been exposed to Asians, African Americans, Jews, and various Eastern Europeans. The combination of the city's sights, sounds, and smells must have been both exhilarating and frightening to the young man from Northfield.

It is simply not possible to know how Moody processed the urban world of Boston, but it is clear it widened his horizons. His letters home are either reminiscent of home or reflect the wonder of a wide-eyed youth. For example, in an 1854 letter to his brothers, Moody wrote, "A steam hot gas ship come in and sutch a site I never seen before. There was a ship from Liverpool loaded with emergrans. All the Greeks in Boston was there. The sung a song when they come in site of their friends. Sutch meetings as there was there I never see."[26] Boston exposed Moody to this new urban world; however, it was not until the Chicago years that he truly grappled with the challenges of the new American city.

During Moody's time in Boston, the most significant event was his religious conversion. Shortly after arriving in Boston, Moody began attending the Mount Vernon Congregational Church.[27] His uncle Samuel Holton agreed to employ Moody on the condition he attended Sunday school. Thus, Moody ended up at Mount Vernon. At Mount Vernon, Moody was befriended by a middle-aged Sunday school teacher named Edwin Kimball. Kimball, concerned about the soul of the new young man in his class, stopped by the store where Moody worked on April 21, 1855. Years later, Moody would recount this event to fellow evangelist J. Wilbur Chapman:

> When I was in Boston I used to attend a Sunday School class, and one day I recollect my teacher came around behind the counter of the shop I was at work in, and put his hand upon my shoulder and talked to me about Christ and my soul. I had not felt that I had a soul till then. I said to myself: "this is a very strange thing. Here is a man who never saw me till lately, and he is weeping over my sins, and I never shed a tear about them." But I understand it now, and know what it is to have a passion for men's souls and weep over their sins. I don't remember what he said, but I can feel the power of that man's hand on my shoulder tonight. It was not long after that I was brought into the Kingdom of God.[28]

Although Moody and others portray this event as definitive, it was more important existentially than intellectually. Moody's newfound Christianity was embryonic, and his conversion was as much a process as an event. Not quite four weeks after his experience with Kimball, the teenager met with Mount Vernon Congregational Church deacons on a Wednesday evening to seek membership. During the interview, the primitive nature of Moody's faith was apparent, and Moody was told he was not yet ready for membership. Kimball, who attended the meeting, later described it in the following manner,

> I remember the chief question and its answer—the longest he gave: "Mr. Moody, what has Christ done for us all—for you— which entitles Him to our love?" "I don't know," he said, "I think Christ has done a good deal for us; but I don't think of anything in particular as I know of."[29]

Despite Moody's dreadful performance, the church remained hopeful about the young man. The minutes of the meeting read:

> Dwight L. Moody. Boards 43 Court St. Has been baptized. First awakened on April 21. Became anxious about himself . . . saw himself a sinner, and sin now seems hateful and holiness desirable. Thinks he has repented. Has proposed to give up sin and feels dependent on Christ for forgiveness . . . loves the Scriptures . . . prays once a day . . . and desires to be useful . . . religiously educated . . . been in the city a year from Northfield in this state. Is not ashamed to be known as a Christian. 18 years old.[30]

Undaunted, Moody continued to work at his faith and sought a second interview in March 1856. Again, the minutes are telling:

> Mr. Moody thinks he has made some progress since he has been here before—at least in knowledge. He has maintained his habits of prayer and reading the Bible. Is fully determined to adhere to the cause of Christ always. Feels that it would be very bad he should join the church and then turn. Must repent and

ask forgiveness, for Christ's sake. Will never give up his hope, or love Christ less, whether admitted to church or not his prevailing intention is to give up his will to God.[31]

Although Moody's theological understanding remained somewhat suspect, the deacons were persuaded by his passion and commitment. So, in May, the Mount Vernon Church added Moody to its membership rolls. Even so, while Moody's faith originated in Boston, it would not be fully mature until his years in Chicago.

The Mount Vernon Congregational Church in Boston would also be the context for Moody's first extended exposure to evangelicalism. A group of Bostonians founded the church in 1842, rejecting the "doctrinal exclusiveness" of Park Street Church and the "free-thinking charms" of King's Chapel.[32] They established Mount Vernon within a few yards of both churches and called Rev. Edward N. Kirk as pastor.

Before coming to Mount Vernon, Kirk had earned a reputation in New England as a revivalist and pastor. He had worked with Charles Finney in upstate New York and would later publish a series of lectures on revivals.[33] The church had invited Kirk intending to promote revivalism in Boston, and Kirk became the one to provide Moody with his initial introduction to evangelicalism and revivalism.

Kirk's brand of revivalism was distinctive. He was an urban revivalist, and his style was decidedly different from others of the day. Kirk was sophisticated, and his preaching was fluent and articulate. Moody later claimed Kirk was "one of the most eloquent men I ever heard."[34] Kirk eschewed crude emotionalism and manipulation, preferring to woo his audiences. His brand of revivalism was urbane and respectable.[35]

Further, Kirk espoused views that would later characterize Moody's work. He was a forceful proponent of charity. In 1843, sensing the threat that urban poverty posed to the Protestant faith, he declared, "Our whole system of education, our modes of life, our very standards of personal piety need great renovation." Charity, in particular, was Kirk's solution. However, Kirk had more in mind than random acts of kindness; he believed charity would drive people to understand poverty and address its root causes. On this, he was explicit: "When men love their neighbors as themselves, the causes of poverty will soon be sought out, and the remedy applied as far as possible." Kirk challenged his Mount Vernon congregation to expose their children to the urban poor, maintaining that "the removal of human wretchedness and elevation of degraded man is the business of life."[36]

Kirk's commitment moved beyond rhetoric. Mount Vernon was involved in forming a YMCA, the Mount Vernon Association of Young Men, from which the Boston YMCA would develop. The Mount Vernon group established a twofold goal of helping men grow in their Christian faith and working to improve the welfare of humanity.[37]

Young women were also part of Kirk's work. Kirk was instrumental in forming the Ladies' Society for the Promotion of Education at the West. Kirk, along with Edward Beecher, delivered the inaugural address. The Society, founded at Mount Vernon in 1846, was designed to provide education for females and female educators in the western part of the United States.

The Society was also a response to Roman Catholicism. Both Beecher and Kirk pointed out the network of Roman Catholic schools in the West and its admirable inclusion of females as students and teachers. Kirk underscored the perceived threat, "The very fact that Rome is so multiplying her machinery in this country, is an indication that we must change our tactics, and meet her on her ground, and adapt our modes of defense to her attack."[38] Although Kirk had deep concerns about Romanism, he was measured compared to other Protestants. As Timothy Smith described it, Kirk, like many other revivalists, "believed the church's task was to save Catholics, not scorn them."[39]

Kirk's impact on the newly converted Moody is hard to measure. However, Pollock argues that Kirk was instrumental in preparing Moody for his fateful meeting with Kimball.[40] The extent of Kirk's impact on Moody's concept of revivalism and his social vision is even less clear. Moody would later express admiration for Kirk's speaking ability, and his approach to evangelistic preaching would reflect some of Kirk's methods. While not smooth and urbane like Kirk, Moody would reject flamboyance and emotional appeals. Further, Moody's approach to social ills would parallel Kirk's. Kirk emphasized charity, education, and temperance, and focused on converting rather than ridiculing Roman Catholics. In addition, Kirk fully embraced the YMCA, an institution that Moody came to hold dear. Admittedly, Moody was a very raw young man with an immature faith, and Pollock notes Moody often slept through Kirk's sermons. Still, Moody saw the energy at Mount Vernon. He saw its ministries and felt their impact personally. Thus, while not significantly influencing Moody, Kirk cannot be dismissed as unimportant in Moody's development.

2

THE FORMATION OF THE CHRISTIAN WORKER

THE FORMATION OF THE CHRISTIAN WORKER: CHICAGO

Rough-and-tumble-business Chicago after the great fire was a regional capital, and in many ways, because of its innovations in industrial method and in architecture, because of its mixture of brutal wickedness and revolutionary newness, the blood of the yards, the showpiece gems of the lakefront, the seething of its immigrant slums, because of its violence, corruption, and creative energy, it was also a world city.[1]

—SAUL BELLOW

Hog butcher for the World, Tool maker, stacker of wheat, Player with railroads and nations' freight handler.[2]

—CARL SANDBURG

The city is the nerve center of our civilization. It is also the storm center. . . . Here is heaped the social dynamite; here roughs, gamblers, thieves, robbers, lawless and desperate men of all sorts, congregate; men who are ready on any pretext to raise riots for the purpose of destruction and plunder; here gather foreigners and wage-workers; here skepticism and irreligion abound;

here inequality is the greatest and most obvious, and the contrast between opulence and penury the most striking; here is suffering the sorest. As the greatest wickedness in the world is to be found not among the cannibals of some far off coast, but in Christian lands where the light of truth is diffused and rejected, so the utmost depth of wretchedness exists not among savages, who have few wants, but in great cities, where, in the presence of plenty and of every luxury men starve.[3]

—JOSIAH STRONG

Water runs downhill, and the highest hills are the great cities. If we can stir them, we can stir the whole nation.[4]

—DWIGHT MOODY

Although he was a child of rural western Massachusetts, Dwight Moody's adult life was defined by cities. He was drawn to cities by the twin prospects of opportunity and excitement as a young man. As he matured, Moody remained attracted to cities, this time for strategic reasons. Moody, like many Protestants, came to see the cities as containing both the most significant opportunity to build up Christian civilization and the greatest threat to tear it down. It is noteworthy that, as much as Moody deeply loved Northfield, he lived in Chicago nine months of the year on average.[5] Undoubtedly, the city shaped Moody. There is also no question that the various urban ills he observed would be integral to his theological formation.

During the nineteenth century, America was transformed from an agrarian society to an urban, industrialized one. Although this shift had begun before the Civil War, it expedited the trend. Between 1860 and 1920, the number of people living in American cities of 8,000 or more inhabitants jumped from 6.2 million (19.7 percent) to 54.3 million (58.9 percent).[6] Three East Coast cities in particular served to illustrate the trend. Between 1860 and 1890, Boston grew from 177,840 residents to 560,892; Philadelphia from a population of 565,529 to 1,293,697;

and New York from 1,080,330 to 3,437,202 citizens.[7] However, even this spectacular growth was dwarfed by Moody's adopted home, the sprawling behemoth on the Midwestern prairie, Chicago. First incorporated in the marshes at the edge of Lake Michigan in 1833, Chicago had grown from a mere seventeen buildings in 1833 to a population of 1,698,575 by 1900, making it the fifth-largest city in the world. Moreover, the city achieved this growth even more remarkably despite having suffered a devastating fire in 1871.[8]

More than 28 million immigrants entered the workforce between 1860 and 1920, roughly equal to the country's total population in 1850.[9] From 1860 to 1900, during Moody's work, 14 million immigrants arrived.[10] By 1900, fully two-thirds of the urban population was foreign-born.[11] They were a mixture of Roman Catholics and Protestants from Europe, Jews from Europe, and Chinese. Some were fleeing difficulties in their homeland, others seeking new opportunities their homelands did not afford.

The largest group of immigrants was Roman Catholic. The rise of the Roman Catholic population during the nineteenth century was meteoric. In 1820, Roman Catholics comprised less than 1 percent of the population; by 1830, 3.8 percent; by 1840, 5.8 percent; and by 1850, 12.5 percent.[12] Sydney Ahlstrom observes, "During the first half of the nineteenth century, the Roman Catholic Church in the United States ceased to be a persecuted, numerically insignificant body and became the largest church in the country."[13] This trend would continue throughout the nineteenth century. By 1870, 40 percent of all churchgoers were Roman Catholics.[14] Shortly after that, in 1875, the Vatican appointed the first American cardinal.

In addition to immigrants, those who were born in the U. S. flocked to the city from the countryside.[15] Moody was typical of this group. Drawn by the opportunities of the newly emerging cities, many young men and women left the farm and struck out for the city. Not surprisingly, overcrowding, low economic standards, and illiteracy gripped urban areas. Class wars erupted with the rise of industrialization and the massive influx of immigrant workers. Riots, boycotts, and strikes rocked the country.[16] These traumas produced exceedingly complex economic, social, moral, and religious problems.

The city shaped Moody's vision for ministry. The United States and the United Kingdom cities were Moody's parish. These cities, saturated with immigrants, racked with poverty, plagued by labor unrest and religious tension, and scarred by slums, formed the young convert.

While Boston was the scene of Moody's first exposure to urban life and ills, Chicago was formative. Chicago was also where Moody became fully immersed in evangelicalism. While his faith began in Boston, it was in Chicago where his new religious sentiments matured and where Moody was made into a fully fledged evangelical.

Chicago was significant in three ways relative to Moody's theology and social vision. First, Moody was immersed in the evangelical community in Chicago. While Moody began his conversion in Boston, it was completed and solidified in Chicago. In Chicago, Moody became fully immersed in the teachings, practices, and personalities of the evangelical faith. Second, Chicago defined the problem of urbanization for Moody. As we have seen and will see, Moody was personally and intensely involved with Chicago's poor. He knew their concerns firsthand. Urban poverty and its accompanying ills were not abstract concepts for Moody. He lived in the stench and served the sick. He saw the squatters—especially their children. He saw the families devastated by alcoholism. He saw the labor unrest and the turmoil and chaos it was creating. He knew the fear of both the laborer and the owner. These events framed his understanding of urban social ills. The third was his relationship with Roman Catholics. Moody's openness is all the more remarkable when seen in the context of the hostility directed toward Catholics in Chicago. Moody had possibly imbibed some of Kirk's moderate response to Catholics in Boston; however, Moody's tone was even less strident.[17] Regardless, Moody broke with the cultural norm and most of his peers on this question.[18] On this point, Moody distanced himself from the Protestant, middle-class values of the day.

The religious faith Moody professed in Boston began to develop in Chicago, but as his interview at Mount Vernon had demonstrated, he was far more zealous than wise. During his first months in Chicago, he pestered his coworkers about their lives, railing against billiards, cards, theater, and the like. Some of his colleagues expressed frustration with his imperious attitude, and later in life Moody would acknowledge his overbearing ways.[19]

However, Moody began to mature as well. His early letters home from Chicago reflect the maturing of the initial changes in Boston. On September 25, 1856, Moody wrote to his mother,

> I went into a prayer meeting last night, and as soon as I made myself known, I had friends enough. After meeting they com to me and seemed to be as glad to see me as if I were their earthly brother. God is the same hear that He was in Boston and in him I can find piece.[20]

In October of the same year, he wrote his brother Warren,

> Warren I wish you could know more about Christ who is the same everywhere although the people don't think much of him out here but I want to have you pray for me night and day for I am in a very wicked city where many of the folks keep the stores open on the holy Sabbath and that is enough to sicken anyone.[21]

During these early days, Moody came into contact with Mrs. H. Phillips. Mrs. Phillips was referred to as "Mother" at her home church, First Baptist Church. Beginning sometime in 1857, Moody started rooming at the Phillips' home. She encouraged Moody to memorize Scripture, be faithful in prayer, and witness and pray for the lost. She was also involved with Chicago's poor children, working in Sunday school. She may have been the inspiration for Moody's own Sunday school work.[22] Phillips's impact was apparent in his letters home. A letter to his mother in 1858 reveals his burden for prayer. Moody pleads for prayer on his behalf, for the lost young men of the city, and for the ability to witness to those young men around him.[23]

The letters from the early 1860s confirm Moody's deepening religious commitment. In February 1860, he wrote to his mother and asked her "not forget to pray for him."[24] In April, he wrote to his brother George on hearing of the death of George's wife.

> I have just received news from home that you have met with a great affliction. One that was nearer to you than any other living person on earth has been called to her rest but all is well. I have thought of how I should like to have the death messenger for me when I think that there is rest on the other side of Jordan for the weary in the sweet fields of Eden. . . . The world has no charms for me when I look up but the trouble with God's children is they do not look up enough. . . . Your sweet wife is beckoning you on to a higher holy life. . . . I hope you will look to Jesus for comfort. Go to your closet in secret prayer and there you will find peace in your soul. . . . God will bless you if only you will look to him. Jesus my all to heaven has gone, his track I see and I will pursue.[25]

The letters from 1861 continue these themes. From a letter in February: "Tell all my friends there is nothing like the religion of Jesus

Christ and I am in hopes the family altar is kept up thar to home."[26] In June, he wrote to his mother about his siblings, encouraging her to "tell them to love the Lord Jesus Christ with all their hart and we will all meet in heaven. Tell them to pray for me."[27] In November, again to his mother, he told of his burden for his siblings:

> I would like to see you all and talk with you about my Savoir that seems so near to me. Oh what would life be without Christ. I sometimes get to looking down on the dark world of sin but when I look to Jesus it makes me look up. Mother I often think of you and say shall we meet in heaven. Oh it is a solem question to think of. Have made up my mind to make it my lifes business to get to heaven. I want to invite all my brothers and sisters than oh, I often pray for them and hope you do the same. I wish you would write to Luther and urge him to come to Jesus. Oh I would like to see him a converted man.[28]

The seriousness of Moody's commitment is apparent. Also conspicuous are the evangelical themes: biblical imagery, a passion for the lost, a sense of sin, and the hope of heaven. Evangelicalism had taken root in the young Dwight Moody.

Shortly after he arrived in Chicago, Moody's newly established spiritual inclinations were reinforced by religious fervor sweeping through the city as the 1857 New York City revival made its way west to Chicago. This revival would be the initial means by which Moody would be drawn into the evangelical community in Chicago. It would also be one of his first lessons on how revivals were done and their impact on communities.

The First and Second Great Awakenings often overshadow the 1857–1858 revival in America. The definitive work on the revival is by Kathryn T. Long. Long argues that the neglect of the 1857–1858 revival results from several factors. First, it falls outside the parameters of the Second

Great Awakening and thus is lost amid the significant amount of work around that event. Second, it just predates the Civil War and is overshadowed by it. Finally, there has been very little work done on religion and the Civil War until recently.[29] However, the 1857–1858 revival was seen as important in its time, viewed as an important event of nineteenth century American religious history. It was variously described as "our American Awakening," "the event of the century," America's third "great awakening," and simply "the Great Revival."[30]

The revival was reported to have started in the North Dutch Church at the corner of Fulton and William Streets in lower Manhattan.[31] This strategic location was just a short walk from both Broadway and the business corridor on Wall Street. The key figure was a layperson, an ex-businessperson named Jeremiah Calvin Lamphere (b. 1809). In 1857, Lamphere turned his back on the pursuit of wealth and joined the staff of the North Dutch Church as a city missionary.

Lamphere was determined to start weekly prayer meetings designed to attract businesspersons in light of the church's location.[32] Within six months, the prayer meetings were said to have spread to "every nook and corner of the great republic."[33] The movement would not be confined to North America. As Richard Carwardine points out, it is hardly surprising this revival would "soon be followed by spectacular revivals in Ulster, Wales, and many parts of Britain."[34]

Moody was already active in daily prayer meetings in Chicago before the revival. In a letter to his mother dated January 6, 1857, he described his experience: "I go to meeting every night. Oh how I enjoy it. It seems as if God were here himself."[35] A similar refrain was found in a letter to his brother George later in the same year. Moody spoke of the effect the meetings were having on his life and reflected his growing emphasis on God's love:

I have enjoyed more religion hear than I ever have in my life. Oh George I wish sometimes you were out hear although we did not youst to get along very well but I think we could live together well enough now. Do you enjoy as much religion as you have I hope you will holde on to the promises in the Bible. I find the better I live the more enjoyment I have & the more I think of God & his love the less I think of this worlds troubles. George don't let anything keep you from the full enjoyment of Gods love. I think we have things sometimes come a bo(?) us to try ower faith and God likes us to cling on as the Samest sais in one place God likes to chastise them whome he loves so let us pray for each other. I have brout you befor God in my prayers & hope you have done the same.[36]

As these letters indicated, Moody was already quite active in religious meetings by the time the revival hit Chicago. The revival heightened Moody's growing spiritual consciousness. Commenting on the effect of these meetings just before his death, Moody remarked, "I would like before I go hence to see the whole church of God quickened as it was in '57 (sic)."[37]

One of the unique characteristics of this revival was the prohibition against discussing what were described as "controverted points."[38] Chief among these controverted points was slavery. Later, we shall learn of Moody's involvement with the abolitionist movement in Boston and note the deep anti-slavery sentiments of his home and surrounding towns in northwest Massachusetts. Despite this, Moody never complained about this prohibition in his comments about the revival.[39] Clearly, the meetings moved Moody; he observed them carefully and absorbed their methodology. Avoiding "controverted points" became typical of his ministry.

The 1857–1858 revival would shape Moody in several other ways. James Edwin Orr, a distinguished researcher of revivals, describes a conversation he had with another historian. The other scholar asked if Moody started the revival; Orr replied, "No, Moody did not start the '58 Revival.' The '58 Revival' started Moody."[40] Orr went on to say that "Moody was without question the greatest single product of the Revival."[41] Second, this revival would provide a template for the style Moody would employ. Specifically, the revival emphasized decorum and order. For example, signs were posted reminding the attendees that the "Brethren are earnestly requested to adhere to the 5 minute rule," and "Prayers & Exhortations Not to exceed 5 minutes, *in order to give all an opportunity, NOT MORE than 2 CONSECUTIVE PRAYERS or EXHORTATIONS.*"[42] Numerous historians have pointed out Moody's appropriation of Victorian business practice and middle-class sensibilities.[43] But few trace these traits to the 1857–1858 revival. Nevertheless, it seems pretty apparent from the letters that the revival personally moved Moody. Moreover, given Moody's comments during the revival and his nostalgic reflections about the revival toward the end of his life, it is apparent he looked to it as a model for revivals.

Most pertinent to this study is the approach to social questions taken during the 1857–1858 revival. The revival represented a new understanding of the social impact revivals should have in many ways. In a section titled, "Revivalism Without Social Betterment," Kathryn Long describes the shift. She states the revival "produced no groundswell of ethical concern." According to Long, the old New England model had linked "conversionist piety" and "moral reform," meaning that individual conversions and social salvation were linked. The 1857–1858 revival broke this linkage. Specifically, social salvation became a function of individual conversions; that is, "any needed social transformation would result from the cumulative personal reforms of regenerate individuals and from the direct supernatural intervention of God."[44]

While the goal of a righteous republic remained, the means to accomplish it changed. Individual conversions became the only means to bring about meaningful social transformation. The result was socially conservative revivalism.[45] Moody absorbed some of this approach. While it is true that Moody was committed to individual conversion as the best means of bringing about social change, this does not mean Moody opposed reform. Instead, as we shall see, he prioritized it. For Moody, evangelism was always the top priority. The 1857–1858 revival helped to form that prioritization.

Moody's work with the Sunday school movement drew him deeper still into the world of evangelicalism. Moreover, it provided another set of experiences that helped shape his theology, for it was through his work in Sunday schools that he became involved in the life of urban slums.[46]

These early years in Chicago saw the blossoming of Moody's intense love and concern for children. W. H. Daniels describes Moody as having "an intense and almost womanly love for children. He never seemed happier than when in the midst of a crowd of boys and girls, with whom he romped in the wildest fashion, beating them at their own sports and games, until he won their fullest confidence."[47] Consequently Moody tried bringing local boys with him to church. Finally, after several weeks of unruliness from his young charges, Moody was encouraged to find another way to reach young people. This episode foreshadowed what would be an ongoing tension in Moody's life and work. Evangelicalism in the United States during this time reflected middle-class mores and sensibilities. Moody embraced many of these values personally. Yet these same values often hindered interaction with the working masses, the very ones for whom Moody felt most burdened.[48] Faced with the choice of conforming to middle-class sensibilities or pursuing ministry, Moody chose to act on his religious convictions. In this case, the Sunday school provided a way for Moody to follow his burden for poor children without interfering with the sensibilities of the Sunday service.

Sunday schools originated in England when Robert Raikes and Thomas Stock first established a Sunday school for the poor and orphaned in Gloucester in 1780. Because of their efforts, laypeople and clergy began forming similar schools throughout England. Out of these efforts, the Sunday school movement was formed. The movement experienced astonishing growth—by 1800, roughly 200,000 children were enrolled in English Sunday schools. By 1850, this number had risen to 2 million.

By the 1790s, several of these schools had taken root in the United States. Over the next quarter of a century, Sunday schools sprang up as part of a loose network of free schools operated by various religious and philanthropic groups to provide primary education to poor and otherwise disadvantaged children. Although virtually all these schools included religious instruction as part of their curriculum, the amount of religious instruction was a function of the sponsorship of the school. For example, the schools run by the New York Free School Society combined daily academic education with Sunday attendance at Sunday schools.

A critical event in the development of the movement occurred in October 1811, when Presbyterian missionary Robert May opened an evening Sunday school in Philadelphia. Unlike previous free schools, he taught without pay and taught exclusively religious doctrine. May proved to be a trendsetter, and during the decade from 1810 to 1820, schools resembling May's became increasingly common. These institutions were especially popular among young, newly converted Protestants like Moody as a means of expressing their newfound beliefs. By 1820, there were several hundred Sunday schools in the United States, and May's model was dominant. Now Sunday schools emphasized religious instruction over reading and writing, although most taught the latter subjects to inculcate the former. As a result, many Sunday school leaders began arguing for the establishment of a system of free daily schools so that Sunday schools would be free to teach religion alone.[49] Admittedly, the schools also fulfilled a social purpose as they served to control children's activities. Employment of children in industry had brought together youth of similar ages who worked in factories on weekdays and spent their Sundays playing in alleys and wharves, disturbing nearby families and profaning the day. Sunday schools provided an alternative to such rowdiness. The schools also taught proper behavior, enforcing cleanliness, providing Sunday clothing, and reprimanding children for lying, swearing, talking indecently, or other misbehavior.[50]

Still, the primary aim of Sunday schools was teaching fundamental Protestantism to children of the unchurched poor. The Bible provided the text for teaching the truths of the gospel, knowledge of which, Protestants believed, was essential for moral living and good citizenship. Moreover, Protestants felt that knowledge of the Bible would teach pupils the duty required of them as social, rational, and accountable beings.[51]

Moody found the perfect alternative to the Plymouth Congregational Church in the Sunday school movement. In this context, he could work with children without the constraints of middle-class manners. Moreover, the Sunday school would allow him to express his newfound faith aggressively.

Moody hired space in a run-down saloon on the North Side of Chicago and threw himself into the school. In a letter home dated February 12, 1861, he wrote, "I have been holding meetings in my school every night this winter. It has taken all my time."[52] In June, he reiterated the point: "I am drov more now than ever in my life."[53]

The work was located in a notorious area called "the Sands." In 1865, the *Chicago Tribune* described it as home to "the most beastly sensuality and darkest crimes."[54] The *Tribune's* account was confirmed by an early colleague of Moody's named Watts.

Shortly before this (Moody's coming to Chicago), the honorable John Wentworth, mayor of Chicago, had determined to rid that part of North Side designated as the "Sand Lots."

> It was covered by a large number of board shanties, and these were occupied by as miserable a lot of mortals as I ever saw. They were in continual broil and drunkenness and fighting, often accompanied by murder. . . . Moody rented a tumbled-down shack over in the Sands, a poverty-stricken hell in North Chicago. Breweries prospered; It was an abode of thieves, harlots, drunks, and murders. From Moody's Sunday School, his voice could reach 200 saloons, houses of infamy. There were dope fiends, old soaks, streetwalkers, policemen, plug-uglies, tough boys, hard-hitting teamsters, second-story men.[55]

Not surprisingly, because of his efforts in the Sands, many in the religious community dubbed him "Crazy Moody."[56]

They also objected to his methods. Moody often rode through a particularly wretched area of the Sands aptly named "Little Hell," handing out candy to get the children to follow him to his meetings at the school. Some in the religious community accused him of bribery. Moody's defenders retorted that Moody's "missionary sugar" was no different from fine architecture, fresco, and gilding; inlaid pulpits, choirs, rhetoric, three-bank organs, and the like used to entice more elegant sinners.[57]

The religious community was not the only one to consider Moody "crazy." Sometime in late 1859 or early 1860, Moody returned to Northfield for a visit. His uncle Zebulon recorded the following event:

My nephew Dwight is as crazy, crazy as a March hare. Came
on from Chicago last week for a flying visit. I had not seen him
but he drove into my yard this a. m. You know how cold it was
and his face was as red as red flannel. Before I could say good
morning he shouted, "Good morning Uncle Zebulon what are
you going to do for Christ today?" Of course, I was startled
and finally managed to say, "Come in Dwight and we will talk
it over." "No, I can't stop but I want you to think about it," and
he turned the sleigh around and went up the hill like a streak of
lightening. I tell you he is crazy.[58]

Although Uncle Zebulon's comments were not specifically in response to Moody's work with children, they demonstrated how some
processed Moody's zeal for Christian work.

Moody, however, seemed immune to these criticisms. Regardless of
the concerns of the middle-class press and religious establishment, he
was determined to minister to poor children. This phase of Moody's
career became somewhat immortalized by a caricature of Moody riding
on a pony through slums followed by ragged children. William Moody's
biography includes an eyewitness recollection of these days. Moody was
described as riding through the slums and being greeted by the delighted
cries of children. He carried candy in his pockets and generously spread it
among the children. Moody knew the children personally and inquired
by name after those absent.[59]

This account by a witness to Moody's work during this time gives
insight into the school and Moody's approach.

The first meeting I ever saw him at was in a little old shanty that
had been abandoned by a saloonkeeper. Mr. Moody had got
the place to hold the meetings in at night. I went there a little
late; and the first thing I saw was a man standing up with a few

tallow candles around him, holding a negro boy, and trying to read to him the story of the Prodigal Son and a great many words he could not read out, and had to skip. I thought, "If the Lord can ever use such an instrument as that for His honor and glory, it will astonish me." After that meeting was over, Mr. Moody said to me, "Reynolds, I have got only one talent; I have no education, but I love the Lord Jesus Christ, and I want to do something for him: I want you to pray for me."[60]

His daughter recounted another story from the Sunday school days in 1858. She recalled hearing of a particular family with "a giant father habitually drunk, a tiny wife who supported the family and six ill-bred children." Moody almost daily took the family food, coal, or firewood.[61] In this story, Moody's actions were strikingly similar to the care he received as a boy from the young Oliver Everett.

Moody described the early Sunday school years in the following way,

> Sunday was a busy day for me then. During the week I would be out of town as a commercial traveler . . . but I always managed to get back by Saturday night. I would be up by six to get the hall ready for the Sunday School. Every Saturday night a German society held a dance there and I had to roll out beer kegs, sweep out the sawdust, clean up generally. I did not think it right to hire it done on Sunday so I did the work. This took most of the morning and then I would drum up the boys and girls and by two in the afternoon we would have a full hall. After school I would visit the absent scholars and invite the parents to an evening service that I held in a deserted saloon and we would hold an after meeting and I presided. When the day was over I was tired out. I didn't know much at that time. A great many men want to do big things. That is the mistake I made when I

started out. I wanted to preach to intelligent people but I found that they didn't like to hear me. So I began with children but it was years before I could talk profitably to grown people. I talked to children and it was a grand school. It was the preparation I needed.[62]

While targeting children, he also sought out their parents. As we will see, this aspect of Moody's ministry developed and eventually led to the transformation of the Sunday school into a church. It also clearly demonstrated that his commitment to practice his faith was extraordinary. Moody worked tirelessly, teaching, seeking absent students, setting up the hall himself.

The Sunday school would become an extraordinary success. Moody's school flourished by mixing an intense love for the children with simple Bible lessons and practical help for the students' families. In the summer of 1860, Moody wrote to his brother excitedly that the school was "on the incres all of the time."[63] By the end of 1860, the school attendance had grown to about 1,500. It had also become so famous that President-elect Abraham Lincoln chose to stop by the school on the way to his inauguration.[64] In many ways, the Sunday school illustrated what would become essential traits of Moody's ministry. Moody was a man with great zeal and limited education who had a burden for people, impoverished children. While a proponent of middle-class sensibilities, he was also a zealous Christian worker. The Sunday school provided an early illustration of how he would manage those commitments when they conflicted.

The Sunday school also allowed Moody to learn how to evangelize. It forced him to be brief and straightforward in presenting the gospel, traits he carried into his later ministries. The school provided a direct window into life in the slums, providing Moody an opportunity to examine urban poverty. He also observed the impact of personal conversion, and what he saw furthered his conviction. Finally, the Sunday school helped Moody define his gifts. He learned he worked best with working-class, ordinary people. His theology would reflect their concerns: practical, simple, and evangelistic.

The Sunday school would not be the only venue where Moody would develop his evangelistic skills. He also became involved with the YMCA.[65] It would prove equally important to his spiritual and theological formation early in his career. Later, Moody would attest to its role in his life, stating, "I believe in the Young Men's Christian Association with all my heart. It has, under God, done more in developing me for Christian work than any other agency."[66] The YMCA would not only provide a laboratory in which Moody could test his ministry ideas, but it would also be another essential institutional link into the evangelical world.

The Young Men's Christian Association began in Chicago in March 1858. Its arrival was primarily the by-product of the 1857 revival. The Association's records state, "Out of this great revival came the Chicago Association."[67]

In June 1860, Moody left the business world and went into full-time religious work at the YMCA. This decision demonstrated the depth of Moody's faith. Life was hard for him. The daughter of Farwell, one of his early benefactors, recounted that her father said Moody slept under the stairs in the recess of a small room of the YMCA.[68] Another early acquaintance recalled, "I often saw him in old YMCA rooms. It was here he slept on chairs covered with newspapers."[69] This acquaintance also noted Moody had spent his life savings, $7,000, on his Christian work. An 1860 letter to his mother reflected the power of his evangelistic burden. He wrote,

> I was very sorry to hear of the death of Miss Cobb. Tell her father
> and mother that they have my sympathy and that no one can

see God without [change] of heart. Oh mother, it ought to be a warning to us all. We have got to go soon. Then let us be ready. Let us keep our lam[p]s trimmed and burning for we cannot tell the day or hour that the son of man shall come. Let it be the prayer of our heart that we may live nearer our God. I have been anxious that all of my brothers and sisters meet with a change of heart for the Bible says without a change of heart no one shall see God. I am trying in my weak way to live so that when my life is finished I can go home and rest with the people of God.[70]

The letter also reflected a preoccupation with death that was probably tied to Moody's persistent pain over the loss of his father. It is reasonable to assume some of his zeal for evangelism was grounded in this traumatic event.

Like Moody's Sunday school, the YMCA linked material and spiritual aid and was nondenominational and evangelistically oriented. The YMCA and the Sunday school are probably the best illustrations of the young Moody's approach to curing social ills.

During his years at the YMCA, Moody began to learn how to be an evangelist. Given his experience and background, he seemed to be the perfect candidate for the YMCA's approach to ministry. What is more, his experience at the YMCA provided additional hands-on training for the apprentice evangelist. As a result, Moody learned how to talk to working people, and he saw their needs firsthand. As we have seen, Moody credited the YMCA years as pivotal in forming his skills as a Christian worker. In addition, with his time at the Sunday school, Moody's work with the YMCA honed his speaking skills, particularly for the urban working class. These experiences help explain his uncanny ability to connect with everyday people.

Both Moody and the Chicago YMCA flourished during the decade of the 1860s. The seemingly boundless energy and optimism of the young man from Northfield drove the YMCA forward. In turn, the YMCA provided a structured outlet and focused vision for his zeal. Not surprisingly, by 1866, he had risen through the ranks to become president of the Chicago YMCA.

During the years of his involvement, the YMCA engaged in a program of evangelism and public relief. The 1867 annual report of the Chicago YMCA made this clear. "Earnest working Christianity is apt to be comprehensive, and to care for both soul and body. No harm ordinarily comes from doing good in both simultaneously. . . . It was the same Jesus who first preached the Gospel all day to multitudes, that then fed them miraculously."[71] This statement provided the pattern for Moody's approach—keeping evangelism the priority while simultaneously engaging in charitable work.

Under Moody's leadership, the YMCA in Chicago increased its services to the poor. In 1867, the YMCA distributed $24,325.38 worth of bread, clothing, and coal. More than 3,800 families, of which 2,300 were immigrants, received aid. Faithful to its task of combining evangelism and relief work, the association also passed out 42,000 copies of foreign language religious papers during the same period.[72]

What was true of the YMCA generally was true of Moody personally. For example, in an 1862 letter to one of his brothers, he told of his work with the YMCA:

> I am very sorry I have not answered you 3 last letters but I have so much to do I could not find time. . . . I take care of the poore of the city. I have some 500 or 800 people that are dependent on me for their daily food & new ones coming all of the time. I keep a sadall horse to ride around with to hunt up the poore people with & then keepe a nother horse & man to carry around the things with & then I have a man to waite on the

folks as they come to my office. I make my headquarters at the rooms of the Young Mens Christian Association & [I have three meetings to attend each day] besides calling on the sick & that is not all [I] have to go into the countrey about every week to buy wood and provisions for the poore also coal wheet meal & corn then I have to go to hold meetings.[73]

Moody embraced the values of the YMCA. For Moody, urban work meant making evangelism the priority but never excluding relief work. In addition, the approach to social problems demonstrated in the 1857 revival was becoming institutionalized in the YMCA.

The Young Men's Christian Association also provided the context for Moody's introduction to the Chicago business community and John V. Farwell in particular. Farwell led a company that was one of the leading business enterprises in the United States. He had moved to Illinois from New York in 1838, at the age of thirteen. Twelve years later, in 1845, Farwell came to Chicago seeking his fortune. He began as a clerk working for several merchants selling dry goods, clothing, and home furnishings. By 1857, Farwell had worked his way into a partnership in Chicago's largest dry goods firm. The firm changed its name from Cooley, Wadsworth & Co. to Cooley, Farwell & Co. The man who would later become the icon of the Chicago business community, Marshall Field, was one of Farwell's associates in this company. Like Farwell, by 1863, Field had worked his way into the partnership; however, two years later, he left to form his own company. As a result, in 1865, John V. Farwell & Co. was born.

In the following years, Farwell became one of the main drivers of Chicago's business machine. He understood the possibilities Chicago offered and invested accordingly. Astonishingly, by the end of the 1880s, Farwell's company, along with Marshall Field's, ranked as one of the top three wholesalers in the country.[74]

In addition to his involvement in business, Farwell was active in politics. Like Moody, Farwell was a committed Republican. This led to Farwell serving as a presidential elector for Illinois in the elections of 1860 and 1864. President Ulysses S. Grant also appointed him a commissioner for Indian Affairs in 1869.[75]

The other commitment Farwell shared with Moody was to evangelical Christianity. A devout Methodist, he helped build the First Methodist Church in Chicago. Farwell was also active in the YMCA movement, donating the land for its first building in Chicago. At the YMCA, Farwell met and became deeply impressed by young Dwight Moody. This was reflected in Farwell's annual report submitted to the board of the YMCA for the year 1861–1862. He wrote,

> Brother D. L. Moody has given his entire effort and energies in executing the several plans of doing good [charitable distributions of donated food, fuel, and clothing] referred to herein, and to his efforts mainly are we indebted for their practical execution. Not having raised any funds outside of membership dues, we have not been able, as an Association, to make him any remuneration . . . recommend his continued employment as city missionary, for which he is eminently qualified.[76]

Farwell became Moody's lifelong friend and benefactor. Moody counted on Farwell for financial support in his various ministries.

The YMCA was the place where Moody learned practical Christianity. It reinforced what he had started to believe at the Sunday school: serve the needs of the poor but keep evangelism preeminent. He loved it because it had helped him. Moreover, he loved it because it strategically served the city where the church did not.[77]

The YMCA years taught Moody one other vital lesson: the value of a nonsectarian approach. As the YMCA aided thousands of families and distributed tens of thousands of pieces of religious literature in foreign languages among immigrants, Moody observed firsthand what could happen when evangelicals banded together without regard for denominational prejudices. As we shall see, this is a lesson he never forgot.

THE FORMATION OF THE CHRISTIAN WORKER: THE CIVIL WAR

"Thirty years ago war clouds gathered over our land, and the church of God was aroused as I have never seen it since in behalf of the young men of America. . . . Meetings were held everywhere, and many a camp became the scene of a deep and effective revival, and for more than thirty years I have been continually meeting men who were converted in those army meetings."[78]

—DWIGHT MOODY

In many ways, the American Civil War became the defining moment in the life of the United States. Driven by the issue of slavery, the war was a deeply contentious and costly affair.[79] In many homes, it pitted brother against brother. This was true even in the home of the First Family, as several members of Abraham Lincoln's family by marriage served in the Confederate armed forces.

Moody was deeply involved in the American Civil War. He made nine trips to the battlefront to minister to Union troops. These trips would span the length of the war, from 1861 to 1865. Moody and his wife would be with General Grant as he entered the Confederate capital of Richmond, Virginia, at the end of the war. He also worked with Southern prisoners at Camp Douglas, a prisoner-of-war camp just south of Chicago.[80]

What Moody witnessed firsthand was dreadful. Moreover, the human cost of the conflict was staggering. At least 618,000 Americans died in the Civil War, and some experts say the toll reached 700,000. To put these figures in context, these casualties exceed the nation's loss in all other wars combined from the Revolution to Vietnam.[81]

In addition to the cost of human life, the war also took a terrible economic toll. The best estimates indicate that the war cost about 7 billion dollars ($133 billion in current dollars). The per capita burden on Southerners was almost three times that of the North.[82] Researchers later described the infrastructure damage, especially in the South, as "burned or plundered homes, pillaged countryside, untold losses in crops and farm animals, ruined buildings and bridges, devastated college campuses and neglected roads and train tracks all left the South in ruins."[83]

The effect on Protestant churches was equally devastating. Like the nation, the prominent Protestant churches were bitterly divided by the issue of slavery. In an ominous sign of what was to come for the country, the slavery question divided the Presbyterians in 1838, the Methodists in 1844, and the Baptists in 1845.[84] The war embittered the factions, further isolating the divided churches.[85]

It was the YMCA that took Moody into the war. Reflecting its commitment to ministering to young men, the YMCA established the Christian Commission in early September 1862 and called for "volunteers or delegates [who] were willing to serve in any capacity to bring spiritual or physical comfort to Union or Confederate soldiers."[86] As the first historian of the Commission put it, "From the beginning the army was recognized as a field for evangelistic effort."[87]

The average delegate, who was in his teens, would leave a YMCA headquarters with a badge and a shouldered blanket; dried food and medical supplies for wounded soldiers; a bucket for water, coffee, or stimulants; and a Bible for religious work and use in the burial of the dead. Delegates' activities included passing out Bibles, hymnbooks, and tracts; holding prayer meetings; helping write letters or delivering letters from home; purchasing items forgotten by the soldiers; cooking homemade meals; and providing emergency rations. Often during and after battles, they assisted surgeons by changing bandages or bathing wounds.[88] During the war, nearly 5,000 delegates volunteered to serve without pay, and they distributed an estimated 2.5 million pieces of literature, preached almost 50,000 sermons, and held over 75,000 prayer meetings.[89] Farwell was named the head of the Christian Commission in Illinois, and the first delegate commissioned nationally was Dwight Moody.

Camp Douglas, a Union training camp just south of Chicago, was Moody's first assignment with the Commission. He immediately threw himself into working among the recruits. Moody launched a series of religious meetings at the camp. The meetings quickly became popular and well attended. They escalated to the point that eight to ten different meetings were held every twenty-four hours.[90] Within weeks, Moody had overseen the printing and distribution of 3,500 Union Sunday school hymnals. Thousands of Bibles and other pieces of religious literature were disseminated as well. Still unsatisfied, Moody decided each regiment in the camp should have its own Christian Commission tent. In addition to being stocked with religious literature, each tent contained writing materials to encourage the men to write home. By the end of the conflict, over 1,500 religious services had been held at the camp.[91]

After his initial work at the camp, Moody began making trips to the front. At least one of his early trips was to the Battle of Shiloh in 1862. Shiloh was one of the bloodiest battles of the early years of the war; in fact, it was perhaps the costliest in U. S. history up to that time.[92] The images Moody saw on the battlefield were burned into his mind. Writing to his mother after another battle, he lamented,

> I am at Cairo with things to relieve the wants of the sick & wounded soldiers. I was sent to Fort Donelson Tenn—last week & as soon as I got hom they sent me back with 7 or 8 hundred dollars worth of things for the wounded. One hospital has

about 1400, another 800, etc. I tell you mother as I was going through the hospitals today I remarked to a lady that was with me if I was going to be sick I would want to be home for there is nothing like home. Who could take so good care of me as you could? The sympathy goes a great ways too, I tell you, you do not know how roughly the poor fellows are treated. Our army are very healthy as a general thing. Some sickness among them, not much. I was on the battlefield before they had buried the dead. It was awful to see the dead lying around without being anyone to bury them. They are buried now. The prisoners are up to Chicago, a good many of them. So we have meetings with them daily.[93]

Another time he recalled, "I could hear the groans of dying men, and I helped bear away some of the wounded, and I saw the scene in all its terrible reality."[94]

If the horror of the battlefield were not enough, Moody worked at a Union prisoner-of-war camp as well. As the war progressed, both sides had collected thousands of prisoners of war. Since neither side expected a protracted conflict, they were not prepared to deal with a large number of prisoners. Camp Douglas was hastily converted into a prisoner-of-war camp beginning in February 1862 (note Moody's comment about prisoners sent to Chicago in the above letter).[95] The haste of the process is illustrated by the fact that, for some time, the camp housed both Union recruits and Confederate prisoners. A letter from Moody's brother Sam describes this and gives us a glimpse of Moody's work during the transition days at the camp.

Dwight is run from morning to night. He hardly gets time to eat. Camp Douglas is situated here (there is bout 17,000) he holds meetings down there most every night. It is a treat to go down there and hear the soldiers sing which is about 300 or 400 gathered as they come from most every state. The Rebel prisoners are among them.[96]

Writing the same day to his mother, Moody said, "I have been trying for a long time to find time to write you but so many things to do and so few to do them. I am drove from piler to post. I wish I had time to write you my feelings but I must go to Camp Douglas now."[97]

Despite the availability of resources, conditions at the camp quickly degenerated. The monthly mortality rate was at 10 percent within one year, a rate unsurpassed by any other prison in the North or South.[98] At its worst, estimates for the mortality rate range from 20 to 30 percent, establishing Camp Douglas's reputation as an extermination camp. This makes the mortality rate at Camp Douglas comparable to the rate at the notorious Confederate camp of Andersonville.

Three traits distinguished Camp Douglas from other Northern prison camps: extreme acts of cruelty, high mortality rates, and a low official count of prisoners who died. Although the official count was around 4,000 deaths, others put the number as high as 6,129. Many men died of exposure, scurvy, and smallpox.[99]

It is hard to measure the effect the war had on Moody. His son William, in his biography, noted that "the record of these years is fragmentary."[100] The few letters available from this time provide only a glance into his psyche.[101] Indeed, though, anyone exposed to this amount of gore and inhumane behavior could not walk away unscathed. One reasonable assumption is that these experiences soured Moody on human nature and the progress of human civilization. The war, combined with the urban ills of Chicago and Boston, predisposed him to a more dubious view of humanity and society. What he had been taught about human sinfulness by Edward Kirk and others seemed to be confirmed by what he observed on the battlefield and in the prison camp. Further, it is hardly surprising that Moody became an enthusiastic proponent of premillennialism shortly after the war's end.

The Civil War would also bring an important man into Moody's life, General Oliver Otis Howard. He was born in Maine in 1830 and was educated at Bowdoin College (1850) and the U. S. Military Academy (1854). Upon leaving West Point, he served in the Seminole War in Florida. While in Florida, he underwent a profound religious conversion after attending a Methodist tent meeting. With the outbreak of the Civil War, Howard joined the Union Army, eventually rising to the rank of major general. General O. O. Howard met Dwight Moody in 1864. Moody led a meeting among Union troops, and Howard's troops were assigned to the encampment Moody was serving.[102] As Howard recalled it, Moody's "preaching was direct and effective."[103] Consequently Howard joined Moody in leading services among the men for a few days before they went into action.

General Howard was a social reformer in many ways: he believed in temperance, racial equality, and education for women. Howard earned a reputation as a committed and zealous Christian throughout the war, often demanding his men attend prayer meetings and temperance gatherings. Howard taught Sunday school and was an enthusiastic supporter of the YMCA.[104] He also sparked controversy by showing kindness to defeated Southern troops and citizenry, often meting out severe punishment to any of his forces engaged in looting or wanton destruction of property.[105] Throughout their days together during the Civil War, Howard reinforced what Moody had heard and seen during his days in Boston at Edward Kirk's church. Moreover, by his zeal for evangelism and concern for the physical needs of others, Howard reinforced the lessons Moody had learned through the Sunday school and YMCA in Chicago.

Howard was also a forward thinker on racial questions. As he put it, "I never could detect the shadow of a reason why the color of the skin should impair the right to life, liberty, and the pursuit of happiness."[106] Howard lived out his convictions. When soldiers took Indian wives, Howard viewed these as legitimate marriages in the eyes of God. When soldiers returned East, abandoned their wives, and married white women, Howard viewed this as bigamy. He also invited African American children to join the Sunday school in his church in Washington, DC, resulting in a church split. Howard's views often brought him into conflict with his colleagues in the Union Army. As his biographer put it, "The anomaly of Howard's position as advocate of racial equality and as a high-ranking officer in the United States Army had proved so impossible of comprehension that more than one person, and often this meant a fellow officer, simply never understood him at all."[107]

Near the end of the war, Abraham Lincoln selected Howard to lead the Freedmen's Bureau. After the war, President Andrew Johnson confirmed Howard's role with the Bureau. Central to Howard's vision for helping the newly freed slaves was education. Howard wrote, "The burden of my efforts ... may be condensed into the words: Educate the children. That was the relief needed. Is it not always the relief which in time becomes a permanency?"[108] In his report to the secretary of war in 1869, he wrote, "The most urgent want of the freedmen was education; and from the first I have devoted more attention to this than any other branch of my work."[109]

Howard believed education was a critical component in addressing poverty. Speaking in 1866, he said, "The only way to lift the ponderous load of poverty from the houses of poor whites and blacks, and keep it lifted is by instruction."[110] Howard pushed not only for male education but also for the education of females of all races.[111]

For various reasons, 1872 brought the dismantling of the Freedmen's Bureau. During his tenure at the helm, Howard had used Bureau monies to establish thousands of multiple types of schools.[112] The most notable was Howard University, the brainchild of a missionary society meeting Howard attended on November 20, 1867. Initially envisioned as a school to train pastors, the goal was quickly broadened to include lawyers, teachers, doctors, and dentists. Howard became the president of the university, and it was named in his honor.

While Howard saw education as a means to address poverty, his motive was religious. Speaking on his work at the Freedmen's Bureau in 1866, he clarified this. Howard proclaimed he was taking love as his motto. He argued that only love could restore the country, rebuild communities, and bring families back together. Love was "the fundamental law; it is the very bottom of a true reconstruction." Moreover, in Howard's definition, this love was Christian. "The fundamental truth of the whole Gospel is love," he said. "This fundamental truth requires us to love one another." Howard believed that the practical spirit of the Lord Jesus Christ was love and that such a spirit was "required in this country."[113]

Moody's relationship with Howard continued after the war, and Moody called on Howard to speak at YMCA and Sunday school conventions and various revivals. He also asked Howard to speak at his schools in Northfield and Chicago. William Moody's biography declared Moody maintained a lifetime intimacy with Howard, and Dorsett described them as close friends.[114]

Moody was shaped by the character traits he saw in Howard. Howard was an older man who acted on his convictions. His peers respected him. Both Generals Grant and Sherman trusted him and gave him significant responsibility on their staff. He had served as superintendent at West Point, and he had been awarded the Congressional Medal of Honor for bravery in combat.[115] Howard's actions reinforced Moody's evangelical convictions, especially his enthusiasm for evangelism and temperance. It is also likely that Howard influenced Moody's beliefs concerning education. It hardly seems coincidental that Moody's first school was for women and that all his schools were multiracial. Indeed, Dorsett claimed that Howard taught Moody much about leading an educational institution and instructed him on the complicated and delicate issues of race in the United States.[116] By linking education to Christian charity, Howard echoed what Moody had heard from his first pastor at Northfield, Oliver Everett.

By the advent of Moody's first trip to the United Kingdom in 1867, a number of the elements that would shape his social vision were already in place. As a boy, he had learned about God's love and what Christian charity could do to help those in need. As a young man, he had experienced a conversion, been nurtured in the revivalist evangelical tradition, and served in institutions where he had learned to balance evangelism and charity. The deplorable conditions of the slums of Chicago and the carnage of the Civil War tempered Moody. He had begun forming relationships with the business community in Chicago from whom he would draw financial support. Now, as a young adult, he would interact with a number of the evangelical giants of the United Kingdom.

THE FORMATION OF THE CHRISTIAN WORKER: THE TRIP TO THE UNITED KINGDOM

I want to tell you how thankful I am forever going to London; it seems to me that I was almost in darkness until I went over there. I have enjoyed myself much more in Christ since I got back. I would not take anything for what I learnt while in your city. I love the dear friends in London more than I can express with this pen, and my heart goes out to you all very much.[117]

—DWIGHT MOODY TO R. C. MORGAN

Although scholars often overlook this trip, Moody's first trip to the United Kingdom proved pivotal in forming his theology and social vision. During this trip, evangelicals in the United Kingdom reinforced Moody's developing ideas about theology and social action. Some of these figures were people whom Moody already admired. Others were individuals he would come to admire.

As noted earlier, the trip was occasioned by the exhaustion of Moody and his wife, Emma. The couple had been married in 1862. Although theirs appears to have been an excellent marriage, the new couple also had little time together. If anything, being husband and wife seems to have led to a redoubling of their efforts in ministry. Emma's diary reflected this: "D. L. Moody and Emma C. Revell married on August 28, 1862. D. L. busy with his work among the soldiers."[118] We have already noted Moody's work in Chicago and his heavy involvement with the Civil War. On top of this, the couple had their first child, Emma, in October 1864. Mrs. Moody's recovery from the birth was slow, and yet, within six months of the delivery, Emma would leave the baby at home and join Dwight with General Grant's army during the final stages of the Civil War. Unfortunately, shortly after returning from the front, the Moodys received news that Emma's father had died. The death was unexpected and dealt a blow to the couple. In a letter to Dwight's mother, Emma expressed her grief.

> I suppose Mr. M has written to you of father's death. I have felt so sad I could not write before. It was so dreadful. I had hoped so much that I might see him living and it was so hard when coming to the house to see the [black] crepe on the door. At the funeral it seemed hard to bear but it has been so much harder since. Father was so afraid of spoiling my pleasure that tho he wanted to see me so much he would not send for me till the doctor said "there was no hope." He told mother he knew he should not see me here but he should in Heaven. He told her to tell me he would like to have seen me but he loved me and wanted me to meet him in heaven. Father's last words were,

"Perfect Peace." I have thought of the passage when my trial seemed so hard to bear, "Shall not the judge of all the earth do right?" I know He does and yet I cannot help thinking of father. It is my first great trial.[119]

In addition, by Christmas of 1866, Emma's health had taken a turn for the worse with the development of some sort of respiratory ailment.

Moody was struggling as well and beginning to show severe signs of burnout. He was struggling with forgetfulness and bouts of anger, at one point pushing a heckler down a short flight of stairs. He lost track of his schedule and at times doubled-booked himself. Moody's fragile state was evident to his friends as well. Major Whittle had met Moody during the Civil War. He would become a fast friend and a coworker in Moody's revivals. Whittle observed Moody's state of mind and commented in his diary, "He had become mixed up with building Farwell Hall and was on committees for every kind of work and in his ambition to make his enterprises succeed because they were his, had taken his eyes off the Lord."[120]

Although neither Dwight nor Emma mentioned it, both must have been affected by the years of slaughter they had seen during the Civil War.[121] It is hard to believe both were not profoundly traumatized.

Stressed by Emma's health, Moody's workload, and the residual effect of the war, the couple heeded the advice of Emma's doctor to take a trip. The physician had prescribed rest and ocean air for her continued respiratory ills. A trip to the United Kingdom would provide not only ocean air and time away; it would give Emma a chance to visit some of her extended family. For Dwight, the trip also held potential meetings with several men he had come to admire, including George Müller, George Williams, and Charles Spurgeon. Baby Emma was left with Grandma Revell, and the couple set sail in the fall of 1867.

Moody would spend four months in the United Kingdom. He spent most of the time connecting with other evangelicals. There were natural ties with the YMCA that he strengthened and leveraged. In addition, he observed Sunday schools, prayer meetings, and various other ministries eager to exchange ideas.

George Müller and Henry Moorhouse

Shortly after Moody arrived in Chicago, J. B. Stillson, a devoted Christian businessperson, introduced Moody to the writings of George Müller. Stillson came alongside Moody and began intentionally sharpening the desire for ministry that he saw in this young businessperson's life. W. H. Daniels wrote that Stillson was greatly impressed by Moody's passion but believed his desire lacked direction and depth. Stillson saw Moody as "a young man of earnest purpose, plain habits, and not very much education."[122]

In the late 1850s, Stillson told Moody, "If you want to draw wine out of a cask, it is needed first to put some in. You are all the time talking, and you ought to begin to study." Moody concurred, and Stillson "proceeded to mark out for him a course of reading, intending to assist him in enlarging his education."[123] Among the books selected was Müller's autobiography, *The Life of Trust*. Eventually business took Stillson away from Chicago and, in the somewhat comical words of Daniels, "thus did Moody escape becoming a bookish man."[124] While he may have escaped becoming "bookish," Moody was left with what his son Paul describes as "an earnest desire to hear and meet" Müller.[125] Moody's goal was to "imbibe a heady draught of Müller's faith."[126]

On September 27, 1805, George Müller was born in Kroppenstadt, Prussia, near modern-day Halberstadt, Germany. He was educated at the University of Halle, the heart of German Pietism. While at Halle, Müller underwent a religious conversion and decided to pursue a career in foreign missions. However, the Berlin Missionary Society rejected him. Müller then moved to England, and, in 1829, illness prompted a trip to Devon to recuperate. In Devon, Müller was introduced to the fledgling Plymouth Brethren movement. Subsequently he was appointed to pastor a small chapel in Teignmouth. During this pastorate, Müller began practicing a radical kind of faith, choosing to forgo his salary and rely on God alone to provide for his needs. In his autobiography, Müller had expressed that he "began to have conscientious objections against any longer receiving a stated salary."[127] Although he had several reasons, one of his primary reasons came from James 2:1–6. Since it was the general practice of the day to provide for a minister's salary through pew-rents, Müller rejected the notion on the grounds such a practice was "against the mind of the Lord, as in general, the poor brother cannot have so good a seat as the rich."[128] Furthermore, it was essential to Müller that givers be motivated out of a cheerful free will, citing that "God loveth a cheerful giver."[129]

In 1832, Müller moved to Bethesda Chapel in Bristol. It was in Bristol that Müller's vision for ministry fully blossomed. He began by adding work with orphans and teaching Sunday school to his pastoral duties. By 1834–1835, Müller had founded his two significant endeavors: the Scriptural Knowledge Institution for Home and Abroad, a mix between a Bible school and a mission society, and The Bristol Orphanage Mission Work. The orphanage began small, but it eventually housed over 2,000 children.

The story of Müller's life captured the imagination of the young Dwight Moody. Throughout his autobiography, Müller stated that he and his wife never regretted trusting God completely for their financial resources.[130] He further claimed, "All our needs had been met more abundantly than if I had received a regular salary."[131] His reminder that the Lord would provide for them *"by the day . . . and almost by the hour*"[132] served as a moving illustration of God's ability to provide for those who trust Him.

Moody applied a version of Müller's approach to his own life. S. A. Kean, the treasurer for the YMCA from the beginning of Moody's work there, recalled, "Mr. Moody was fertile in schemes and expedients for raising money for the Lord's work; but of the many tens of thousands of dollars which he secured for the Association, he received nothing whatever for himself."[133] Furthermore, he explained that Moody refused a salary because "it would embarrass him, and limit his freedom to go at a moment's notice wherever the Lord might call him."[134] This appeal to go without a salary to maintain the freedom to follow the leading of God sounds similar to Müller's concern that man's money would lead to man's control. Müller wrote, "If money was paid, [the patron] is a member and has a right to vote."[135] Kean expressed the depth of Moody's commitment to refusing a salary for his work in that he did not "remember to have paid him a dollar either for his services or the expenses incidental to his work. Neither [did he] remember any appropriation being made for his assistance, though he often needed and always deserved it."[136] Like Müller, who repeatedly affirmed that the Lord was able to "richly supply all [his] temporal needs,"[137] Moody proclaimed to his friends, "God is rich, and I am working for him."[138]

It was not only the unique nature of George Müller's life that inspired Moody; it was also their shared passion for poor children. In essence, Müller served to shape Moody because Müller embodied the passions that Moody was already pursuing. Müller's burden for caring for orphans is evident throughout his writing. On one occasion, Müller recounted being moved by "a poor little orphan boy" who attended one of his schools but was recently taken to the poorhouse. Almost despondent, Müller wrote, "May this lead me to do something to supply the temporal needs of poor children!"[139] Müller's journals displayed the same passion as his vision to begin an orphan house moved closer to reality. He wrote of desiring "to be used by God to help the poor children and train them in the ways of God."[140] Furthermore, the very fact that Müller's two significant endeavors—the Scripture Knowledge Institute and the orphanage—were both established to meet the needs of children would have demonstrated to Moody the focus of Müller's heart.

Müller's example undoubtedly provided hope and vision for the young and impressionable Moody. After seeing the school in Bristol, Moody wrote to his mother,

> The great orphan schools of George Müller are at Bristol. He has 1,150 children in his house but never asks a man for a cent to support them. He calls on God, and God sends money to him. It is wonderful to see what God can do with a man of prayer.[141]

Müller also revolutionized Moody's approach to Bible study. As we shall see, Moody had a fierce devotion to the Bible that characterized and shaped his entire ministry. Before meeting Müller, Moody's Bible study, while extremely fervent, lacked structure and direction. Moody apparently flipped open his Bible and studied at random. While Daniels and Dorsett attribute the development of D. L. Moody's Bible study formation to Stillson, Moody himself made a different claim. In his book *Pleasure and Profit in Bible Study*, Moody directly attributes the drastic change in his study to Müller.[142] Moody wrote, "I received from George Müller the idea of taking one book of the Bible at a time. I found that plan was very helpful to me. If I hadn't much time, I would take a short epistle or one of the Minor Prophets, and read it at one sitting."[143] In a sermon, Moody explained the value of this method by paralleling the Scriptures to a letter from his wife. In his comparison, Moody noted that if he only read one page a day, he would "forget what was on the first page before [he] got to the eighth."[144] While Moody eventually moved beyond Müller's technique, Müller's method remained foundational.[145]

Müller also influenced Moody indirectly through the life of one of his converts, Henry Moorhouse.[146] Moorhouse was a profligate—a wild drinker and gambler who was converted through the ministry of Müller in Manchester in 1861.

Shortly after his conversion, Moorhouse embarked on his career as an evangelist and, by 1867, was a leading revivalist in the British Isles. Moorhouse became interested in Moody and traveled to Dublin to hear Moody preach. Moody did not make much of an impression on Moorhouse, whose analysis of Moody's preaching was blunt. Moorhouse remarked to Moody afterward that he did not use the Bible enough.[147] Further, Moorhouse informed Moody that he was coming to America to preach with him.

Shortly after arriving in Chicago, Moody received a note indicating Moorhouse had just arrived in New York and was coming out West to preach. Though miffed, Moody arranged for Moorhouse to speak in Chicago for several days while he was gone. Moorhouse arrived at the prearranged time, and Moody left to attend business. Upon returning, Moody ventured out to hear Moorhouse preaching a seven-part series on John 3:16. In closing that seventh sermon, Moorhouse said, "For seven nights I have been trying to tell you how much God loves you, but this poor stammering tongue of mine will not let me."[148] After the sermon, Moody confided to a friend,

> I never knew up to that time that God loved us so much. This
> heart of mine began to thaw out; I could not keep back the
> tears. I just drank it in. So did the crowded congregation. I tell
> you there is one thing that draws above everything else in the
> world and that is love.[149]

Moody repeatedly told the story of Moorhouse preaching and noted the dramatic impact it had on him. It is possible Moody exaggerated the influence of this event; however, Dorsett goes so far as to claim that it utterly transformed Moody and that only his conversion had a similarly dramatic effect.[150] What is clear is that Moorhouse's teaching reinforced what Moody had learned as a child from Oliver Everett, seen as the driving force in General O. O. Howard's life, and observed in the ministry of George Müller. From this point on, the love of God would be the central theme of his ministries.[151] And the Bible would be the centerpiece of his preaching.[152] As William put it in his biography of his father, "Mr. Moorhouse taught Moody to draw his sword full length, to fling the scabbard away, and enter the battle with the naked blade."[153]

The Plymouth Brethren and John Darby

George Müller and Henry Moorhouse were both Plymouth Brethren. Moody was probably drawn deeply into the Brethren fellowship while visiting the United Kingdom through his admiration for Müller. In addition, he spent significant time with one of the original Plymouth Brethren, John Darby, even inviting him to come to America to preach at Moody's Illinois Street Church.[154] Moody met other Plymouth Brethren notables, including F. C. Bland and Henry Varley, and was also introduced to the writings of C. H. Mackintosh.

The Plymouth Brethren emerged out of Anglicanism in the 1820s, taking a primitivist approach to Christianity. The movement grew out of the concerns of four men—John Nelson Darby, Edward Cronin, John Bellett, and Francis Hutchinson. During the winter of 1827–28, they began meeting in Francis Hutchinson's home in Dublin, Ireland, to practice their new convictions, coming together on the Lord's Day and remembering the Lord Jesus in the breaking of bread. This simple service, patterned after the New Testament church, was the product of several years of study in which the four men compared what they found in the Bible with what they saw in the Church of England. They concluded there was no biblical justification for a national church or even for various dissenting bodies. They rejected some Anglican practices, including a distinct clergy and its accompanying ecclesiastical structure, as well as elements of the liturgy. This conviction led them to withdraw from the Church of England to practice their simple form of faith. The movement spread in Dublin and eventually to England. The group began to flourish in Plymouth in the early 1830s and people in the area began to call them "brethren from Plymouth," eventually becoming known simply as the Plymouth Brethren. When the Brethren split in the 1840s, Darby emerged as the leader of the Exclusive Brethren.[155]

John Nelson Darby was born to a wealthy Anglo-Irish family on November 18, 1800.[156] Despite his father's objections, Darby pursued a career in the Anglican Church, was ordained as a deacon in 1825, and became a priest in 1826. Darby was installed as curate in Calary, near Enniskerry, County Wicklow, and reportedly distinguished himself for his successful ministry among the Roman Catholic peasants of his parish. Throughout these years, Darby remained spiritually restless, at one point flirting with Roman Catholicism. Later he described himself as looking "for the Church. . . . I too, governed by a morbid imagination, thought much of Rome, and its professed sanctity, and catholicity, and antiquity. I held apostolic succession fully, and the channels of grace to be there only."[157] Shortly after his brief consideration of Catholicism, Darby left the Anglican Church and eventually joined the newly formed Brethren movement.

Under Darby's tutelage, the Plymouth Brethren became known for their unique practices and doctrinal emphases, such as the authority of the Bible, an instantaneous conversion experience, and premillennialism. Darby and the Brethren have been described as preaching the "absolute inerrancy of the Scriptures."[158] For example, in his synopsis of 1 Timothy, Darby wrote, "The scriptures are the permanent expression of the mind and will of God furnished as such with His authority . . . but this is not all—they are inspired. It is not only that the truth is given in them by inspiration. It is not this which is here stated. They are inspired."[159]

This belief concerning the inspiration and reliability of the text was coupled with a robust conception of perspicuity and a literal hermeneutic. Darby had begun studying the Bible independently about 1820. This independent study became a critical component in his religious life. Darby's religious conversion stemmed directly from reading the Holy Scriptures alone or, as he put it, "independent of any assistance from man."[160] He therefore insisted "that individual Christians, not intermediaries, such as churches, priests, or pastors were qualified to act as the final arbiters regarding interpretation and appropriation of the Bible."[161] Individuals could derive the meaning of the text using a literal hermeneutic.[162]

Moody's relationship with John Darby was complicated. Commenting on Moody's work in Edinburgh in 1873, Darby wrote, "As to the work at Edinburgh, I dare say there may have been conversions, and one must bless God for that. But Moody before he came to England denied openly all work of grace in conversion, and denounced it as diabolical in his own pulpit."[163] Dorsett wrote of Darby, "One day while doing a Bible reading time at Farwell Hall in Chicago he and Moody had a verbal exchange on free will. The session ended when Darby, in disgust with Moody's emphasis on 'whosoever will may come,' closed his Bible and walked out; and he never returned."[164] Earlier, Robert T. Grant, a Brethren evangelist, had been sent to Chicago to proselytize. His report to Darby stated, "Moody is quite in a pet about so many of them leaving him who were his best workers."[165]

Despite Moody's conflict with Darby, the Brethren remained a force in Moody's life, shaping not only his hermeneutic and personal Bible study but also his understanding of inspiration. However, Darby was not the only Brethren leader to influence Moody's understanding of the Bible. Concerning C. H. Mackintosh, Moody wrote,

> I had my attention called to C. H. M.'s notes, and was so much pleased and at the same time profited by the way they opened up Scripture truth, that I secured at once all the writings of the same author, and if they could not be replaced, would rather part with my entire library, excepting my Bible, than with these writings. They have been to me a very key to the Scriptures.[166]

The Brethren also introduced Moody to a doctrine that would distinguish him from earlier American revivalists: premillennialism, or the doctrine of the imminent return of Christ. While we do not know precisely when Moody was first exposed to premillennialism, it is apparent that by the end of 1867, Moody had embraced premillennialism, and the doctrine became standard fare in his preaching.[167]

Dwight Moody was born about the time premillennialism was gaining strength in the British Isles and the United States, and he would play a critical role in its ascendance.[168] After Moody, virtually every prominent evangelist in the United States would espouse premillennial theology, including George Needham, W. J. Erdmann, Major D. W. Whittle, J. Wilbur Chapman, Leander Munhall, Reuben A. Torrey, and Billy Sunday. A similar pattern emerged among prominent pastors and leaders of the evangelical world missions movement, such as James H. Brookes, Robert Speer, A. T. Pierson, A. B. Simpson, A. J. Gordon, Charles Blanchard, and C. I. Scofield.[169]

At least four factors predisposed Moody to the premillennial position. First, given the difficulty of his boyhood, it is not surprising he would be drawn to a position that emphasized otherworldly hope. While he and his family emerged from the loss of his father, he had no illusions about other families who did not recover. Second, Moody knew the harshness of life most urban dwellers faced—the enormous problems in the cities and their seemingly overwhelming nature. Third, he saw the catastrophic effects of the Civil War. He tended to the dead and wounded, and saw the devastation and the lingering bitterness. Based on these experiences, it is understandable Moody would be drawn to premillennialism's pessimism concerning the trajectory of society. Fourth, men whom he deeply admired like Müller and Spurgeon were committed to premillennialism.[170] It is hardly surprising Moody became an enthusiastic proponent of the doctrine.

Premillennialism emerged in opposition to postmillennialism.[171] Postmillennialism was the dominant view in America from the time of the Puritans to early in the twentieth century, and was well established in England. According to Bebbington, in England, "the postmillennial theory was evidently widespread."[172] Men like William Carey, Thomas Chalmers, and others spread the view. A crucial work delineating the postmillennial view was David Brown's *Christ's Second Coming: Will It Be Premillennial?* (1846). In this work, Brown, who became the principal of the Aberdeen Free Church College, presented the classic view of postmillennial eschatology in England.[173]

Postmillennialism emphasizes the present aspects of God's kingdom that will come to fruition in the future. It asserts that the millennium will be ushered in through Christian preaching and teaching, resulting in a more godly, peaceful, and prosperous world where many economic, social, and educational problems will be solved. The new age will come about as more people are converted to Christ.[174]

By comparison, premillennialism asserts that the kingdom of Christ will be inaugurated in a cataclysmic and supernatural manner. The premillennialist believes the return of Christ will be preceded by declension, including wars, famines, and earthquakes. The Antichrist will appear, and there will be a great tribulation. These events will climax in the second coming, followed by a thousand-year reign by Christ and His saints that will be established suddenly and supernaturally rather than gradually through the conversion of individuals. The curse will be removed from nature, and even the desert will produce abundant crops. Jewish people will be converted in large numbers and will again have a prominent place in God's work. Christ will restrain evil during this millennial rule. Despite the idyllic conditions of the golden age, there will be a final rebellion of wicked people, followed by a final judgment, when humans will be consigned to heaven or hell.[175]

At first blush, it might appear logical for premillennialists to shy away from social agendas. They could perhaps be uncaring or even fatalistic about the affairs of this world because of their belief that real improvement can only take place after the second coming. In fact, premillennialists maintain that things must get worse before they get better—that wars, pestilence, and chaos must precede the second coming. By contrast, postmillennialists could logically become paternalists or activists in world affairs because of the crucial role of human involvement in building the New Jerusalem. In practice, though, premillennialists have responded to social needs in various ways. One notable variance appeared between the premillennial approach to social issues in the United Kingdom and the United States.

In *Age of the Atonement*, Boyd Hilton pointed out an apparent role reversal between premillennialists and postmillennialists in the nineteenth century. He noted that some premillennialists, like Shaftesbury, were the ones to lead the call for social intervention in the United Kingdom.[176] Ralph Brown best explained this interventionist premillennialism in the United Kingdom. He pointed out that premillennialists in the United Kingdom were hardly monolithic on the question of social intervention due to the varied theological frameworks from which they approached the issue. These frameworks provided alternative ways of viewing the world, society, and the role and responsibility of individuals and the church. Thus, Brown concluded that premillennialism was less determinative than other theological convictions in explaining the behavior of Shaftesbury and similar premillennialists.[177]

However, in the United States, premillennialists took a more hands-off approach to social issues. Timothy Weber concluded that premillennialism often shied away from social concerns because of its "hopeless view of the present order."[178] In a similar vein, Martin Marty maintained, "Premillennialists often give up on the world before God does. . . . As a result, the social conscience of an important part of American evangelicalism has atrophied and died."[179]

However, there are three caveats concerning Moody's premillennialism. First, as we have seen, Moody's initial exposure to the doctrine was to the British variety. This experience may help to explain why some of his British colleagues were more activistic than Moody.[180] Second, both Weber and Marty's comments are specific to a mature form of premillennialism.[181] In the early twentieth century, premillennialism in America became entangled in the modernist/fundamentalist debates and reflected the militant separatism of the fundamentalist movement in its maturity.[182] On the other hand, Moody interacted with American premillennialism in its infancy, when it was less inclined toward militancy. Third, though American premillennialists tended to avoid engaging with social ills, they were hardly uniform in this stance. Weber identified three different responses within American premillennialism. Citing Jonathan Butler's study of the Adventist movement, Weber argued that the categories Butler used for Adventists applied to premillennialists as well.[183]

Butler defined the first category, *apolitical apocalyptic*, as those who withdraw from political issues and involvements. Weber cited James

Brookes as an example of this position. Brookes was a pastor in St. Louis who became a close friend of Moody. Moody would later recruit Brookes to write a title for a series on premillennialism.[184] Brookes would also mentor C. I. Scofield for several years after Scofield's conversion.[185] Brookes made his position clear in an address to other premillennialists in 1880: "Well would it be if the children of God were to keep aloof from the whole defiling." He added that, since believers were "dead to the world," they should stay out of all political involvement, even voting, since "dead men don't vote."[186] However, Brookes's position was the minority position among American premillennialists.[187]

Butler called the second position *political apocalyptic*. He populated this category with those who are politically engaged, but purely for the purpose of verifying their position. These premillennialists engage in a kind of self-fulfilling prophecy. They are observers rather than regular participants. Their interaction is limited by their firm belief that the current age is in inevitable decline.[188]

Butler's final group, called the *political prophetic*, assumed social and political responsibility. However, their involvement in these realms is highly selective and emphasizes individualistic and moralistic short-term goals. In other words, those who fit into the *political prophetic* category tend to eschew long-term programs that are attempting a social transformation. They do believe they can effect some essential change, but they also think that any long-term attempt at transformation will prove to be doomed until the return of Jesus.[189]

One thing is clear: the premillennialism with which Moody interacted was not monolithic, and there were a variety of approaches to social ills among its followers. Moody closely interacted with proponents of the different methods, and, as we shall see in the next section, Moody's premillennialism was not thoroughly developed. Nonetheless, while Moody did not articulate a nuanced premillennialism, he was a man of action, and as we shall see in future chapters, his behavior fits best with the *political prophetic* category. Therefore, while it is evident that premillennialism shaped Moody, it was just one among a host of theological influences. Premillennialism must be seen as one of several doctrines shaping his social ills approach.

Charles Spurgeon

Another premillennialist to whom Moody had a particular attraction was Charles Spurgeon. Dorsett went so far as to describe Spurgeon as Moody's "hero," while David Bebbington called Moody "one of Spurgeon's most ardent admirers in the United States."[190] This assessment was reinforced in an 1881 letter from Moody to Spurgeon. He wrote, "I have for years thought more of you than any other man preaching on this earth."[191] From the time of his conversion, Moody claimed to have heard of Spurgeon. He also claimed that "everything I could get hold of in print that he ever said, I read."[192] This is particularly telling given Moody's general lack of reading.[193] When Moody arrived in England in 1867, Spurgeon's Metropolitan Tabernacle was one of the first places he went. Finding he could not get in without a ticket, Moody determined to find a way in and ended up in the gallery, soaking in Spurgeon's every word. As Moody described it, when Spurgeon "walked down to the platform, my eyes feasted upon him, and my heart's desire for years was at last accomplished."[194]

Moody followed Spurgeon for several more days, listening to Spurgeon speak during a series of special meetings at the Agricultural Hall.[195] Moody endeared himself to Spurgeon, and the two ended up spending four days together, a remarkable amount of time given Spurgeon's schedule. At the end of the trip, Moody is purported to have said, "He sent me back to America a better man."[196]

The 1867 trip to Spurgeon's church would be the first of many such visits by Moody. Each time, Moody demonstrated his high regard for Spurgeon. Moody went to the Tabernacle again in 1872, remarking, "I thought I would come back over again to learn a little more."[197] In 1874 and 1875, Spurgeon wrote to Moody inviting him to speak at the Tabernacle. In response to Spurgeon's 1874 request, Moody replied, "In regards to coming to your Tabernacle, I consider it a great honor to be invited; and in fact I should consider it an honor to black your boots."[198] Spurgeon spoke at Moody's campaign in 1875.[199] Moody agreed to speak again at the Tabernacle in 1881 and remarked, "I do not know of a church in all the land that I shrink from as I do from yours; not but what your people are in sympathy with the gospel I preach, but you can do it so much better than I can."[200] Speaking at the Tabernacle in 1884, Moody noted, "I have been here a great many times since (1867), and I never come into the building without getting a blessing to my soul."[201] Dorsett concluded that Moody "studied at Spurgeon's feet whenever he visited Britain."[202]

The feeling of admiration Moody held for Spurgeon was mutual. Spurgeon defended Moody's work.[203] Speaking publicly about Moody, Spurgeon said,

> I want you now to hear me a moment while I say the brother who is about to speak, Mr. Moody, is one whom we all love. He is one whom we not only all love, but he is evidently one whom God loves. We feel devotedly grateful to Almighty God for raising him up and for sending him to England to preach the gospel to such great numbers with plainness and power. We shall continue to pray for him when he has gone home. Among the things we shall pray for will be that he may come back again. I might quote the language of an old Scotch song with regard to Prince Charlie—"Bonnie Moody's gaun away, Will ye no come back again? Better loved ye canna be, Will ye no come back again?"[204]

Moody was even a guest in Spurgeon's home. In fact, Spurgeon rearranged his schedule to accommodate Moody's schedule.[205] When Spurgeon died in the early 1890s, his widow, Susie, sent Moody a duplicate of his pulpit Bible with the following inscription.

Mr. D. L. Moody from Mrs. C. H. Spurgeon,

In tender memory of the beloved one gone home to God. This Bible has been used by my precious husband and is now given with unfeigned pleasure to one in whose hands its blessed service will be continued and extended.

S. Spurgeon, Westwood,

November 20, 1892[206]

In fact, Mrs. Spurgeon sent Moody two Bibles. In addition to his pulpit Bible, she sent him a copy of Spurgeon's study Bible. In this Bible, Spurgeon had marked in red passages that he had preached. In William Moody's biography of his father, he notes that after Moody received it, as he prepared a sermon, he constantly checked that Bible first to see if Spurgeon had preached the text. If he had, Moody would immediately look it up in the collection of Spurgeon's sermons.[207]

Moody clearly looked to Spurgeon as a model for ministry and as a theological sounding board. He read Spurgeon, carefully observed Spurgeon, and checked his sermons against Spurgeon. No other figure influenced Moody in this way. That is not to say Moody had blind allegiance to Spurgeon. On the contrary, Moody would never adopt Calvinism like Spurgeon, and he was not above criticizing elements of Spurgeon's ministry.[208] However, Moody made it a point to see Spurgeon whenever he was in the United Kingdom. Further, by Moody's testimony, he began reading Spurgeon shortly after arriving in Chicago and continued reading him throughout his life. Spurgeon is probably the only person he consistently read; therefore, it is reasonable to assume Spurgeon played a significant role in Moody's thinking. For this reason, Spurgeon's social vision, as well as his understanding of conversion, premillennialism, pneumatology, and the Bible, warrants a somewhat more extended examination.

Given the shape of their early lives, a friendship between Moody and Spurgeon seemed quite unlikely. Born in 1834, Spurgeon, unlike Moody, was reared in the evangelical Protestant faith.[209] As a boy, he lived with his paternal grandparents, and his grandfather was a minister. Also, unlike Moody, Spurgeon began reading at an early age. Patricia Kruppa wrote that "his first playthings were books, and even before he could read he was put in a chair, given a copy of *The Evangelical Magazine* to examine, and admonished to remain quiet and not to disturb his grandfather."[210] While Spurgeon's youth was inundated with works such as *Foxe's Book of Martyrs* and *Pilgrim's Progress*, his conversion occurred later due to a lay minister's sermon at a Primitive Methodist church in 1850.[211] Though Spurgeon's doctrinal position for the majority of his ministry was Baptist with a Puritan heritage, Spurgeon would frequently allude to that snowy morning that he spent in the Methodist church.[212] Spurgeon's ascent to the pulpit seemed the logical ending given his rearing in many ways.

Spurgeon espoused premillennialism and Calvinism; he also preached extensively on the Holy Spirit. In sermons from 1859, Spurgeon asserted that the Spirit's work in the believer does not come to an end at conversion. As he put it, "The acceptable acts of the Christian's life, cannot be performed without the Spirit."[213] In the 1864 sermon "The Superlative Excellence of the Holy Spirit," Spurgeon challenged his hearers: "Do not say that we want money; we shall have it soon enough when the Spirit touches men's hearts. Do not say that we want buildings, churches, edifices; all these may be very well in subservience, but the main want of the

Church is the Spirit, and men into whom the Spirit may be poured."[214] This absolute need for the Spirit by the church and the individual believer was a constant refrain in Spurgeon's sermons and writings until his death in 1892.[215]

Spurgeon was particularly concerned about the role of the Holy Spirit in ministry. He was adamant about this when speaking to his charges at his Pastor's College, which he founded in 1857. In 1877, as part of his Friday afternoon lectures, he noted, "The Holy Spirit is absolutely essential. Without Him, our office is a mere name. . . . We ought to be driven forth with abhorrence from the society of honest men for daring to speak in the name of the Lord if the Spirit of God rests not upon us. . . . Little wonder that the root cause of many useless ministries lies in the lack of distinctly recognizing the power of the Holy Ghost."[216]

Spurgeon was not just a preacher; he was active in his community. Spurgeon's approach to social activity was unique. Generally, social concern was displayed in three distinct ways in Victorian Britain: individual charity, reform, and calls for restructuring society.[217] Of these three options, Spurgeon falls into the first. Yet he and the Metropolitan Tabernacle maintained a remarkable record of community involvement. Specifically, they provided training for poor ministers, an orphanage, a book distribution society, an almshouse, and numerous societies and missions. In addition, Spurgeon supported public education, Shaftesbury's schools for the poor, temperance movements, and suffrage for the poor. Moreover, he preached against slavery, imperialism, and war. On a personal level, he spent one day a week going door-to-door with a Bible and a pocket full of shillings ministering to the community.[218]

David Nelson Duke argued that theology grounded Spurgeon's response to the social ills of London. Specifically, Duke maintained that Spurgeon's actions are traceable to three theological pillars: absolute devotion to God in Christ; the salvation of individual souls; and the belief that a distinct Christian character develops from the new nature found in Christ.[219]

By "absolute devotion to Christ," Spurgeon meant living and acting in a way that glorifies God and extends His kingdom. In applying this principle to social ills, Spurgeon said, "Be on the side of temperance and sobriety; be on the side of peace and of justice; be on the side of everything that is according to the mind of God, and according to the law of love."[220] Elsewhere he proclaimed, "God grant that the day may come when the mischievous division between the secular and the religious things be no more heard of, for in all things Christians are to glorify God."[221] For Spurgeon, this extended into the realm of politics. He reasoned that Christians should use even their citizenship for Christ's glory.[222]

Though Spurgeon was premillennial, his Christianity was not otherworldly. Christians were meant to glorify God by obeying Him in life; the commands to feed and clothe the poor or care for widows and orphans could hardly be fulfilled in heaven. Consequently they must be observed in the world where these evils exist.[223] As Duke put it, for Spurgeon, "care for one's fellow human beings was not a secondary item for Christians, something to be done if time remained after church activities and private devotions. It was a daily obligation commanded by God, a duty one abandons at one's eternal peril." He then cited Spurgeon, "The chief business of one whom God has called is that he should live as the elect of God."[224] It is hardly surprising Spurgeon named his magazine *The Sword and the Trowel; A Record of Combat with Sin and Labour for the Lord.*

Duke calls Spurgeon's second pillar the "concern for the salvation of individual souls." The key to understanding this lies in what Spurgeon meant by salvation. Spurgeon was a thoroughgoing Calvinist. To use theological terms, Spurgeon was not interested in mere justification; he was interested in justification and sanctification. Speaking to a group of people converted under Moody's ministry, he remarked, "Salvation from hell is not the salvation they ought to cry after, but salvation from sin."[225] For Spurgeon, salvation involves the transformation of the person. He was not given to counting converts or devising methods to get professions of faith. Instead, Spurgeon was concerned with the totality of a person's life.[226]

Moreover, Spurgeon saw the poor as the focus of evangelism. In a sermon from January 1857 titled "Preaching for the Poor," Spurgeon said, "It is a mark of Christ's gospel that the poor are gospelized—that they can receive the gospel. True it is, the gospel affects all ranks, and is equally adapted to all; but yet we say; 'If one class can be more prominent than another, we believe that in the Holy Scripture the poor are most of all appealed to.'"[227] Later, speaking to the men at his Pastor's College, he said, "The world is full of grinding poverty, and crushing sorrow; shame and death are a portion of thousands, and it needs a great gospel to meet the dire necessities. Do you doubt it? Go and see for yourself."[228]

This helps explain Spurgeon's decision to start an orphanage, his zeal for relief for the poor, and his support of Gladstone's Liberal party.[229] Although he had been a moderate imbiber of alcohol, Spurgeon came to back abstinence.[230] However, his response to war was the most striking illustration of his concern for individual souls. He believed war diverted resources away from children and the poor.[231] Further, the carnage appalled him. Although not a pacifist, his criticism of war was graphic and visceral.

> Ever see a man's head smashed, or his bowels ripped open?
> Why if you are made of flesh and blood, the sight of one poor
> wounded man, with the blood oozing out of him will make
> you feel sick. . . . Where's your hearts [sic] if you can think of
> broken legs, splintered bones, heads smashed in, brains blown
> out, bowels torn, hearts gushing with gore, ditches full of blood,

and heaps of limbs and carcasses of mangled men? Do you say my language is disgusting? How much more disgusting must the things themselves be? And you make them! . . . [The souls of soldiers] are as precious in God's sight as yours, they suffer as much pain when bullets pierce them as ever you do; they have homes and mothers and sisters. . . . Before the deep curses of widows and orphans fall on you from the throne of God, put up your butcher knives and patent men-killers, and repent.[232]

Spurgeon's comments echo Moody's. These men were not merely engaging in hyperbole; their comments were based on firsthand experience. Moody saw the slaughter of the American Civil War. Spurgeon spent time visiting prisoners and the wounded from both sides during the Franco-Prussian War.

Spurgeon's third theological pillar was the belief that a distinct Christian character develops from the new nature found in Christ. Spurgeon conceived of Christianity as an inside-out religion. On this point, Spurgeon's affinity with the Puritans is evident. He believed that Christian practice is the inevitable product of Christian conversion and that those who are genuinely converted will live the faith. Functionally this meant that true Christians love their neighbors.[233] As he explained in a sermon:

Many of the sermons of Christ—and what sermons shall compare with them—have not what is now currently called "the gospel" in them at all. Our Saviour did not every time he stood up to preach declare the doctrine of election, or of atonement, or of effectual calling, or of final perseverance. No, he just as frequently spoke upon the duties of human life, and upon those precious fruits of the Spirit which are begotten in us by the grace of God. Mark this word that I have just uttered. You may find I am correct in stating that very much of our Saviour's time was occupied in telling the people what they ought to do towards one another.[234]

These theological beliefs drove Spurgeon's social actions. Thus, while Spurgeon was an individualist and a social conservative, he was ultimately a follower of the Bible. Spurgeon maintained that poverty was the product of individual moral failing. He was undoubtedly no social engineer. However, he knew what the Bible said about wealth, justice, widows, and orphans. Spurgeon spoke to these issues, and warned against equating wealth with righteousness.[235] He railed against the treatment of the poor. "Think," Spurgeon exclaimed, "how the poor are oppressed and ground down with awful poverty in many parts of this great city. Shall not God avenge the cry of starving women?"[236] Addressing the issue of voting, he said, "Whenever topics which touch upon the rights of men, righteousness, peace, and so on, come in my way, I endeavour to speak emphatically as I can on the right side. It is part of my religion to desire justice and freedom for all."[237]

Spurgeon is particularly instructive for understanding Moody. Moody deeply admired Spurgeon, and Spurgeon was someone he read regularly. Spurgeon functioned as a model for belief and practice for Moody. They were kindred spirits in their premillennialism, and when Moody was challenged on his premillennialism, he appealed to Spurgeon.[238] Moody saw Spurgeon working among the poor of London while maintaining that evangelism must be the priority of ministry. Moody knew Spurgeon believed mass conversions could only effect social change. Moody observed Spurgeon's commitment to the Bible and how Spurgeon sought personally to apply its teaching about the poor. Moody read and heard Spurgeon's insistence on the ongoing work of the Holy Spirit, especially concerning ministry. Therefore, as we shall see, it should not be surprising that many of Moody's ministries would hearken back to what he saw during his times with Spurgeon, especially Moody's emphasis on conversion, the Holy Spirit, and the poor.[239]

The Mildmay Conference and William Pennefather

Moody was also introduced to the Mildmay Conference in England during this trip. Seeing a need for prayer in London, Moody started a noon prayer meeting. Through these prayer meetings, he was brought into contact with the Mildmay Conference. The conferences, an annual gathering for Christian workers, were the result of the work of William Pennefather. Pennefather, an Irish Anglican and nephew of John Darby, was the minister of St. Jude's Mildmay Park. The conferences brought Moody into contact with most of the evangelical Anglicans and nonconformists. One of his most important contacts was R. C. Morgan. Morgan was a nonconformist who ran a periodical titled *The Revival*, which later became *The Christian*. Morgan's support through the magazine would be crucial during Moody's 1873–1875 campaign. In addition, Moody later invested in R. C. Morgan's British publishing firm, Morgan and Scott, which issued his sermons.[240]

The Mildmay Conference influenced Moody in three ways. First, it reinforced his emerging premillennialism. One of the conference themes was the impending return of Christ and the urgency for Christian service and personal holiness, themes that would be prevalent in Moody's work. Second, it provided a model for the Northfield Conference Moody organized in 1880.[241] By observing Mildmay, Moody was convinced of the value of conferences and learned how to develop similar ones. Third, the Mildmay conferences provided ideas for women's religious education. Specifically, Moody was impressed with Pennefather's work establishing an order of deaconesses in the Church of England. These women served among the poor by providing practical help and conducting Bible studies. The idea of training women for practical missions stayed with Moody, and when he returned to Chicago, he was instrumental in forming a similar endeavor there.[242] These experiences and his early conversations with General O. O. Howard were the origins of what would become a growing desire for women's religious education.[243]

Moody met Pennefather in a subsequent trip to Great Britain in 1872. Pennefather, then fifty-seven, deeply impressed the thirty-five-year-old Moody. This trip would be their only meeting. Later Moody would say, "I well remember sitting in yonder seat looking up at this platform and seeing the beloved Mr. Pennefather's face illuminated as it were with Heaven's light. I don't think I can recall a word that he said, but the whole atmosphere of the man breathed holiness. . . . I thank God that I saw and spoke with that holy man; no one could see him without the consciousness that he lived in the presence of God."[244]

The young Moody also impressed Pennefather. Pennefather believed London needed revival, and Moody was the man to lead it. He wrote Moody asking him to return. Pennefather's letter would be the impetus for the 1873–1875 revival, making Moody a household name.

THE FORMATION OF THE CHRISTIAN WORKER: 1871

"What a Mistake!" he said in relating the story to a large audience on the twenty-second anniversary of the great fire in that city in 1871, "I have never dared to think to give an audience a week to think of their salvation since."[245]

—DWIGHT MOODY

Ah, what a day!—I cannot describe it, I seldom refer to it, it is almost too sacred an experience to name—Paul had an experience of which he never spoke for fourteen years—I can only say God revealed Himself to me, and I had such an experience of His love that I had to ask Him to stay His hand.[246]

—DWIGHT MOODY

The year 1871 was a difficult but defining year for Moody. By the end of the year, Moody would have a renewed focus that would drive the rest of his life. The direction came from two very different but powerful events: the Great Chicago Fire and a powerful personal religious experience.

The Chicago Fire

The Chicago Fire of 1871 was arguably the worst urban disaster of the nineteenth century. It burned from the morning of October 8 until the 10th. On the first evening of the fire, Moody conducted a meeting in Chicago. Approximately 2,500 people were in attendance. Moody preached on Pilate from Matthew 27:22, "What then shall I do with Jesus which is called the Christ?" As the meeting ended, Moody challenged his listeners, saying they had a week before the next meeting to decide for Christ. The meeting ended with a hymn during which many noticed the sounds of fire engines.[247]

The Chicago fire department proved to be no match for the fire raging through the city. By the time it was over, Chicago had been decimated. Property damages were estimated at over $190 million. Over 100,000 people were homeless, about one-third of the city's population. The fire had consumed over three and a half square miles of the city, making it twice the size of the 1666 London fire. The fire reduced eighteen thousand buildings and fifty churches to ashes.

The coroner reported finding 127 bodies. However, this count was far from accurate, as many were simply incinerated, leaving no trace of their demise. Many others drowned in the Chicago River or Lake Michigan, trying to avoid the conflagration. Most of these bodies were never recovered. City officials finally estimated the total death toll to be around three hundred. However, this number was also guesswork; many of the dead came from the city's poorest areas, where records were sketchy at best. Further, many were immigrants, some with no family ties.[248]

Moody survived the conflagration but not unscathed. Although he and his family escaped harm, his ministry did not fare well. The YMCA and the Sunday school were destroyed, and the flames claimed his own home. His daughter Emma recalled Moody poking through the house's ashes with his cane and finding only a toy iron stove of hers.[249]

The net effect of the fire on Moody was threefold.[250] First, Moody was no longer bound to Chicago. In a sense, he was now free to pursue a much larger venue in which to ply his skills. Second, it brought a new urgency to his evangelism. He described his handling of the meeting the night of the fire as one of the biggest mistakes of his ministry career. Moody often wondered how many of those 2,500 people died that night or the next day in the fire. He later said, "I want to tell you of the one lesson I learned that night: . . . that is, when I preach, I press Christ upon the people then and there and try to bring them to a decision on the spot. I would rather have that right hand cut off than to give an audience now a week to decide what to do with Jesus."[251] Third, it provided focus. Moody began to concentrate on evangelism. One of his later sermons reflected this commitment: "Concentrate your life upon some one thing and it will cut a channel so deep that your influence will be felt."[252]

Baptism in the Holy Spirit

Immediately after the fire, Moody threw himself into raising funds for the rebuilding of his church and the YMCA. A letter from New York dated November 24, 1871, typified the kinds of monetary appeals Moody was making. In the letter, Moody described the "sad state of things in Chicago so far as the spiritual work." He wrote of churches and missions in ashes, including his work. Reflecting his difficulties, he stated, "I have no earthly possessions and apply to those in sympathy with God's work who have the means of helping." He concluded his appeal, "My plan is to raise $50,000 and put up a Tabernacle to accommodate seven or eight burnt out missions."[253]

Eventually Moody went to New York personally to raise funds. While there, Moody began to struggle spiritually. Although he received generous support from many in New York, he remarked, "My heart was not in the work of begging, I could not appeal."[254] Along with the external effect of the fire, Moody was struggling internally. William describes his father as "crying all the time that God would fill [him] with His Spirit."[255] A close confidant wrote later in his diary, "For a year or more before Moody left for Chicago he was continually burdened and crying to God for more power."[256] Looking back on that time later, Moody described himself as being in a "cold state." He felt that "it did not seem as if there was any unction resting on his ministry." Moody talked of God "just showing me myself" over a period of four months. He confessed to "preaching for ambition" rather than "preaching for Christ." He concluded, "For four months a restling went on in me. I was a miserable man."[257]

Moody's rhetoric bears a striking resemblance to Spurgeon's exhortations and denotes Spurgeon's influence on Moody. Specifically, Moody's self-professed lack of unction and power hearkens back to Spurgeon's assertion that much ministry was ultimately useless because it was not being done in the power of the Holy Spirit. The Baptist preacher from London cast a long shadow over the American evangelist.

Ironically, while the staunchly Calvinist Spurgeon shaped Moody's understanding of his spiritual burden, two Free Methodist women from Chicago were instrumental in lifting that burden. The two women, Sarah Cooke and Mrs. W. R. Haxwurst, attended a Free Methodist camp meeting during the summer of 1871. During one of the meetings, Cooke reported that "a burden came upon me for Mr. Moody, that the Lord would give him the Baptism of the Holy Ghost and of fire."[258] After listening to Moody preach for weeks, they approached him and told him, "We have been praying for you." Somewhat miffed, Moody replied, "Why don't you pray for the people?" Their response was, "Because you need the power of the Spirit."

Moody later recalled his reaction. "I need the power! Why, I thought I had power. I had the largest congregations in Chicago, and there were many conversions. I was in a sense satisfied."[259]

However, the women kept up their prayer vigil and constantly urged him to seek extraordinary power from the Holy Spirit.[260] Eventually, persuaded of their sincerity, Moody agreed to sit down with the women. According to Torrey, the women introduced Moody to the concept of baptism in the Holy Spirit.[261] Because of that conversation, Moody agreed to pray with the women concerning the matter. He described the event in the following manner: "There came a great hunger into my soul. I did not know what it was. I began to cry out, as I never did before. I really felt that I did not want to live if I could not have this power for service."[262] Cooke described Moody as being in such great agony "that he rolled on the floor and in the midst of many tears and groans cried to God to be baptized with the Holy Ghost and fire."[263]

This yearning finally came to a head in New York. Moody described the event as follows:

> It came upon me as I was walking in the streets of New York. Many a time I have thought of it since I have been here (England). At last I had returned to God again and was wretched no longer. I almost prayed in my joy, "Stay Thy hand" I thot this earthen vessel would break. He filled me so full of the spirit. If I had not been a different man since I do not know myself. I think I have accomplished more in the past four years than in all my life. But oh it was preceded by a wrestling and a struggle. . . . There was a time when I wanted to see my little vineyard, Chicago, blessed and

I could not get out of it. But I could work for the whole world now. I would like to go around the world and tell the perishing millions of a Savior's love.[264]

Moody's experience was just the cusp of a burgeoning wave among evangelicals in the United States in the late nineteenth-century. C. I. Scofield would remark at the end of the century, "Within the last twenty years more has been written and said upon the doctrine of the Holy Spirit than in the preceding eighteen hundred years."[265] While certainly an exaggeration, Scofield's claim accurately reflects what was happening among evangelicals from the late nineteenth century until the First World War.[266]

As American evangelical interest in the work of the Holy Spirit developed, different positions began to emerge. Most evangelicals believed in a work of the Holy Spirit after conversion that was usually referred to as "baptism in the Holy Spirit." However, they disagreed on the meaning or purpose of this baptism. One group argued the purpose of the baptism was for holiness or eradication of sin. This position reflected the idea of personal purity or perfectionism and was rooted in the teaching of John Wesley. A second group, sometimes referred to as higher life or Keswick theology, maintained that the purpose of baptism in the Holy Spirit was power for service.[267] This group was predominantly rooted in the Reformed tradition.[268] By the end of the 1880s, these two were engaged in a strenuous battle for supremacy.[269]

As Moody indicated, this event, along with the fire, was the impetus for expanding his ministry beyond Chicago. It was the last step in his decision to become a traveling evangelist. His experience also fused Spurgeon's teaching on the necessity of the Holy Spirit for effective ministry with the conception of baptism in the Holy Spirit and brought him into the vortex of the swirling debates among evangelicals about the Holy Spirit's work.

CONCLUSION

As Moody looked to 1873, he determined to head to the United Kingdom. By the time he left, his theology was in place. It had been formed initially in the United States by the Christian charity he experienced as a boy in Northfield from the young Oliver Everett. Through the ministry of Edward Kirk in Boston, he was exposed to the revivalist evangelical tradition. The specter of the Civil War, and the nineteenth-century phenomena of urbanization, especially in Chicago, provided the context in which Moody synthesized these ideas. Moody's experience as a Christian worker with various nonsectarian evangelical movements and his relationships with men like O. O. Howard and John Farwell also contributed to this thinking. Moody's first trip to England added premillennialism, a conservative view of the Bible, and a new approach to Bible study learned from the Plymouth Brethren and the redoubtable Baptist preacher Charles Spurgeon. Evangelicals in Britain also allowed Moody to observe different types of ministries that he would seek to replicate later in his life. In short, British evangelicalism reinforced what he learned in America while adding new theological ideas and ministry models that would be a part of Moody's work for the rest of his life. The Chicago Fire would bring focus to Moody's life, and a second powerful religious experience energized this focus. With all of this in place, Moody set sail for Great Britain. By the time he returned, Moody would be one of the most famous men in the English-speaking world.

3

MOODY'S THEOLOGY

A Survey of His Basic Commitments

If a man should ask me up to his house for dinner tomorrow, the street would be a very good thing to take me to his house. But if I didn't get into the house, I wouldn't get any dinner. Now a creed is the road or street. It is very good as far as it goes, but if it doesn't take us to Christ, it is worthless. . . . Faith [is] in a person, and that person is Christ. It isn't a creed about him, but it is himself. [1]

—DWIGHT MOODY

He keeps close to the essentials, and is free from such crotchets as often narrow the sphere and destroy the influence of evangelists . . . he has stuck to simple old truths. [2]

—E. J. GOODSPEED

Some people would smash up a work like this in 24 hours. I have not come to preach this or that doctrine; I preach "the whosoever." Some are always asking, "why I don't specifically preach election or sanctification or baptism" or this or that. I would say to them, "Why don't you go and preach them yourselves?" [3]

—DWIGHT MOODY

The previous chapters examined the various factors that formed Moody's theology. Special attention was paid to contexts, individuals, and movements that shaped Moody's faith. In this chapter, there will be no attempt to sum up all of Moody's theological convictions or even place Moody relative to other evangelicals of his day. Instead, this chapter will focus on those parts of Moody's doctrine that drove his social vision. Those doctrines will be examined in detail, with the next chapter given to a demonstration of how these doctrines manifested themselves in Moody's social vision and social work. As such, this chapter seeks to explain the theological foundation for Moody's social vision fully.

Moody is a complicated figure to categorize theologically. He was not given to creedalism, denominationalism, or theological speculation, instead concentrating on practical religion.[4] Further, Moody was primarily an evangelist. As his son William pointed out, Moody "preferred to devote his energies to evangelistic work, yielding to the denominational churches the function of indoctrinating the Christian faith."[5]

Therefore, some have opined that Moody was indifferent to theology, did not like it, or possessed little of it.[6] However, this is simply not true. Moody did not believe that sincere faith alone was sufficient. He thought that faith must also have the correct object. This is where doctrine came into play. For example, at Northfield in 1899, he made the following statement:

> People have an idea now that it makes very little difference what a man believes if he is only sincere if he is only honest in his creed. I have had that question put to me many a time: "Mr. Moody, you don't think it makes any difference what a man believes if he is only sincere?" I believe that is one of the greatest lies that ever came out of the pit of hell. Why they virtually say

you can believe a lie just as well as you can believe the truth, if only you are earnest, you know and stick to it.[7]

Additionally, as early as the 1870s, Moody had preached sermons that laid out his concept of faith, which followed a traditional approach: knowledge, intellectual assent, and trust—what he referred to as "laying hold."[8]

By closely examining the life and work of Moody, a fundamental theological framework emerges. For our purposes, I will not attempt to provide a thorough survey of Moody's theology. Instead, in this chapter, I will concentrate on six essential elements that framed his social vision and work. First, Moody evidenced a profound understanding of the love of God. This was a core belief that became a defining doctrine for Moody. Second, Moody aggressively pursued a nonsectarian approach to religion. This approach was part of his strategy to broaden the gospel's impact. It also reflected his concept of love. Third, he demonstrated a deep commitment to the Bible and a literal hermeneutic. While Moody did not have a highly developed and nuanced doctrine of the Bible, he revered it and sought to make it normative in his life and work. Fourth, he embraced the revivalist evangelical tradition. Specifically, Moody taught salvation as the "Three Rs": Ruined by sin, Redeemed by Christ, and Regenerated by the Holy Ghost. This revivalism underscored his concept of conversion and put him in line with past evangelical revivalists. The fifth doctrine, the Holy Spirit's role in Christian service, and the sixth doctrine, premillennialism, served to separate him from earlier generations of revivalists. This chapter takes a close look at these six essential elements.

1. THE LOVE OF GOD

The sun is light, and can't help shining; God is Love, and he can't help loving.[9]

—DWIGHT MOODY

Love was the motive of his life, the essence of his religion, the center of his message, the incentive of his achievement and the secret of his power.[10]

—JOHN MCDOWELL

The love of God was a central theme of Moody's evangelistic preaching.[11] It was arguably the central theme of his life. In fact, as we shall see, love was the central tenet of his social vision. His doctrine of God's love hearkened back to what he saw and heard from Everett, Moorhouse, and Müller, and what he experienced in 1871. It was also grounded in the Bible.

Moody believed the central attribute of the Godhead is love. He wrote of the Holy Spirit,

> We read that the fruit of the Spirit is love. God is love; Christ is love. . . . What a blessed attribute is this. May I call it the dome of the temple of the graces. Better still, it is the crown of crowns worn by the Triune God. Human love is a natural emotion which flows forth towards the object of our affections. But Divine love is as high above human love as the heaven is above the earth. The natural man is of the earth, earthly, and however pure his love may be, it is weak and imperfect at best. But the love of God is perfect and entire, wanting nothing. It is as a mighty ocean in its greatness, dwelling with and flowing from the Eternal Spirit.[12]

For Dwight Moody, the God of the Bible was preeminently a God of love.[13] When he described heaven, he talked of the souls of the departed as drinking "from the living streams of love that roll by God's high throne."[14] Again, in the same work, he reiterated this point: "Another want that we feel here is love. Heaven is the only place where the conditions of love can be fulfilled."[15]

Moody saw the work of the Holy Spirit as predominantly displaying the love of God. Findlay wrote, "For Moody, the third person of the Trinity manifested himself in the world chiefly as the love of God shining in and through individual Christian lives. As he once put it: 'You can sum up all the fruits of the Spirit in one word—Love.'"[16]

Moody believed that love is a critical Christian virtue. He wrote, "Love is the badge that Christ gave His disciples. Some put on one sort of badge and some another. . . . But love is the only badge by which the disciples of our Lord Jesus Christ are known."[17] Moody believed the first impulse of a young convert is to love. It is also one of the first effects of conversion. In his words, "Do you remember the day you were converted? Was not your heart full of sweet peace and love?"[18]

Moody's comments on 1 Corinthians 13 illustrated the importance he placed on the virtue of love,

> I would recommend all Christians to read the thirteenth chapter of First Corinthians constantly, abiding in it day and night, not spending a night or a day there, but just go in there and spend all our time—summer and winter, twelve months in the year, then the power of Christ and Christianity would be felt as it never has been in the history of the world.[19]

Elsewhere he wrote, "The first of the graces spoken of in Galatians, and the last mentioned in Peter, is charity or love."[20]

Writing to the Chicago Avenue Church, he pleaded with its members to make love central in the congregation's life. He wrote, "I found a verse in 1 Peter, iv. 8, today. I never saw it before: 'Above all things put on love.'" He went on to urge them, "Think much of that one expression. Put it at the head of the list. Faith is good, but this is above it. Truth is good: but what are we if we do not have love? May the dear church get such a flood of love from on high that it will fill all our hearts."[21]

He expressed frustration with the evangelical church's lack of emphasis on this virtue. He wrote, "Now in this age, ever since I can remember, the Church has been very jealous about men being unsound in the faith. If a man becomes unsound in the faith, they draw their ecclesiastical sword and cut at him; but he may be ever so unsound in love, and they don't say anything."[22]

He addressed this again in a personal letter written to the Rev. Dr. W. J. Erdman, pastor of the Chicago Avenue Church. "I do hope you will hold the people to the thought of love. I am sure that is where the churches have all gone astray. We must have it above all things. Let us put that first. If the church is sound in love, I think it will be sound in everything else."[23]

As we shall shortly see, work was also among the core principles Moody emphasized, but it was subservient to love, which provided the only sound basis for work. Moody made this point emphatically and repeatedly. One of his most widely published sermons was simply titled "To the Work! To the Work!" In this sermon, Moody proclaimed,

> It is not always more work that we want so much as a better motive. Many of us do a good deal of work, but we must remember that God looks at the motive. The only tree on this earth that can produce fruit that is pleasing to God is the tree of love.[24]

Elsewhere, commenting on Romans 5:5, he reiterated the point, emphasizing the unique need for love in ministry. He maintained that a person might find success in law or medicine or business without love, but "no man can be a co-worker with God without love. If our service is mere profession on our part, the quicker we renounce it the better. If a man takes up God's work as he would take up any profession, the sooner he gets out of it the better."[25] Again, in a sermon published under the title "Charity," Moody argued that many ministers lacked converts in their ministry despite having excellent preaching skills because they did not have love as their motive. As he put it, "A man though he is deep in learning and theology, if he has no love in his heart, he will do no good." Moody then concluded,

> Is love the motive power that urges us to go out and work
> for God? This is the first question we ought to ask ourselves.
> Without it, a great deal of work will go for naught. The work
> will be swept away like chaff without it. Christ looks down and
> examines our hearts and actions, and although our deeds may
> be great in the eyes of the world, they may not be in His eyes.[26]

Moody reemphasized this point in 1881 in a work tellingly titled *Secret Power: Or, The Secret of Success in Christian Life and Work.*

> We cannot work for God without love. If I have no love for God
> nor for my fellow man, then I cannot work acceptably. We are
> told that the "love of God is shed abroad in our hearts by the
> Holy Ghost." Now, if we have had that love shed abroad in our
> hearts, we are ready for God's service; if we have not, we are not
> ready. It is so easy to reach a man when you love him; all barriers
> are broken down and swept away.[27]

In this same work, Moody went on to claim that "God cannot use many of His servants, because they are full of irritability and impatience. . . . Their mouths are sealed; they cannot speak for Jesus Christ, and if they have not love, they cannot work for God."[28]

Moody then went on to explain that, by love, "I do not mean love for those that love me; it don't take grace to do that. It takes the grace of God to love the man that lies about me, the man that slanders me, the man that is trying to tear down my character; it takes the grace of God to love that man." [29] As Moody understood it, Christian love was the supernatural ability to love the unlovely, especially those who were his enemies.

Moody believed this love was the product of the work of the Holy Spirit. As he put it, "The Holy Ghost is to impart love," and "The fruit of the Spirit, as you find it in Galatians, begins with love." This love was supernatural in origin, so he cautioned against people "trying to get this love; and . . . trying to produce it of themselves. But therein all fail." He maintained, "When the Holy Spirit kindles love in your heart, you cannot help loving God; it will be spontaneous. . . . When the Spirit of God comes into your heart and mine, it will be easy to serve God." He concluded, "Some one comes along and treats us wrongly, perhaps we hate him; we have not attended to the means of grace and kept feeding on the word of God as we ought; a root of bitterness springs up in our hearts; then we are not qualified to work for God." [30]

For Moody, love was a critical component in successful evangelism. As he explained it,

That is the key which unlocks the human heart. If I can prove to a man that I come to him out of pure love; if a mother shows by her actions that it is pure love that prompts her advising her boy to lead a different life, not a selfish love, but that it is for the glory of God, it won't be long before that mother's influence will be felt by that boy, and he will begin to think about this matter, because true love touches the heart quicker than anything else. [31]

In 1877, Moody exhorted his listeners, "Let the young men go plead with them, bring them to the Tabernacle, and don't let them go out without presenting the claims of Christ, and showing them His never-dying love." [32] In the same year, he told the following story.

Look what that teacher did in Southern Illinois. She had taught a little girl to love the Savior, and the teacher said to her: "Can't you get your father to come to the Sunday-school?" This father was a swearing, drinking man, and the love of God was not in his heart. But under the tuition of that teacher the little girl went to her father and told him of Jesus' love, and led him to that Sunday-school. What was the result? I heard before leaving for Europe that he had been instrumental in founding over 780 Sabbath-schools in Southern Illinois.[33]

Moody was unusual among revivalists in his lack of emphasis on God's wrath.[34] In fact, Moody placed God's wrath in the context of God's love. In his sermon "Love," he said, "It is because God loves the sinner that He gets angry with him," and God's anger "is one of the very strongest evidences and expressions of God's love."[35] This emphasis on love does not indicate that Moody denied the doctrine of eternal damnation; he simply found it unhelpful. He once remarked, "Terror never brought a man in yet."[36] Further, he saw love as God's method. Moody noted, "He [God] loves them in spite of their sin, and it is this love which, more than anything else, brings hard-hearted sinners to their knees."[37]

While Moody may not have believed the doctrine of hell had practical value as an evangelistic tool, it did serve as a motivating factor for his work. Preaching in the United Kingdom, he admitted, "If I believed there was no Hell, I am sure I would be off to-morrow for America." He added, "You would not find me here, going from town to town, spending day and night preaching and proclaiming the Gospel, and urging men to escape the damnation of Hell."[38]

Practically, his conception of God's love shaped his approach to theological debates. Moody avoided using harsh critiques in theological disputes, arguing that "Christ's teaching was always constructive."[39] Elsewhere, Moody claimed that Christians should follow Christ's example in dealing with error by largely ignoring it, thus "letting it melt away in the warm glow of the full intensity of truth expressed in love. . . . Let us hold truth, but by all means let us hold it in love, not with a theological club."[40] For Moody, most, if not all, of the issues of life should be viewed through the prism of God's love.

2. NONSECTARIANISM

For denominations he cared nothing; for Christianity he would give up his life. Every one believed in him, no matter of what faith or unfaith; all knew that Dwight L. Moody was an honest, sincere, devoted Christian.[41]

—*THE INDEPENDENT*, DECEMBER 28, 1899

I would like to know to what denomination the Savior would belong. I tell you, my friends, these denominational names do not come from on high. They are devices of the evil one.[42]

—DWIGHT MOODY

A dogged commitment to nonsectarianism characterized Moody's work. Three factors fed into this belief. First was his early experience with nonsectarian ministries, specifically the 1857–1858 revival, the Sunday school movement, and the YMCA. The second was his commitment to the doctrine of love, and the third was the trauma of losing his father.[43]

What Moody saw modeled as a young man in Boston and Chicago became a matter of conviction for the mature evangelist. An 1876 article in *Scribner's Magazine* described Moody's ideal mission: "It brings all the churches together upon common ground. The Presbyterian, the Baptist, the Methodist, the Episcopalian sit on the same platform. . . . They learn toleration for one another. More than this: they learn friendliness and love for one another. They light their torches at a common fire."[44]

One of Moody's reasons for nonsectarianism was his commitment to God's love. Moody believed the doctrine of God's love must mitigate sectarianism:

> Oh, yes, let us sink this party feeling and contend for Christ only. Oh, that God may so fill us with His love, and the love of souls, that no thought of minor sectarian parties can come in; that there may be no room for them in our atmosphere whatever; and that the Spirit of God may give us one mind and one spirit here to glorify His holy name.[45]

Further, in Moody's opinion, sectarianism undercut evangelistic efforts. Speaking in Chicago in the late 1870s, he addressed the issue, directly claiming a sectarian spirit had subverted the work in Chicago. Moody argued that Methodists, Baptists, and Presbyterians were condescending toward each other and more interested in converts to their denomination than to Christianity. He described this attitude as a significant stone hindering the work. He concluded, "Let us have none of that spirit in this meeting. Talk not of this sect and that sect . . . but solely and exclusively of the great comprehensive cause of Jesus Christ."[46]

An illustration from one of his sermons reinforced this point. Commenting on 1 Timothy 1:12, Moody told of a meeting between a dying soldier and a chaplain during the Civil War. The soldier asked the chaplain to what persuasion he belonged. The chaplain answered, "Paul's persuasion." The soldier replied by asking if he was Methodist, Presbyterian, or Episcopalian. The chaplain replied "no" to all these options, then said, "I am persuaded that He is able to keep that which I have committed unto Him against that day." Moody ended the story by proclaiming, "It is a grand persuasion; and it gave the dying soldier rest in a dying hour."[47]

Friendships with Roman Catholics

In addition to his wariness of Protestant sectarianism, Moody maintained many friendships with Roman Catholics—a stark contrast to many Protestant brethren. Josiah Strong spoke for many Protestants when he wrote in 1891,

> The growing spirit of charity which thinketh no evil, is slow to recognize the fact that most Roman Catholics are Catholics first and citizens afterward. The fact remains, however, and makes it possible to throw the Roman Catholic Church into a single political scale. Those who do not believe that the priesthood has both the power and the disposition to cast a substantially solid Catholic vote simply do not know what some others do know.[48]

Given this anti-Catholic sentiment among evangelicals, the cordial relationship Moody maintained with Roman Catholics was remarkable.

As previously discussed, Moody formulated this approach early during his time in Chicago, where he frequently reached out to Roman Catholics. One of the more interesting and illustrative events during the early years of the Sunday school was Moody's interaction with Bishop Duggin, the Roman Catholic prelate of the Chicago diocese. After having several meetings disrupted by Catholic boys from the area who were throwing stones through the meeting room's windows, Moody visited the bishop, who invited him to join the Roman Church. Moody declined, saying that he would not be allowed to work or pray with Protestants. The bishop replied that such would not be the case. Moody then asked to pray with him there in the bishop's home. They knelt in the bishop's hall together and prayed for Moody's Sunday school.[49]

A similar story comes from August Fry's 1955 BD thesis, which recounted his father's story. Fry's father grew up on Chicago's Near North Side during Moody's ministry in that part of the city. He recalled the

Irish boys in the neighborhood referring to Moody as "Father Moody" and how they all enjoyed the times he would stop by to share stories.[50]

Those early episodes would set the tone for Moody's interaction with the Roman Church and individual Roman Catholics throughout his ministry. During his career, he received what was, for those times, exceptional support from Roman Catholics. Moody made numerous preaching tours of the American East Coast. Cities like Brooklyn, Boston, Philadelphia, and New York contained large numbers of Roman Catholic immigrants, and the Roman Church in these areas generally welcomed Moody. *The Tablet*, a Northeastern-based Roman Catholic newspaper, provided evidence of this attitude in a lengthy editorial that was generally favorable toward Moody. It stated, "The work of Mr. Moody is not sin. It cannot be sin to invite men to love and serve Jesus Christ. It is irregular, unauthorized, but it may bring multitudes to a happier frame of mind, in which the Church may find them better prepared to receive her sublime faith."[51] It also published statements by some prominent Catholics in support of Moody.[52]

Moody also traveled to Ireland as part of his first campaign in the United Kingdom. He went straight to Dublin and ran a series of meetings for five weeks. He astonished the Irish by refusing to attack the Roman Catholic Church and, in turn, received a measure of support from the Roman Catholic newspaper in Dublin. The paper covered the meetings and editorialized,

> The deadly danger of the age comes upon us from the direction of Huxley and Darwin and Tyndall, rather than Moody and Sankey. Irish Catholics desire to see Protestants deeply imbued with religious feeling rather than tinged with rationalism and infidelity, and so long as the religious services of our Protestant neighbors are honestly directed to quickening religious thought in their own

body without offering aggressive or intentional insult to us, it is our duty to pay the homage of our respect to their conscientious conviction: in a word, to do as we would be done by.[53]

As a result, the mission produced a series of meetings described as "the most remarkable ever witnessed in Ireland."[54]

A personal letter Moody received in 1875 from a monk in Wales demonstrated a poignant illustration of the response by some in the catholic tradition. The monk's commitment is evident in his description: "I and my people are what you would call 'High-Lows,' for we are extreme Catholic and ritualists and have in our Houses the perpetual adoration of the holy sacrament." His admiration for Moody was evident as he wrote, "In these days of tribulation surrounded by rationalism and infidelity without, and secularism within, yours is a work to confound the one and break down the other." He concluded, "I have prayed and shall pray for a blessing upon you."[55] Moody believed this brother's prayer was one of the reasons his campaign was going so well.[56]

Moody's openness to evangelizing Roman Catholics continued throughout his life. In his published sermon "Love," Moody told of an imprisoned Roman Catholic archbishop who traced a cross in his cell. Moody concluded, "Ah, that Catholic bishop had been to Calvary. He could realize the breadth and length and depth and height of God's love, and that Christ gave Himself up freely for us all."[57]

In Northfield, he employed a Roman Catholic man who struggled with alcoholism. Moody worked with him and always encouraged him to attend the local Catholic church.[58] He made a personal donation to help the parish church in Northfield purchase a new organ.[59] His son Paul recounted the event in his biography of Moody in the following manner.

He gave a substantial donation to the Catholic Church when it was in the process of erection in Northfield and also an organ, and the dear old pinhead people attacked him in print and otherwise. For years afterward, he received letters, mainly from England, that he had been fellowshipping the anti-Christ, and they consigned him to the outmost hell. He chuckled over these.[60]

While Moody may have faced chastening from "dear old pinhead" Protestants, the local Catholic parish in Northfield displayed no rancor toward Moody. Indeed, when his mother died, the church asked "that they might furnish a pallbearer" as a token of respect.[61]

As late as January 1899, the year of his death, he wrote to his son-in-law, A. P. Fitt, about a planned book on the doctrine of the atonement. He noted that he was eager to get the book out, suggesting it would be "well to see what Luther, Wesley, Spurgeon and others said." He encouraged Fitt to get C. I. Scofield to help. He then wrote, "And I would get some strong statement from the Roman Catholic Church— the Episcopalian Church—and all the different denominations."[62]

However, it would be wrong to conclude Moody endorsed Roman Catholicism without criticism. As Gundry pointed out, Moody was not afraid to draw distinctions between himself and the Catholic Church on the essential issues of confession, priestly absolution, works, and the sacraments.[63] For Moody, the critical point was a person's relation to Jesus and their essential understanding of the gospel. He fittingly described his approach in 1898: "Now the way I get a Catholic I say everything good I can about them. There is such a thing as tact, and if you can say a good word for the Catholic Church, say it, and at the same time you want to put the truth in."[64]

In a memorial address he delivered shortly after Moody's death, F. B. Meyer likely summed up Moody's approach aptly: "What were Roman Catholics, or Congregationalists, or Baptists to him? The one thing he cared for was the glory of God. These were the things that attracted people."[65]

Friendships with Liberal Theologians

In the previous chapter, we noted the tensions developing among evangelical Protestants over the emergence of liberal theology. While it is true that the modernist-fundamentalist debates would not fully emerge until after Moody's death, differences were already noticeable, nonetheless. Despite the tensions, Moody maintained personal relationships within both parties.[66]

Moody maintained cordial relationships with Washington Gladden, Lyman Abbott, Henry Drummond, and William Rainey Harper while befriending R. A. Torrey, James M. Gray, A. T. Pierson, and A. C. Dixon.[67] These men reflected the spectrum of belief among Protestants. For example, some consider Washington Gladden, a Congregationalist minister, the father of the social gospel movement.[68] He embraced liberal Christianity and sought to bring it to bear on the social ills besetting America at the turn of the century. A Congregationalist like Gladden, Abbott combined liberalism and Darwinism to form an optimistic progressivism. He was fond of exclaiming, "What Jesus was, humanity is becoming."[69] Henry Drummond later authored one of the most famous books attempting to reconcile evolution with Christian doctrine, *The Ascent of Man*. William Rainey Harper was the first president of the University of Chicago. As a liberal, he was a devoted advocate of higher criticism.

On the other end of the spectrum was R. A. Torrey, a leader in the fundamentalist movement and a Congregationalist. Torrey served as president of the Moody Bible Institute and the Bible Institute of Los Angeles and conducted worldwide evangelistic tours. A prolific writer, Torrey was instrumental in the publication of *The Fundamentals*, a series of conservative booklets on the faith. James M. Gray, a Reformed Episcopalian, also served as president of Moody Bible Institute. He collaborated with Torrey on *The Fundamentals*. A staunch dispensationalist,

Gray also served as an editor of the *Scofield Reference Bible*. A. C. Dixon, a Baptist, was a resolute fundamentalist who vigorously objected to the methods of higher criticism. He is most noted for serving as pastor of Spurgeon's Tabernacle in London. Finally, a Presbyterian, A. T. Pierson, was active in the cause of foreign missions. As a contributor to *The Fundamentals*, Pierson was well known for his pietism and premillennialism.

An incident Washington Gladden recorded illustrates how Moody sustained these contradictory friendships. A dispute had broken out at Northfield between an evangelist and a higher critic. The cantankerous debate had moved into Moody's study. After listening to both men, Moody called them to prayer. He prayed, "God bless our brother higher Biblical critic and qualify him for his great work. God bless our brother listener and strengthen him for the load that has been laid upon him. God bless our brother accuser and give him more love. Amen." Gladden concluded, "That was the end of the matter."[70]

Nonsectarianism characterized Moody's revivals and distinguished the institutions he developed. For example, as the Illinois Street Church was formed, he determined it was to be an independent, evangelical church with "the most aggressive evangelism program in Chicago."[71] Commenting on the church's nondenominational status, Moody remarked, "If I thought I had one drop of sectarian blood in my constitution, I would open a vein and let it out."[72] Even the architecture reflected his views; the sanctuary contained both a baptistery and a baptismal font to provide for both adult and infant baptisms.[73]

His schools would be no different. All four in the United States were nonsectarian—two in Northfield, one in Mount Hermon, and Moody Bible Institute in Chicago. His remarkable openness to Roman Catholics was demonstrated especially at the two Massachusetts schools. Roman Catholics attended the schools, and the school newspapers contained stories celebrating the Jesuits, Ignatius Loyola, and Bernard of Clairvaux, among others.[74]

Centrality of the Local Church

It would be a mistake to conclude that Moody's nonsectarianism led him to dismiss the local church. Speaking to the leaders of the YMCA, he advised, "Do not, however, put the Association in place of the church; it is only a handmaid and a feeder of the church."[75]

In fact, in the 1879 Cleveland campaign, he began holding more meetings in churches rather than in large tabernacles. As he explained, "The plan of holding meetings in the tabernacle centralizes the interest and possibly draws out larger crowds, but the churches are the place to do effective work."[76] Moody believed the local church was the end of his work. As he put it, "No man in the world should be so happy as a man of God. It is one continual source of gladness. He can look up and say, 'God is my Father, Christ is my Savior, and the Church is my mother.'"[77]

Perhaps *interdenominational* is the best word to summarize Moody's attitudes—a better description than *nondenominational*. Moody was a man of conviction, but he was also a man with a generous spirit and a singular focus on evangelism. Lyman Abbott probably best summed him up when he said, "Not the least of the many services which Mr. Moody rendered to the age has been this practical demonstration that . . . a true Christian catholicity is always possible."[78]

3. THE BIBLE

He knew only two books, the Bible and Human Nature. Out of these he spoke; and because both are books of life, his words were afire with life.[79]

—HENRY DRUMMOND AND GEORGE ADAM SMITH

I have one rule about books. I do not read any book, unless it will help me understand the Book.[80]

—DWIGHT MOODY

An old writer said that some books are to be tasted, some to be swallowed, some to be chewed and digested. The Bible is one that you can never finish with. It is like a bottomless well; you can always find fresh truth gushing forth from its pages. . . . I thank God there is a height in the Book that I have never been able to reach, a depth that I have never been able to fathom.[81]

—DWIGHT MOODY

At a meeting held at Carnegie Hall in 1937 to celebrate the centenary of the birth of D. L. Moody, Henry Sloane Coffin gave one of three keynote addresses. Coffin had become friends with Moody at Yale and would later be a regular speaker at the Northfield conferences. After Moody's death, he became one of the leading spokespersons for Protestant Liberalism and served as president of Union Theological Seminary. He recounted a conversation he had while riding with Moody in his buggy in his address.

"Harry Coffin, do you swallow this higher critic stuff?"

I said: "Mr. Moody the evidence seems to me to indicate that the general outlines of it are correct."

He said: "Do you believe there were two Isaiahs?"

I said: "Well, it appears that the historical background indicates that parts of that book come from different situations."

"Well," he said, "that is what my dear friend, George Adam Smith thinks, but what is the use of talking about two Isaiahs when people do not know what one said?"

And then he pinched me on the knee—he had a way of doing that when you were next to him in the buggy—and said: "See here, it doesn't make much difference who wrote the book anyhow, God could have used a half dozen Isaiahs. The important thing is what is there—do you believe it? Do you live it? Will you teach it?"

With that came another pinch on the knee.

That was Moody (laughter).[82]

Coffin's version of the story seems to indicate that Moody's view of Scripture was somewhat pragmatic and ambivalent. At first glance, several pieces of evidence support this interpretation. First, there are numerous stories of Moody taking notes during lectures by scholars like George Adam Smith and William Rainey Harper. In addition, *Christian Century* attempted to cast Moody as a moderate in the 1920s.[83] What's more, his youngest son, Paul, in another *Christian Century* article, claimed his father was more in sympathy with men like Harry Fosdick than the fundamentalists.[84] Finally, as we have seen, Moody maintained cordial relations with many liberals. However, these facts reveal more about Moody's affection for individuals and his desire to avoid conflict than they give us insight into his beliefs.

Although some have expressed uncertainty about Moody's view of Scripture, his views reflect what he saw and heard during his interaction with Müller, Darby, and Spurgeon. Even if they were not articulated in a sophisticated fashion, as we shall see, his views paralleled theirs. Moody's belief in the Bible was the center of his life and work, so much so that a colleague and early biographer, J. Wilbur Chapman, claimed it was one of the "three cardinal truths with which his ministry was particularly identified."[85]

Moody's first formal statement on the Bible was found in the 1867 *Manual of the Illinois Street Independent Church*. The church grew out of Moody's Sunday school and was located on Illinois Street between LaSalle Boulevard and Wells Street. The statement of faith consisted of six articles. The second article read as follows: "We believe that the Scriptures of the Old and New testaments were given by inspiration of God, and are the only perfect rule of faith and practice."[86]

The *Manual* was the work of a committee. Specifically, "Messrs. D. L. Moody, J. H. Thayer, and J. H. Harwood were appointed to draft articles of faith and covenant for the proposed church."[87] While the actual wording might not be Moody's, he certainly shared their intent.

Moody was committed to the reliability of the Bible. In Boston, he said, "Men may go on scoffing and making light of the Bible, but you will find it out to be true by and by."[88] Writing to his son William in 1888, Moody expressed his frustration with those who called into question the reliability of the text.

> I cannot understand how Munger could differ with me about
> Jonah, for twice Christ says he was in the belly, so should he be
> in the bowels of the earth. I am sure Christ believed it, and so
> shall the servant, the master. I hope you will have the courage
> to stand up against any man who does not preach all the truth.
> I have little sympathy with any man who would attempt to
> undermine any man in the Bible.[89]

In a published sermon titled "What Is Christ to Us?" Moody noted, "People say this Bible was good enough for ancient days; but we have men of culture, of science, of literature now, and its value has decreased to the people of our day. These men want us to give up the Bible . . . the Bible of our fathers and mothers is true." He concluded the section by claiming, "Look at the history of the nations where the Bible has been trampled underfoot. Only a few years ago France and England were pretty nearly equal. England threw the Bible open to the world; and France tried to trample it. Now the English language is spoken around the world, and its prosperity has increased. But look at France. It has gone down and down with anarchy and revolution."[90]

Later, in 1894, commenting to a newspaper in Montreal, Moody said, "I notice if a man goes to cut up the Bible and comes to the one truth and says, 'I don't believe this and I don't believe that'—I notice that when he begins to doubt portions of the Word of God, he soon doubts it all."[91]

When interviewed by the *Boston Traveler* regarding his views on Scripture, Moody's reply was telling. "I cannot understand what these people mean who come to me and say that they cannot believe in the Old Testament, but can believe in the New. Now, both Testaments come from the Lord, and both are entitled to the same credence. . . . If you can't rely on this book, what can you rely on?"[92]

Clearly, Moody's understanding of scriptural reliability brought him into conflict with proponents of higher criticism.[93] However, as the Coffin story indicated, Moody often tried to avoid polemics on the subject. For example, his son Paul recounted a discussion with Moody regarding the divergent accounts of the death of Judas found in the Gospels. Moody's response to the problem was, "What difference does it make what happened to a rascal like Judas?"[94] While he avoided polemics, it would be wrong to conclude that Moody was unclear about his beliefs concerning the Bible. For example, when asked by a reporter to comment on the contention of a liberal preacher that the story of Jonah was a myth, Moody replied, "I stand by Jonah."[95] Preaching in Boston in 1877, he commented, "That is the kind of men we want nowadays—men who won't take and cut the Bible to pieces, like the king who took out his penknife and said, 'I don't like that. Cut that out. . . .' And so they cut and slashed away at the Bible until they haven't got hardly anything left."[96]

Because of his commitment to the Bible's reliability, he chose to live with a degree of ambiguity regarding complex issues. J. Wilber Chapman recounted a conversation that illustrated Moody's belief.

A man came to me with a difficult passage some time ago and said, "Moody, what would you do with that?" I answered, "I don't do anything with it." "How do you understand it?" "I don't understand it." "How do you explain it?" "I don't explain it." "Well, then, what do you do with it?" "I don't do anything with it." "But you believe it, don't you?" "O, yes, I believe it, but there are lots of things that I believe that I cannot understand and that I cannot make plain. I do not know anything about higher mathematics, but I believe in them, with all my heart. I do not understand astronomy, but I certainly believe in astronomy."[97]

In fact, Moody pointed to difficult passages as a kind of proof for the Bible's reliability.[98]

Not only was Moody committed to the reliability of the Bible, but he also saw it as authoritative. For Moody, the Bible rebutted all skeptics. When asked about the authority of the Bible, he remarked, "I am not here to defend the Bible; it will take care of itself."[99] Preaching in Boston, Moody remarked, "The Bible is a match for all infidels; that is the reason so many Christians are overcome by infidels because they do not know their Bibles well enough." Indeed, it was the final authority for Moody on all issues. As *The Free Church Monthly Record* put it, "An appeal to Scripture is with them [Moody and Sankey] the end to all controversy."[100]

Part of Moody's commitment to the Bible can be explained by what he believed about the Bible's role in human life. Specifically, Moody was a traditional Protestant; he thought that the Bible was the means God used to transform humanity. Thus, for Moody, the Bible was foundational. As a result, Moody composed the following list of how the Bible works in a person's life in *Notes from My Bible*, in a section called "What the Word of God Does."

1 Peter 1:23. By it, we are born again.

1 Peter 2:2. By it, we grow.

John 15:3. By it, we are cleansed.

John 17:17. By it, we are sanctified.

Psalm 119:105. By it, we get light.

Ephesians 6:17. By it, we are defended.

John 12:48. By it, man is judged.[101]

In the same work, his note on 1 Timothy 3:15 read, "Scripture knowledge is the candle without which faith cannot see to do its work."[102] At the end of the work, he expanded the "candle" theme in a section titled "The Candles of Scripture":

1. The candle of the law: Conscience. Proverbs 20:27; Ps. 18:28.

2. The candle of grace: Love. Luke 15:8.

3. The candle of Testimony: Life. Matthew 5:15.

4. The candle extinguished: Death. Job 18:6; 21:17.

5. The candle outshone: Glory. Revelation 22:5.[103]

Reflecting on his own life, Moody observed, "I wish I had spent a little more time during the first years of my Christian experience in studying the Bible."[104] While he may have lamented not spending a little more time, Moody tried to study the Bible immediately following his conversion. His early letters home reflect his study. For example, in a March 17, 1857, letter to his brother George, he wrote, "I hope you will holde on to the promises in the Bible . . . and God likes us to cling on as the Samest sais in one place God likes to chastise them whome he loves so let us pray for each other."[105] In an 1862 letter to his brother Samuel, Moody encouraged him, "You know the Bible says that if any man will be my disciple let him take up his cross & follow me."[106]

By all accounts, Moody had limited education and was hardly a voracious reader as a young man. We have seen how difficult it was for Moody to read the Bible. Nevertheless, the fact that he pushed himself to read it, and absorbed it enough that it became part of his vocabulary, indicated his commitment to the book. By 1861, he had picked up the habit of using a concordance to help with his study.[107] This habit would remain part of his mature study of Scripture.

By 1862, he was preaching up to three times a day. In a letter to his brother that same year, he lamented his lack of study: "I do not get 5 minutes a day to study so I have to talk just as it happens."[108] In his biography of Moody, Daniels describes these early sermons. "Though often founded upon a text of Scripture, [the sermons] were largely made up of personal incidents . . . appeals to Christians, inciting to greater activity; and earnest calls to sinners, urging them to repent and believe the Gospel."[109] We have seen how Moody attempted to make up for his lack of study by constantly plying those around him with Bible questions. One acquaintance recalled a dinner in Peoria, Illinois, during the Civil War. He remarked on Moody's "intense thirst for the knowledge of the Bible, for the entire dinner time was taken by Mr. Moody in quoting verses and in asking the ministers to tell him, 'What does this verse mean?'"[110]

Moody's personal study habits did improve. The 1867 trip to London provided the key for Moody's later private Bible study. Moody synthesized his teaching from George Müller with the instruction of others and eventually developed a multifaceted approach to studying the Bible that involved reading a single book through three separate times; first for the story, second for the thought, and third for the literary style. He also incorporated completely different methods, such as studying the Bible topically within a single chapter.[111]

Given his approach to Bible study, it is not surprising that his son wrote after his death, "He knew his Bible as very few have done, and was always wearing out Bibles, covering the margins with references and notes, and allowing them to pass freely among his friends. His Bible school and the Chicago seminary have filled hundreds of young minds with the same enthusiasm."[112] One cannot study the life of Moody and not gain an immediate sense of the central role Scripture played in his life.

The Bible played a prominent role in Moody's later letters. A survey of Moody's letters reveals a plethora of Bible references. One commentator goes so far as to claim that "in every piece of writing the Lord's name appeared; in all his conversations with intimate friends he praised the Lord and the Bible."[113] While probably an exaggeration, it cannot be far from the truth.

Moody's letters to his children also show the Bible's role in his relationship with them. Writing to his son William from Harrisburg, Pennsylvania, in January 1885, he urged, "I hope you grow up to love the Bible . . . and I would like to say of you as Paul did of Timothy, that from your youth you have known the scriptures for they are able to make you wise unto salvation."[114] A year earlier in London, he wrote to William, "I trust the new year before you will be the best year and that you will grow in all the graces, Galatians 5:22–23."[115] Later the same year, he wrote to William urging him to memorize Romans 8: "It is one of the grandest chapters in the Bible."[116] Finally, toward the end of the year, he urged both William and Paul to "learn Isaiah 57:15."[117]

Moody would use the same approach with his grandchildren. Shortly after the birth of his first grandchild, Irene, Moody presented her with a Bible. The inscription read,

> The Bible for the last forty years has been the dearest thing on earth to me, and now I give a copy as my first gift to my first grandchild, Irene Moody, with a prayer that it may be her companion through life and guide her to those mansions that Christ has gone to prepare for those who love and serve Him on earth.[118]

The Bible was at the forefront of Moody's revival work. One observer of his work in Scotland credited his reliance on the Bible in his work and preaching as one of the keys to his success among the Scots. He remarked, "The preaching won the Scotsmen's hearts by its loyalty to the Bible and its expository character."[119] Another account concluded, "It was said that Moody's preaching abounded with nothing so much as with the Scripture."[120]

Not only was the Bible crucial in his preaching, but it was also equally vital in personal work. He wrote, "If we are going to be successful, we must have hand to hand work, singling out some one person at a time and presenting to them the truths of the Bible."[121]

The Bible played a critical role in Moody's educational enterprises. John McDowell, commenting on the Northfield schools, made this clear: "[Moody] made the Bible central in all the work of his schools, going so far as to put a Bible in the cornerstone of every major building erected on the campus of the Northfield Schools." McDowell maintained that three principles drove all of Moody's schools. The third principle was that "the schools were to embrace the Bible as their foundation. . . . [Moody] declared more than once that were it not for Christ and the Bible the Northfield Schools never would have existed."[122] McDowell's assertion is supported by the first seminary announcement, which stated, "The Bible is intended to form the basis not only of the belief but of the life, of the institution."[123]

What was true for the Northfield enterprise was doubly true for the Bible Institute in Chicago. Describing his vision for the school, Moody said, "Give them [the students] plain English and good Scripture. It is the sword of the Lord and cuts deep." He envisioned a typical day as mornings given to Bible lectures while the afternoon and evenings consisted of preaching and other evangelistic meetings throughout the city.[124]

Moody believed the Bible was crucial in sustaining conversions and sobriety. He was fond of saying, "This book will keep you from sin, or sin will keep you from this book," and "The Word alone makes us sure."[125] In the late 1870s, he said, "I have noticed a great many that have been brought out commence right off to study their Bible; but those who have been brought out, and do not study their Bible, do not love their Bible, I notice they have turned back."[126] In the same revival, he said, "I pity those young converts who do not get in love with their Bibles. If you hear these skeptics and scoffers all the time, before you know it you will begin to believe what they say and be just like them; but if you do believe your Bible, the more they attack it, the more they scoff at it the more you will love it."[127] Shortly after his triumphant return from the United Kingdom in 1875, Moody wrote an open letter to new converts printed in *The Christian* magazine. In part, the letter read, "Do not above all, forsake your Bibles."[128]

This commitment to Scripture is partly explained by Moody's belief in the moral power of the Bible. He once remarked, "The more refined, as a rule, people are, the fonder they are of flowers, and the better they are, as a rule, the more they love the Bible. The fondness for flowers refines people, and the love of the Bible makes them better."[129]

It was Moody's constant habit to encourage new believers in their Bible study. His instruction to them was simple. It was what he called "the law of perseverance." By way of explanation, he quoted the psalmist: "I have stuck unto thy testimonies." Moody explained, "Application to the Word will tend to its growth within and its multiplication out. Some people are like express-trains; they skip along so quickly that they see nothing."[130] He ended this first piece of advice by encouraging people to "read the Bible itself—do not spend all your time on commentaries and helps. If a man spent all his time reading up the chemical constituents of bread and milk, he would soon starve."[131]

He told converts to get three books. First, he recommended a large-print Bible. They should not get one "you have to hold right under your nose in order to read the print; and if the church happens to be a little dark, you cannot see the print."[132] He said it should also be a good Bible so that they would take care of it, but not so good that they would be afraid to write in it (he also expressed distaste for gilt-edged Bibles that look as if they have never been used). Second, he advised getting a *Cruden's Concordance*. He pointed out, "You can find any portion or any verse in the Bible by just turning to this concordance."[133] Third, Moody recommended purchasing a topical textbook. He maintained these books would help one study the Word of God with profit. The topical textbook should include *The Bible Text Cyclopedia*, a complete classification of Scripture texts in the form of an alphabetical list of subjects.[134]

Elsewhere, Moody proposed a fourfold study strategy. First, he suggested praying earnestly for divine illumination (Ps. 119:18). Second, meditate devoutly on the truths revealed (Ps. 119:97). Then inquire honestly, with a readiness to do the will of God when revealed (Acts 8:31–38). Finally, he said, compare Scripture with Scripture (1 Cor. 2:13).[135]

It is evident from the advice Moody gave others on Bible study that he was fully committed to the notion of perspicuity.[136] He acquired this belief from the Plymouth Brethren, specifically John Darby and George Müller. Perhaps nothing illustrated Moody's commitment to perspicuity and a literal hermeneutic more than his practice of Bible reading, the public reading of the Bible organized by topic with a few connecting comments added to making the readings flow. As James Brookes, the noted premillennialist minister from St. Louis, described the practice:

> Have your leader select some word, as faith, repentance, love, hope, justification, sanctification, and with the aid of a good Concordance, mark down before the time of the meeting the references to the subject under discussion. These can be read as

called for, thus presenting all the Holy Ghost has been pleased to reveal on the topic.[137]

Some credited Moody with devising this practice of Bible reading.[138] However, while it did play a prominent role in his revivals and later conferences, he learned this practice from the Plymouth Brethren, specifically Henry Moorhouse.[139] Regardless of its origins, Moody was an enthusiastic proponent of the practice. However, this technique of Bible reading assumed a very radical commitment to the notion of the perspicuity of the Scripture and the priesthood of all believers.[140]

At times, Moody seemed to equate belief in the Bible with belief in Christ. For example, Moody once asserted, "You can never separate Jesus the Word made flesh from the written word. He, who proclaimed Himself the way, declared also he was the Truth."[141] In a similar vein, in Boston he preached "that Boston may be brought back to its Bible and that this city may come to know and love the person of the Lord Jesus Christ."[142] Goodspeed tells us that Moody's preaching in Philadelphia contained a similar refrain. "Mr. Moody says truly, that the test of a revival is the prominence it gives to Bible study. . . . From the days of Nehemiah down to the present time, every true revival of pure religion has shown itself in a new interest in God's law and testimonies."[143] Moody also stated this proposition negatively: "An infidel is one who doesn't believe in the inspiration of Scripture."[144]

The Bible was the center of Dwight Moody's life and work. He saw the Bible as inspired, reliable, and authoritative. It was the key to effective Christian work and living. It was to be read literally, studied carefully, believed thoroughly, and lived comprehensively.[145] While Moody may have been friends with and shared pulpits with those who had a more liberal view of Scripture, he disagreed with their views. Therefore, any attempt to explain Moody's theology or social vision must look at the Bible's role in Moody's thought or action.

4. SALVATION AND THE "THREE RS"

"There are three R's in the Bible: Ruin by sin, Redemption by Christ, and Regeneration by the Holy Ghost."[146]

—DWIGHT MOODY

Moody's faith was formed and nurtured in the womb of evangelicalism.[147] Its basic teachings formed the backbone of his doctrine. Therefore, the basic tenets of revivalist evangelicalism supported Moody's doctrine of God's love. The core elements of evangelicalism as Moody articulated them in his preaching were the "Three Rs," namely, "Ruin by sin, Redemption by Christ, and Regeneration from the Holy Ghost."[148] In fact, W. H. Daniels argued these "Three Rs" not only framed his preaching but, "according to this triad of topics, he lays out all his campaigns."[149]

Moody defined human beings as "ruined by sin," meaning that they were both sinful and sinners, a condition traceable to Adam. As he put it in 1870, "You may say the earth is a vast hospital. Every man and woman coming into it needs a physician. If you search, you will find everyone wounded. By nature we are sinners."[150] A little over a decade later, he restated his position, "Men are all bad by nature; the old Adam stock is bad, and we cannot bring forth good fruit until we are grafted into the one True Vine."[151] In another of his published sermons, he put it this way, "I don't care where you put man, everywhere he has tried he is a failure. He was put in Eden on trial; and some men say they wish they had Adam's chance. If you had you would go down as quickly as he did."[152] Clearly, for Moody sin is a matter of human nature, not environment.

He believed, because we are sinners by nature, we all sin. As he put it in his sermon on "Repentance,"

> Is there a man here who can say honestly, "I have not got a sin
> that I need ask forgiveness for, I haven't one thing to repent of"?
> A man who has broken one commandment of God is as guilty

as he who has broken ten. If a man don't feel this, and come to Him repentant and turn his face from sin toward God there is not a ray of hope. Nowhere can you find one ray from Genesis to Revelation. Don't go out of this Tabernacle saying, "I have nothing to repent."[153]

Given the fallen state of humanity, Moody argued for the necessity of redemption by Christ. His concept of redemption was very basic: "Being bought back, we sold ourselves for naught, and Christ redeemed us and bought us back."[154] Humanity's only escape is through the work of Christ. As Moody explained it, "You ask me what my hope is; it is, that Christ died for my sins, in my stead, in my place, and therefore I can enter into life eternal."[155] Elsewhere in the same sermon the point was reiterated: "If you ask me what you must do to share this blessing, I answer, go and deal personally with Christ about it. Take the sinner's place at the foot of the cross. Strip yourself of all your righteousness and put on Christ's."[156] Moody argued, "If the Word of God don't teach that, it don't teach anything."[157]

For Moody, the blood of Christ played a vital role in human redemption. In a sermon based on Hebrews 12:22, he stated, "We are not redeemed by such corruptible things [gold and silver], but by the precious blood of Christ."[158] He amplified this claim in his comments on 1 Peter 1:9. He wrote that the blood of Christ is precious,

1. Because it redeems us. (1 Peter 1:19)

2. Because it brings us nigh. (Ephesians 2:3)

3. Because it blots out our sins. (Revelation 1:5)

4. Because it brings peace. (Colossians 1:20)

5. Because it justifies. (Romans 5:9)

6. Because it cleanses from all sin. (1 John 1:7)

7. Because it gives boldness in the Day of Judgment.[159]

Because of the central role God's love played in Moody's preaching, there has been some debate about Moody's concept of atonement. James Findlay, in his academic biography of Moody, argued that Moody did not hold to substitution, and claimed that a moral influence model suits Moody far better. In fact, he went so far as to describe Moody as varying from "both the standard expressions of evangelical theory and from the Anselmic, penal theories still characteristic of certain groups of scholastic Calvinists in this country."[160]

Findlay traced the moral influence model back through Arminianism, to Socinianism with its origins in the work of Peter Abelard. He then appealed to B. B. Warfield for a definition. The moral influence theory "has always been that in which the stress is laid on the manifestation made in the total mission and work of Christ on the ineffable love of God for sinners, which being perceived, breaks down our opposition to God, melts our hearts and brings us prodigals home to the Father's arms."[161] Findlay assumed that a substitutionary view is categorized by a primary emphasis on the tremendous wrath of God, while the moral influence view is far more concerned with the love of God. Noting Harry Moorhouse's popular tagline, "Love them in," Findlay went on to quote Moody himself in order to show Moody's apparent congruence with the moral influence model. Moody preached:

> I remember for the first few years after I was converted I had a good deal more love for Christ than for God the Father, whom I looked upon as the stern Judge, while I regarded Christ as the Mediator who had come between me and that stern Judge and appeased His wrath; but when I got a little better acquainted

with my Bible these views all fled. . . . I began to see that God was to be loved just as much as His Son was.[162]

It is certainly not surprising that Findlay noted Moody emphasis on God's love. However, many of Moody's other sermons offer a strikingly different picture. For instance, Moody preached, "You and I have lost life by the fall, and what we want is to get back that life we lost, and we have it offered to us by the atonement of Christ. . . . Let us thank God we have a refuge, a substitute for the sin we are groaning under."[163] Another account of Moody's thoughts on the atonement comes from the diary of Mrs. Jane MacKinnon. She wrote, "Mr. Moody had said at breakfast: 'What shall I preach today? You know all my sermons.' . . . I was very thankful when Mr. Wylie replied . . . 'Oh, let us hear "The Blood," just the sermon to give to people already well grounded in the doctrine of the Atonement.'"[164] According to his sermon on "The Blood," one of his most celebrated, "people say we ought to preach up Christ's life and moral character. . . . But Christ died for our sins. He didn't say we were to preach His life to save men. Christ's death is what gives us liberty."[165]

Moody proclaimed the power of the blood of Jesus to restore the soul, "so the soul is restored to its full beauty of color when it is washed with the blood of Jesus Christ."[166] He also believed it covered sins. He told the story of a boy in Ireland who was asked by his teacher if there was "anything God cannot do; and the little fellow said, 'Yes, He cannot see my sins through the blood of Christ.' The blood covers them."[167] Moody reinforced the point in one of his illustrations, "Look at that Roman soldier as he pushed his spear into the very heart of the God-man. What a hellish deed! But what was the next thing that took place? Blood covered the spear! Oh! Thank God, the blood covers sin."[168]

In fact, for Moody, teaching on the saving role of the blood of

Christ was nonnegotiable. Preaching in London in 1875, he made his point clearly and forcefully. "If you are in a church, either Dissenting or Established, and the minister doesn't preach the blood, get out of it as Lot out of Sodom."[169]

What is significant is that Moody repeatedly linked the blood of Jesus with substitution. This was particularly true in his sermon "The Blood." As he put it, "I have learned that the man who makes much of the blood in his preaching, much of the atonement, and holds up Christ as the substitute, God honors his preaching."[170] Moody made clear his commitment to substitutionary atonement when he declared, "That is the doctrine of the Bible, the glorious doctrine of substitution. Christ paid the penalty, Christ died in our stead."[171] He also said, "Substitution! If you take that out of the Bible you can take the Bible along with you if you wish to. The same story runs all through the book. The scarlet thread is unbroken from Genesis to Revelation. Christ died for us, that's the end of the law."[172]

Two conclusions can be drawn from Moody's words. First, both the ideas of the blood of Christ and of Christ functioning as a substitute for humanity were central to Moody's concept of salvation. Second, the idea of substitution for Moody included the notion of penalty.

Findlay's claim that Moody held to the moral influence theory was simply an overstatement and illustrates the kind of theological ambiguity one finds at times in Moody. It is fair to note that Moody raised themes that are compatible with the moral influence position. Nevertheless, he also used penal substitution language. Moody was not a careful theologian, for he was an evangelist who simply used the language of the Bible. As such, he defies a clear categorization. The ultimate problem with Findlay's view may simply be that Moody could hold the wrath and love of God in tension, while Findlay evidently could not.[173]

Moody's final "R" was regeneration by the Holy Ghost. Moody believed while the cross is something done *for* humanity, regeneration by the Holy Spirit is something done *to* humanity. The Holy Spirit causes a necessary change in human nature. Moody considered this synonymous with conversion, the new birth or being born again. He claimed, "We must be born of the Spirit, hearts must be regenerated—born again." He believed that every conversion was a supernatural work done by God.[174]

Moody saw this as a crucial doctrine. As he put it, "This doctrine of the New Birth is therefore the foundation of all our hopes for the world to come. It is really the A B C of the Christian religion . . . if a man is unsound on this doctrine he will be unsound on almost every other fundamental doctrine in the Bible."[175]

Moody was also quite clear about what regeneration is not. He asserted that it is not attending church, making a resolution to change one's ways, praying, partaking of the Eucharist, or being baptized.[176] For Moody, "there must be a new creation. Regeneration is a new creation; and if it is a new creation it must be the work of God."[177]

Regeneration, as Moody understood it, was an inside-out event. It was not an outside-in moral reformation. He explained it this way, "I cannot help believing in the regeneration of man, when I see men who have been reclaimed. . . . Old things have passed away, and all things have become new. They are not reformed only, but regenerated—new men in Christ Jesus.[178] Conversion from the inside out was Moody's ultimate goal. As we shall see, this was a key piece in his urban strategy.

In turn, these doctrines were run through the pervasive American democratic and Arminian grid of the day. That is, every woman and man was encouraged to choose to accept this message of the "Three Rs,"[179] thus, Moody's consistent call to men and women to respond to the gospel.

This is not to say that Moody was a committed Arminian. Indeed, we have seen his indebtedness to the giant of Calvinist apologists, Charles Spurgeon. Nevertheless, William McLoughlin argued that

Moody extended Finney's new measures into the urban scene in the later nineteenth century, and Dorsett argued that Moody's theology was closer to Wesley's than Calvin's.[180] However, Gundry convincingly showed that this was not the case. Bebbington, citing Gundry, argued, "Moody actually held certain distinctly Calvinist positions. For example, in *Notes from My Bible*, he distinguished between the position of believers, which is eternally secure, and their condition, which might lapse into sin. The implication of this was that Moody upheld the doctrine of perseverance of the saints. Furthermore, he was attacked by Methodists as well as by Calvinists. It seems clear that he had forged an uncomplicated soteriology designed to cater to both parties." Bebbington noted that Moody once remarked, "I don't try to reconcile God's sovereignty and man's free agency."[181] Nineteenth century American culture lent itself to a more Arminian approach to the question of human freedom in salvation. Moody's approach reflected that culture rather than a well-developed theological commitment.

5. THE HOLY SPIRIT

"The Holy Spirit is closely identified with the words of the Lord Jesus. 'It is the Spirit that quickeneth; the flesh profiteth nothing, the words that I speak unto you, they are spirit and they are life.' The Gospel proclamation can not be divorced from the Holy Spirit. Unless He attend the word in power, vain will be the attempt in preaching it. Human eloquence or persuasiveness of speech are the mere trappings of the dead, if the living Spirit be absent; the prophet may preach to the bones in the valley, but it must be the breath from Heaven which will cause the slain to live."[182]

—DWIGHT MOODY

Moody's belief about the work of the Holy Spirit played a unique role in his theology. He developed his ideas in a period where there was strong interest in the work of the Holy Spirit. Earlier in the century, Charles Finney and Asa Mahan promoted their ideas on the role of the Holy

Spirit post-conversion in their revivalist work.[183] By the time Moody was introduced to the revivalist tradition, the thinking of Finney and Mahan was prevalent. In Moody's case, his own experience in 1871 served as the grounding for his teaching. That experience reflected Spurgeon's teaching and the practical instruction of the two Free Methodist women cited earlier.

We have already noted the role that the Holy Spirit played in Moody's concept of regeneration. In that sense, Moody was certainly not unique. However, what does distinguish him is his concept of the role of the Holy Spirit in sanctification. Specifically, Moody argued for victory over sin and a baptism in the Holy Spirit empowering the Christian for service.[184]

Moody addressed his concept of victory over sin in two books: *Secret Power: or, The Secret of Success in Christian Life and Christian Work* (1881) and *The Way to God and How to Find It* (1884). As he put it, "Whatever the sin is, make your mind up that you will gain victory over it without further delay."[185] However, this does not mean Moody was an advocate for perfectionism or entire sanctification.[186] Speaking at a Keswick convention in 1892, he made this clear. "I dare not make any professions of being holy. I have peace in Christ and I trust Him, but I don't know what I might be left to do and I never trembled more in thinking of the power of the devil and my own weakness than now. And for a man to make a profession that he is without sin and then fall is an awful stumbling block." Moody went on to reference the fall of Pearsall Smith and summarized the crux of the "whole doctrine of perfection: What is the standard? 'X' makes his own conscience or consciousness the standard and does things God's law and Man's law condemn as wrong and yet claims to be without sin. Right there it seems to me is the danger of the teaching."[187] Moody was not a perfectionist.[188]

He explained his reasoning in an 1876 sermon, "For twelve or fifteen years . . . I thought when a man was converted God changed his whole nature. . . . I now believe that every child of God has two natures. Because we have two natures; there is a battle always going on between the world of light and darkness."[189] Thus, while Moody believed in victory over specific sins, he denied the removal of the sinful nature.

In addition to victory over sin, Moody preached a baptism in the Holy Spirit as a means of empowerment for Christian service. Moody asserted there are "about three classes of Christians." The first class was what he called "3rd chapter of John" Christians, "who had got to Calvary and there got life. They believed on the Son and were saved, and there they rested satisfied. They did not seek anything higher." The second class was "4th chapter of John" Christians, who had a "well of living water bubbling up." He claimed, "There are a few of these, but they are not a hundredth part of the first class." The third or best class was the "7th chapter of John" Christians. These are Christians, "Out of whose belly shall flow rivers of living water."[190] What differentiated these classes was their relationship with the Holy Ghost. The third class was like a glass filled to the brim with water, "so full that merely touching it makes the water pour out."[191] Clearly, Moody believed that a higher level of Christian living which involved a relationship with the Holy Spirit was possible and desirable.

In the previous chapter, we discussed the debate surrounding the role of the Holy Spirit in a believer's life after conversion. Moody made his position on this matter clear in a sermon published in 1877. In this sermon, Moody first asserted a second work by the Holy Spirit postregeneration. He explained, "In some sense, and to some extent, the Holy Spirit dwells with every believer; but there is another gift which may be called the gift of the Holy Spirit for service. This gift, it strikes me is entirely distinct and separate from conversion and assurance."[192]

Explaining further, Moody maintained, "There is a difference between the indwelling of the Holy Ghost and His filling one with power. Every true child of God, who has been cleansed by the blood of Christ, is a temple or dwelling-place of the Holy Ghost. But yet he may not have fullness of power."[193] In essence, Moody drew a line between the work of the Holy Spirit on and in the believer. As he explained it, "The Holy Spirit in us is one thing, and the Holy Spirit on us is another. . . . A man working without this unction, a man working without this anointing, a man working without the Holy Ghost upon him, is losing his time after all."[194]

The need for Holy Spirit power was a consistent theme in his preaching. In an 1877 sermon he remarked, "God has a great number of children who have no power, and the reason is, they have not the gift of the Holy Ghost for service. God does not seem to work with them, and I believe it is because they have not sought this gift."[195]

Moody explained his position in various ways, but he always linked it to power from God. For example, "God" he exclaimed, "has got grace enough for every one of us, and if we were only full of the Holy Ghost what power we would have!" And later, "How many times we have preached and taught, and it has been like the wind! And why? Because our hearts were not full, and we did not have that anointing."[196] In another sermon, he applied the teaching to himself. "I want more of this power. Pray for me that I may be so filled with the Holy Spirit when coming on this platform that men may feel I come with a message from God."[197] Further, Moody believed that being baptized with the Holy Spirit not only empowered existing Christian service, it also created new service, especially evangelism.[198]

Accordingly, Holy Ghost-empowered ministry was a doctrine Moody prized.[199] After Moody's death, R. A. Torrey, a close associate, wrote a book entitled, *Why God Used D. L. Moody*. In it, Torrey recorded two incidents that reflected Moody's earnest belief in the doctrine. The first involved an incident at Northfield where Moody asked Torrey to meet with some of the speakers at a Northfield Conference who did not believe in baptism in the Holy Spirit. Apparently, Moody and Torrey reasoned with these men deep into the night, without success. After the meeting, Torrey recalled Moody's response. Almost in agony Moody exclaimed, "Oh why will they split hairs? Why don't they see this is just the one thing they themselves need? They are good teachers . . . but why will they not see that the baptism with the Holy Ghost is just the one touch that they themselves need?"[200] Secondly, Torrey recalled the advice Moody gave to him every time he was invited somewhere to speak. "Now Torrey," Moody enjoined, "be sure and preach on the baptism with the Holy Ghost." On one of these occasions, Torrey asked Moody if he was aware Torrey had other sermons. Moody replied, "Never mind that."[201]

Moody's position is best described as a version of the Keswick movement. He shared their commitment to a second work and the need for Spirit-empowered service. Nevertheless, he was less sanguine about victory over sin. While he agreed with Keswick about the Spirit's ability to give victory over sin, he was not in full agreement with their notion that the struggle against sin could be diminished.[202]

Moody's understanding of the work of the Holy Spirit played a key role in his theology. In Moody's mind, the Holy Spirit connected his doctrines of love, regeneration, and empowerment for service. In this way, the Spirit functioned as a backbone for his theology. It is no wonder Moody's teaching on the Spirit was a distinctive of his ministry.

6. PREMILLENNIALISM

"I look on this world as a wrecked vessel. God has given me a lifeboat and said to me, 'Moody, save all you can.' God will come in judgment and burn up this world; they are in it but not of it, like a ship in the water. This world is getting darker, and ruin is coming nearer and nearer. If you have any friends on this wreck unsaved, you had better lose no time in getting them off."[203]

—DWIGHT MOODY

Drawn to a negative view of human history because of the carnage of the Civil War and the chaos of the city, premillennialism provided Moody with an interpretative schema for these events. Spurgeon and the Plymouth Brethren also propagated this schema. Further, premillennialists were noted for their commitment to the reliability of the Bible and a literal reading of the text, two tenets Moody fully embraced.[204] Accordingly, it is hardly surprising Moody became a committed premillennialist. Along with Moody's belief in the Bible, Chapman called premillennialism one of his three cardinal truths.[205]

His premillennialism was a distinguishing characteristic of his ministry. Gundry claims Moody was "the first noteworthy premillennial preacher of revival and evangelicalism in America."[206] Findlay noted that Moody preached on Christ's return at least once every revival campaign.[207]

Nevertheless, as might be expected, Moody did not sharply define his belief, nor did he assert it in a polemical fashion. His response to the postmillennialist position typically reflected his nonsectarian spirit, simply stating, "We will not have division."[208] He also objected to any attempt to lay out a precise pattern for the second coming of Christ, declaring, "I don't know! I don't think any one knows what is going to happen."[209] At another point he urged, "Don't criticize if our watches don't agree about the time we know he is coming."[210] Even so, Moody was not afraid to assert his belief in general terms.

As has been noted, Moody came to his evangelical convictions when premillennialism was just becoming popular on both sides of the Atlantic. In fact, he acknowledged, "At one time I thought the world would grow better and better until Christ could stay away no longer." However, after 1867, he was a strong proponent of premillennialism, and he and his lieutenants would play a prominent role in its spread.[211] The Northfield Bible conferences played a strategic role in the promulgation of premillennialism. In fact, from its inception in 1880 until

Moody's death in 1899, premillennialists dominated the pulpit in Northfield.[212]

Moody often spent time explaining and defending this belief. One of the obstacles he faced was the perceived newness or novelty of the doctrine. In a published sermon from 1877, he responded to this charge, "Now some of you think this is a new and strange doctrine, and that those who preach it are speckled birds; but let me tell you that most of the spiritual men in the pulpits of Great Britain are firm in this faith. Spurgeon preaches it."[213]

Moody believed the Bible contained clear teaching on the Lord's return. Speaking on prophetic teachings in the Bible, he said, "The Bible does not say, as many seem to think, that prophecy is a dark place which we do well to avoid, but rather that it is like a light shining in a dark place."[214] He began a sermon entitled, "The Return of the Lord," by citing 2 Timothy 3:16, "All scripture is given by inspiration of God, and is profitable for doctrine, for reproof, for correction, for instruction in righteousness"; Moody pointed out this passage said "all Scripture," not some Scripture. He then questioned those who said prophecy is unintelligible or inscrutable. He concluded matter-of-factly that "if God didn't mean to have us study the prophecies, he wouldn't have put them into the Bible."[215] Further, he argued that when you study the Bible carefully, it does not align with the postmillennialist claim that the world will get better and better. On the contrary, Moody believed the Bible plainly taught the world will get worse.[216]

Moody's enthusiasm in preaching premillennialism can partly be explained by his understanding of the role the doctrine played in Christian living. In fact, he believed "the devil does not want us to see this truth, for nothing would wake up the church so much." He held that a firm belief in the premillennial return of Christ would cause worldly things like "gas stocks, and water stocks and stocks in banks" to lose their grip on humans hearts. The result would be humans whose "hearts are free" and are "looking for the blessed appearing of their Lord."[217] Moody believed the doctrine had the power not only to spur on the individual but also the church. As he put it, "The Church is cold and formal; may God wake us up! And I know of no better way to do it than to get the Church to look for the return of our Lord."[218]

Perhaps even more importantly, Moody believed premillennialism spurred Christian work. Citing himself as an example, Moody claimed, "Some people say, 'Oh, you will discourage the young converts if you preach that doctrine.' Well my friends, that hasn't been my experience. I have felt like working three times as hard ever since I came to understand that my Lord was coming back again."[219]

The Bible also motivated his commitment to the reality of the Second Advent. Moody believed the return of Jesus was one of the major themes of the New Testament. He maintained, "It is taught in the New Testament as clearly as any other doctrine." He pointed out that churches have firm teachings on baptism yet say little on the return of Jesus. He found that perplexing, since by his count baptism was only mentioned thirteen times in the New Testament, while the return of Jesus was mentioned over fifty times.[220] He explained, "Now, don't take my word for it; look this doctrine up in your Bibles, and if you find it there, bow down to it and receive it as the word of God."[221]

Moody consistently likened the world to a wrecked or sinking ship. According to Moody, the demise of that ship "is coming nearer and nearer." "God," he exclaimed, "will come in judgment and burn up this world, but the children of God don't belong to this world; they are in it, but not of it, like a ship in the water. The world is getting darker and darker; its ruin is getting nearer and nearer." "God," he believed, had "given him [Moody] a lifeboat and said to him, 'Moody save all you can.'"[222] This would appear to be a pessimistic picture, but here there is a productive tension in his doctrine. In fact, in an 1899 sermon he declared, "Don't think I'm a pessimist . . . Pentecost isn't over yet. Why shouldn't we have now at the close of this old century a great shaking up and a mighty wave from heaven?"[223]

In fact, Moody was quite optimistic at times. Perhaps the most striking example of this optimism was the immensely influential Student Volunteer Movement, in whose founding Moody played a pivotal role. This movement was enthusiastically given to the cause of "the evangelization of the world in this generation."[224]

Nevertheless, it is apparent that Moody's premillennialism made him pessimistic about the trajectory of society and the ability of anything non-supernatural to alter that trajectory. As he put it in one of his sermons, "Someone will say, 'Do you then, make the grace of God a failure?' No, grace is not a failure, but man is. The antediluvian world was a failure; the Jewish world was a failure; man has been a failure everywhere, when he had his own way and been left to himself."[225] Despite this, Moody was very optimistic about evangelism. Further, although he strenuously preached the imminent return of Christ, he also made long-term plans.

Several factors explain this tension within Moody's words and actions. First, Moody lacked theological sophistication. He had no interest in proposing a theological system. Instead, he was an evangelist who let the churches handle the teaching of theology. Second, Moody embraced a naïve biblicism. He ignored difficult passages in the Bible and issues raised by proponents of higher criticism. Moody was not interested it trying to make all the parts of the Bible fit together perfectly; he was far more interested in living the Bible. Moody was also optimistic about the evangelistic work of the Holy Spirit, not the progress of the human race. This is consistent with his doctrine of the Holy Spirit. Nevertheless, a problem remained. Moody believed regenerated people make society better, but it is not clear how Moody reconciled increasing conversions with a society that continued to decay rapidly. Apparently, he either did not see this tension or he simply ignored it.

CONCLUSION

Dwight Moody was a thoroughgoing evangelical. Revivalism and evangelicalism were the context for his conversion to and formation in faith. Their leading advocates and institutions taught and modelled the tradition to him. He believed in a nonsectarian Christianity that focused on God's love. He believed the Bible was reliable, and a literal reading of the English text shaped his belief and practice. He held to a classic Protestant orthodoxy that emphasized human sinfulness, the atoning work of Christ on the cross, and the necessity of a regenerating work of the Holy Spirit. In the spirit of the times, he came to emphasize an ongoing relationship with the Holy Spirit. Although his views were not developed and nuanced like those of Brookes and Darby, he was at the vanguard of the emergence of premillennialism. These beliefs drove Moody's social vision and social action, the subject of the next chapter.

4

MOODY'S SOCIAL VISION

His Theological Understanding of Social Ills

Whitewashing the pump won't make the water pure.[1]

—DWIGHT MOODY

The previous chapter provided a look at the critical elements of Moody's theology. This chapter will show how that theology shaped Moody's social vision. In short, Moody believed personal conversion was the key to solving the urban social problems of the mid to late nineteenth century. He remarked, "It is a wonderful fact that men and women saved by the blood of Jesus rarely remained subjects of charity."[2] In 1877, he said, "The nation is now crying 'reform' . . . but there can be no true reform until Christ gets into our politics. Men are all naturally bad, and cannot reform until the Reformer gets into their hearts."[3] Preaching at the 1876 revival in New York City, Moody commented, "I know there is great misery and suffering in this great city; but what is the cause of it? Why, the sufferers have become lost from the Shepherd's care."[4] The picture becomes clear: Moody believed that social ills are solved by a change within the hearts of individual women and men. As Moody's son William put it, "He insisted that the most efficacious means of reformation was through the individual."[5]

Three essential points must be established at the outset. First, because Moody believed that individual conversion was the most productive means to bring about social change, it does not automatically follow that he objected to programmatic responses to social ills; he simply believed programs alone were ineffective. Second, Moody's prioritization of evangelism over social action reflected the priorities of earlier evangelicals, including the great evangelist of the mid-nineteenth century Charles Finney and the renowned British preacher Charles Spurgeon. Third, Moody's prioritization of evangelism reflected not only his personal theology and tradition but also his vocation.

CONVERSION, POVERTY, AND SOCIAL VICES

Undoubtedly, Moody believed that conversion was the only solution for urban social ills. For example, Moody firmly believed conversion would solve poverty. He contended that sin was the cause of much poverty; therefore, conversion to faith in Christ would free men and women from the various kinds of sin that held them in poverty. Moody believed two sins, in particular, intemperance and laziness, were primarily responsible for poverty.

Moody mainly focused on alcohol. Preaching in Boston in 1877, he remarked,

> It strikes me this curse of intemperance is worse even than our civil war. That cut off a great many men—ten, twenty, thirty, perhaps forty years earlier than their time; but think of the men that are being ruined body and soul by this terrible curse; and

my only hope is that the nation will get their eyes open to the fact that it is a curse, and that there will be a cry going up to God. I noticed a few days ago in the papers that in Great Britain alone $600,000,000 are spent annually on strong drink, or $18 for each man, woman and child in Great Britain, and yet they are crying out there about hard times, and we are crying out about hard times in this country. I think if it were not for this cursed liquor traffic, we would not have any hard times.[6]

Conversion brought freedom from addiction to drinking. "God," he exclaimed, "is going to destroy the works of the devil, and this appetite for strong drink is one of the devil's works. Taking away a man's appetite for strong drink is a supernatural work, and that is what God does."[7]

The second sin was laziness. Moody believed conversion would make people into energetic, hard workers. To Moody, this meant being a Christian means being a worker.[8] In 1868, he remarked, "I never knew a lazy man to become a Christian. . . . It is the devil whose workers are idlers."[9] In Boston in 1877, Moody made the point explicitly.

I never knew yet a lazy man to be converted. If he was, he soon gave up his laziness. I tell you that laziness does not belong to Christ's Kingdom. I don't believe a man would have a lazy hair in his head if he was converted to the Lord Jesus Christ. If a man has been born of the Spirit of Christ, he isn't lazy, he wants to find something to do, and any manual labor is not degrading.[10]

Moody pointed out that since Jesus worked as a carpenter, manual labor was not beneath Him. The point was clear: if Jesus was not above manual labor, no one else should be either.[11] In explaining the work at the YMCA, he remarked, "Let's keep harping on that word, WORK, until everyone who comes in here will feel perfectly wretched unless he is doing something for Christ."[12] Again, in 1868 he proclaimed, "Every Christian has work to do. It lasts as long as life lasts. When God wants us to rest, He will call us home to heaven."[13] In 1869, while discussing church membership, he said, "When a man wishes to come into our Church, we ask him, what are you going to DO?"[14]

This emphasis on work is sometimes overlooked in studies of Moody. As early as the 1860s, Moody connected conversion and Christianity with work. One of the few works concentrating on Moody's early years made this point. The author August J. Fry attempted to summarize Moody's theology during these years by condensing it into six points. He then added a seventh—work. He wrote, "No idea receives as much attention as this idea—work. It might be said, in spite of the dangerous gauntlet of psychologizing history, that Moody was compulsive about it."[15] Fry was correct. All of Moody's schools included required manual labor for all students.

In fact, Moody literally worked himself to death. He insisted on conducting a campaign in Kansas City, despite suffering chest pains for two weeks before it began. Moody told a confidant that he did not tell anyone in his family because they would have prevented him from preaching. On Tuesday of the first week, he confided in his colleague regarding the pain in his chest, but he still refused to see a doctor for two hours. Finally, after consulting with the doctor, he again refused to stop speaking, although he was forced to travel the two blocks from his hotel to the meeting hall by carriage. He preached again that Friday night but was so exhausted that he was forced to leave on a train that very night. He did make it back to Northfield but died within two months.[16]

CHARITY AND SELF-INITIATIVE

Beyond mitigating the vices of alcohol and laziness, Moody asserted that conversion fills a human with the love of God, and this love, combined with the urge to work, produces charity toward others. In his sermon "To the Work! To the Work!" Moody made this connection clearly. "Christ has taught us very clearly that any man or woman who is in need of our love and help—whether temporal or spiritual—is our neighbor. If we can render them any service, we are to do it in the name of our master."[17]

Moody's disdain for laziness, enthusiasm for work, and regard for the Bible influenced his approach to charity. In an 1880 address to converted men, Moody cautioned against charity to men who will not work. He recounted a story of a man in Chicago who was married with five children. The man showed up at Moody's home on a cold November morning. The man had no work, and the family had been evicted from their residence. When Moody asked the man what the problem was, he admitted he was lazy. Moody told the man, "I pity your wife and children, but I am not going to take care of a lazy man all winter." In the evening, the man returned and asked for shelter for his wife and children. Moody recalled, "He knew I wouldn't let those children stay out all night; he knew he had me." When Moody asked what the man had been doing all day, he "used a great many big words, and said he had been studying the philosophy of pauperism." Moody concluded: "It is not charity to help them. If a man will not work, let him starve. They never die. I never heard of them really starving to death. I never knew them to get out till they worked their way out."[18] As support for his view, Moody cited the Bible.[19] He also provided for the wife and children.

At first glance, Moody's behavior toward the family seemed inconsistent with his rhetoric. Having said men who do not work should be left to starve, he then cared for the man's family. However, his behavior was consistent with his earlier work at the YMCA and the Sunday school. We have seen how he cared for the children and wives of alcoholic men. Moody's reasoning on this was clear and grounded in what he believed the Bible taught. He argued that a man's first job was to care for his family. He said that no one whose family is in want should give away money for charitable purposes. He then cited 1 Timothy 5:8: "If any provide not for his own, and especially for those of his own house he hath denied the faith and is worse than an infidel." Moody concluded, "There is what Paul said to you on that subject. He is worse than an infidel."[20] Moody believed the Bible held the husband responsible for his family; he must work. Therefore, while charity should not be directed toward a lazy husband, his spouse and children should be afforded full Christian charity.

Moody's concern that charity ought not foster laziness also extended to his educational enterprises. Moody started several schools designed to provide educational opportunities for poor children. However, Moody demanded work on the part of his students. When asked why he did not offer free education for poor girls, he responded, "If a student can't do her share, she isn't worth educating. I am ready to meet any ambitious student halfway. . . . It's better to help a person help himself. I find you can do real injury by doing too much for the individual."[21]

Moody's commitment to conversion as the catalyst for personal change explains why he was dubious about social programs not linked to conversion. In 1877, Moody made it clear he had no confidence in voluntary societies or the government to provide an ultimate solution to these problems.

> We have tried a great many methods; we have our temperance
> societies and bands of hope, our lodges and our reform club,
> and we have had the pledge, and I don't know but I am getting
> about discouraged with these things. I am coming to the con-
> clusion that the only hope is that the Son of God is to come and
> destroy man's appetite for liquor. You cannot legislate men to be
> good. We have appealed to our government, and we have failed,

and now it is time to appeal to God. . . . When he comes to their hearts, he will give them victory over their appetites.[22]

Speaking on the same subject in 1880, Moody told the following story:

A man there [Philadelphia] had a house built when he was out of town, and the contractor built it with a brown-stone front, but made the sides an imitation, just on the surface. This stood for a while; but when the winter came, it began to crack, and in the spring, he had to have it repaired. And every year he had to have it fixed over until he put in a wall like the front. And that was like a sinner trying to make himself better, when what he needed was to be made over again, a new creature. How many who heard him had taken their oaths that they wouldn't drink again, had taken pledges, had written their name with their own blood, had promised their wives, and mothers, and friends, they would stop the use of the intoxicating cup, and yet couldn't keep them. It was like painting the pump, expecting to get pure water.[23]

When addressing social problems, Moody believed that any reformation effort must be subservient to evangelism. For example, in 1874, Moody was queried about the issue of drunkenness. He remarked, "It would take a day to answer that," but articulated two sides to the question. On the one hand, Moody stated that he believed every Christian church ought to be a temperance society. In addition, he noted in passing that "some of the ministers and elders in Scotland . . . drink too much wine."

On the other hand, he pointed out that too many temperance people prioritize temperance above all else. In doing so, they became like a one-string violin, annoying and ultimately ineffective. Moody concluded, "And so with temperance; only, when you get the chance of a word, slip it in, and give strong drink a rap."[24]

Moody's attitude toward prisoners is an excellent example of this priority on evangelism as a means for reform. He said,

> We must not suppose that all prisoners are hardened criminals. Many a young man has committed a crime in a moment of anger, or under the influence of liquor. The records show that nearly half the prisoners are under twenty-five years of age. At this time of life a young man is not supposed to have become settled in his character. If he can be reached by the gospel message before he sinks lower and lower, there is every hope for his salvation for this life.[25]

Moody's position reflected earlier American evangelicalism, particularly as Charles Finney expressed it. Like Moody, Finney always made personal conversion the priority of his work. While speaking aggressively and repeatedly against slavery and alcohol, neither took precedence over evangelism. Making the same argument Moody would make a half a century later, Finney maintained that social change was ultimately the product of personal conversion. This is a point that Charles Hambrick-Stowe made in his biography of Finney. Regarding Finney's approach to abolition, he wrote, "The primary work must be to save sinners, for once saved, believers would reject slavery and every form of sin. Finney advocated making abolition an appendage, just as he made temperance an appendage of revival work in Rochester."[26]

We have seen how the Chicago Fire served to focus Moody so that, after 1871, evangelism became his focus. As an evangelist, it followed that Moody would concentrate on conversion. Commenting on Moody's ministry, Charles Spurgeon said:

> I thank God that our dear brethren [Moody and Sankey] do not commit themselves to any particular line of thought other

than the Gospel, and take no concern in various matters which are in dispute with different sections of Christians. I hold that every man should teach the entire truth as he believes it, and if he be a settled pastor, he must not keep back any part of it; but the evangelists are to show forth only the great cardinal truths of the Gospel, and this our friends do.[27]

However, his anthropology was the primary reason for Moody's commitment to conversion as the only sure means of social change. Moody's anthropology was a function of his evangelical theology—specifically, Moody's belief that all humans are ruined by sin. As we saw in the last chapter in the section on the "Three Rs," sin for Moody was personal, and a function of each person's nature—a corrupt nature inherited from Adam.[28] In other words, the nature of an individual, not their environment, determined his propensity to sin. As such, Moody simply could not see how any attempt to change the urban environment could ultimately solve social problems, which he believed were rooted in sin.

As a committed evangelical, Moody believed only Christ could redeem humans from sin. He thought that the sole remedy for human estrangement from God was the sacrificial death of Jesus on the cross. The cross did more than merely demonstrate God's love; it cleared the object of sin out of the way and allowed humans to experience God's love.

Moody believed God's love was transformative. Thus, truly redeemed and regenerated men and women would work hard and love others. Their love would be supernaturally produced by the Holy Spirit and cause them to love those in need, including their enemies. As Moody put it, "The regenerate man loves his enemies and tries to repair all wrong he has done. . . . If this sign is not apparent his conversion has never got from his head to his heart."[29] Moody held that, because of sin, humans needed to be regenerated by the Holy Spirit. He believed humans are in such a condition that only a supernatural act of God can change them. For Moody, Christianity was an inside-out religion that re-created people internally before transforming the external world in which they lived. He, therefore, believed it was useless to attempt outside-in societal transformations.

In a sermon published in 1884, Moody graphically illustrated this belief. He asked his audience to imagine a drunkard's home in any city in America. He described the home as a kind of hell on earth. The place was wretched, the wife and children poorly clothed and fed. The man often came home drunk and beat the family. However, one day the man arrived home and announced that he had been converted at a gospel meeting. Moody continued, "Go down to that house again in a few weeks and what a change!" Moody painted a picture of the wife and the husband sitting in their home together with their children singing hymns. He concluded, "Is not that a picture of Regeneration? I can take you to many such homes, made happy by the regenerating power of the religion of Christ. What men want is the power to overcome temptation, the power to lead a right life."[30]

Because he believed in the power of personal conversion to moderate social evil, Moody sometimes offered advice to the working class that demonstrated a lack of understanding of the complexity of the labor problems. For example, he advised, "Work faithfully for three dollars a week, it won't be long before you have six and then you will get ten dollars and then twelve . . . get these employers always under an obligation to you."[31] He concluded, "You must be so helpful to your employers they cannot get along without you . . . and your employer will increase your wages."[32] While addressing a group of converted alcoholics, he urged, "Get something to do. If you cannot earn more than a dollar a week, earn that. That is better than nothing and you can pray to God for more."[33] While working in Boston, he encouraged reformed alcoholics to leave the city and go out into the country, arguing, "It is not degrading to go out and hoe and shovel in the field, it is noble I think."[34] He added, "I don't see how a man can follow Christ and not be successful."[35] Moody saw this pattern in his own life and often commented, "The whole of my early life was one long struggle with poverty . . . since I began to seek first the kingdom of God, I have wanted for nothing."[36]

Moody believed that a combination of charity and self-initiative was the answer to unemployment and disability. He benefited as a boy from charity and engaged in and supported numerous charitable activities. Moody believed Christians were required by the Bible to be generous toward others, the only exception being the lazy. Moreover, as we shall see shortly, he was willing to criticize businesses and the wealthy for their lack of charity. In Moody's opinion, charity and self-initiative were grounded in conversion.

THE LABOR MOVEMENT AND SOCIAL PROBLEMS

The context of conversion, charity, and self-initiative helps to explain the advice he gave to his coworkers. First, he urged them not to have "anything to say about capital and labor. You don't know anything about it."[37] This attitude was driven by Moody's belief that experts should manage politics and operate the economic system. The evangelist's job was to preach the gospel and save souls.[38] He gave similar advice about using the pulpit to address sociological topics, saying, "I say when we have got all the people to repent of their sins and live as God wants them to live, it'll be time to talk about sociological questions."[39] Despite this, Moody occasionally did raise social issues. For example, in London in 1884, he was asked how Americans might contribute to the understanding and general uplift of the population in Britain. He replied that the greatest need in London was for houses, noting, "At present your poor people shift aimlessly from place to place."[40] Nevertheless, when

Moody did talk about governmental reform, he usually cited the need for conversion. He stated, "You can't reform the government without men who have been themselves reformed, and that reformation must be regeneration through the power of the Holy Ghost."[41]

However, working conditions in American urban centers were appalling and, if anything, worsened during Moody's lifetime. Moody was keenly aware of the unrest among workers. As early as 1869, he engaged in a series of conversations with Samuel Fielden, a leading figure in the labor movement.[42] As Fielden recalled it, Moody initiated an "animated" conversation that lasted over an hour and a half. Despite Fielden's passionate arguments, Moody remained steadfast in his commitment to conversion as the ultimate solution. Fielden concluded, "We parted at the door with the best feeling toward each other. I am only sorry to say that my opponent has persisted in following the wrong path to this day. I am truly sorry for him. I only wish that we both turn to the right before it is everlastingly too late."[43]

Labor leaders like Fielden found particularly fertile ground in Chicago. Within the immigrant class were groups of men well-versed in Marxism and anarchism. In the late nineteenth century, radical labor movements began to emerge so that by the 1880s, Chicago had become the center for the socialist and anarchist movements in America. Other, more moderate forms of labor organizations flourished as well.[44]

Moody's comments on labor issues during these years were particularly telling. In 1883 in Chicago, he compared the conditions among the working class in Chicago with those in England. He described the workers in England as "hard-hearted and hard-headed men who gather in their shops on Sunday, or someplace else, and talk communism or infidelity." He concluded, "We are drifting the same way in this country."[45]

In Chicago, the labor issue came to a head in the Haymarket riot of 1886. Workers gathered at the McCormick reaper plant on the evening of May 4 to protest about working conditions. During the speeches, someone threw a homemade bomb into the crowd of police officers monitoring the gathering. When order was restored, eight police officers lay dead and sixty others wounded. No one has ever determined the exact number of those killed and injured among the crowd. Eight leading figures in the city's anarchist movement were arrested and eventually tried for murder. The business community carefully orchestrated the trial. The jury quickly returned a guilty verdict, and the judge sentenced seven of the eight men to death by hanging. The judgments were met with outrage throughout the country and the rest of the civilized world. International figures like George Bernard Shaw and Leo Tolstoy condemned both the trial and the verdict. Both pleaded for leniency for the convicted. Despite this, the Chicago city leaders remained resolute. Marshall Field, in particular, resisted any call for clemency. Although two death sentences were ultimately commuted, four other defendants were hanged on November 11, 1887. The remaining prisoner committed suicide.[46]

Moody seemed hardly surprised by the event. On the eve of the Haymarket riot, he had warned,

> Either these people are to be evangelized or the leaven of communism and infidelity will assume such enormous proportions that it will break out in a reign of terror such as this country has never known. It don't take a prophet or a son of a prophet to see these things. You can hear the muttering of the coming convulsion even now, if you open your ears and eyes.[47]

The quote illustrates once again Moody's solution to a social problem—mass conversion. He acted accordingly and redoubled his efforts to bring them the gospel.[48]

A letter to A. P. Fitt from Charles Goss dated November 16, 1910, gives more insight into Moody's thoughts. In the letter, Goss recounts to Fitt an episode where he was sitting with Moody and Francis Murphy.[49] He wrote,

> Mr. Moody sat on one side of me, on a lounge, and Francis Murphy on the other: (both weighing, singly, twice as much as I did) and tried to rid me of certain socialistic views. Put together with other statements; one can safely surmise Moody is no friend of the Labor movement.[50]

However, toward the end of his career, Moody began to see things somewhat differently. Accordingly, in the late 1880s into the 1890s, he began to speak out against riches and big business.[51] In 1888, he commented, "It is more profitable to have a clear conscience with God, than to have wealth gathered by defrauding the poor, and grinding the unfortunate."[52] He lashed out against greed and covetousness that "fastened on the hand of Chicago, along with many another Western city."[53] A similar refrain was heard in 1890. "We have too much wealth and too much poverty. Why don't some of the people who have made their fortunes stop and go out into the highways and byways and help the poor? That's my idea of Socialism, and it's founded on the ideas of Christ."[54] He attacked employers in 1894, charging, "We treat our servants just about as we treat our sewing machines, if they do their work well, all right; but if they don't, we kick them out."[55] In the same year, he called A. T. Stewart, a prominent New York department store owner, "supremely selfish," stating, "One of his clerks got sick and couldn't come to the store for two or three or ten weeks; his wages were cut right off." Moody continued saying Stewart thought "he wasn't responsible for aiding the clerk."[56] In 1897, he directed another verbal broadside toward employers. Moody asked rhetorically, "Are you guilty of sweating your employees? Have you deprived the hireling of his wages? Have you paid starvation wages?"[57] Again, in 1899, Moody spoke out, and it is interesting to note that he addressed the structural problem of big corporations: "What can a poor young man do nowadays, unless he goes to work for someone else who is wealthy? ... Trusts, corporations, are bad for young men."[58] Moody believed employers should treat their workers fairly; nonetheless, he never condoned labor unrest. Notwithstanding his misgivings about how workers were treated, Moody was never moved beyond his belief in personal conversion and charity as the ultimate solution to societal problems.

Moody's social vision was a function of his theology. Because of his belief in the "Three Rs," he doggedly maintained individual sin was the cause of the problem and regeneration was the only solution. He appealed to the Bible when dealing with perceived laziness. Moreover, because of his belief in the imminent return of Christ and the inevitable destruction of society, he was unwilling to move away from constantly proclaiming the gospel.

However, for Moody, proclaiming the gospel was never merely a matter of speech alone. Christianity, as Moody conceived it, was about living and doing. Therefore, the following excerpt of one of his published sermons on the topic of "The Good Samaritan" probably best summarized Moody's social vision.

> If you want to get into sympathy, you need to put yourself into a man's place. Chicago needs Christians whose hearts are full of compassion and sympathy. If we haven't got it, pray that we may have it, so that we may be able to reach those men and women that need kindly words and kindly actions far more than sermons. The mistake is that we have been preaching too much and sympathizing too little. The gospel of Jesus Christ is a gospel of deeds not words. May the Spirit of the Lord come upon us this night. May we remember that Christ was moved in compassion for us, and may we, if we find some poor man going down among

thieves, or lying wounded and bleeding, look upon him with sympathy, and get below him and raise him up.[59]

The crux of Moody's social vision was that Christians must love and care for the poor because Jesus loved us, and the Bible demands it. He maintained that part of evangelism consisted of doing good deeds, and this ability to do good was rooted in conversion and the subsequent empowering of the Holy Spirit.

5

MOODY'S SOCIAL ACTION

The Triumphs

If some of you fashionable people would get along with fewer dresses, and spent some of your pocket money relieving the poor, you would show a good deal more wisdom than in spending your lives like so many butterflies.[1]

—DWIGHT MOODY

I want to give you a motto that has been a great help to me. It was a Quaker's motto: "I expect to pass through this world but once. If, therefore, there be any kindness I can show or any good thing I can do to any fellow human being let me do it now; let me not defer nor neglect it, for I will not pass this way again."[2]

—DWIGHT MOODY

Moody's social work reflected his social vision. In addition to his commitment to conversion, Moody supported some social programs and personal acts of charity. As we have already seen, Moody provided aid to the poor, beginning with his early days at the Sunday school and with the YMCA. As his career continued, he was involved with two causes: the temperance movement and education. In addition, Moody was regularly engaged in individual acts of charity.

MOODY AND THE TEMPERANCE MOVEMENT

These grog shops here are the works of the devil—they are ruining men's souls every hour. Let us fight against them, and let our prayers go up in our battle.[3]

—DWIGHT MOODY

The Gospel Temperance is the kind of temperance for me![4]

—DWIGHT MOODY

The relationship between evangelicalism and temperance was close but complex. Indeed, the movement's goals evolved during the early- to mid-nineteenth century.[5] In the 1820s, nascent temperance organizations only advocated moderation and abstention from distilled liquor. Lyman Beecher, who in 1826 founded the American Society for the Promotion of Temperance, best represented this early phase. The society asserted that alcohol consumption was responsible for domestic disturbances, violent crime, and poverty. However, it did not advocate total abstention. On the contrary, as Beecher indicated, he opposed "the daily use of ardent spirits."[6]

By the 1830s, in the face of the rising consumption of wine and beer among the working classes, temperance advocates began calling for total abstinence from all liquor. This was graphically illustrated in a "teetotaler" pledge from the Cleveland Marine Total Abstinence Society dated 1845. Framed by three biblical texts—Romans 14:23, Proverbs 23:29, and Habakkuk 2:15—and accompanied by the quote famously attributed to Constantine, "In this sign conquer," the pledge read, "We the undersigned do hereby promise and agree to abstain from all intoxicating drinks, and in all suitable ways discountenance their use." The "undersigned" included the society president and the pledge. On either side of the text of the printed commitment were columns listing the fruits of temperance and intemperance. "The Fruits of Temperance" included domestic comfort, favor of God and respect of men, peace and plenty, health of body and soul, and eternal happiness. "The Fruits of Intemperance" included the ruin of families, anger of God and contempt of men, poverty in its worst forms, insanity, premature death, and eternal misery.[7] The popularity of such abstinence or "teetotal" pledges signaled the first shift in the goals and strategies of the antebellum temperance movement. The abstinence pledge became a tactic and a public symbol of this sterner sensibility. The Cleveland Marine Total Abstinence Society was only one of the hundreds of temperance societies that flourished in antebellum cities and towns, primarily in the Northeast but also in frontier areas settled by emigrants from the Northeast.[8]

Charles Finney was primarily responsible for the marriage of temperance and revivalism. Moody inherited this emphasis from the revivalist tradition.[9] In addition, as a boy, Moody had seen the strong temperance movement in Northfield.[10] Consequently Moody's embrace of the temperance cause in his adult life was predictable.

Moody was a temperance man. He said, "I am a total abstainer; have never touched liquor and never intend to do so."[11] This was a position he aggressively made known to others. In fact, temperance was a consistent theme in both his revivals and publications.[12] Even a casual glance at any collection of his sermons illustrates his view.

It is also true that some of Moody's ongoing temperance preaching resulted from the continuing problems with alcohol he had seen in urban America after the war. Chicago, his adopted home, illustrated the magnitude of the problem. By some estimates, in the 1890s, Chicago's saloons entertained up to a half million customers daily.[13]

However, Moody's temperance fervor was moderated by his theological convictions. Temperance had a place in his life's work, but it was never the dominant theme of his ministries. The best illustration of this is his relationship with Frances Willard. Willard was instrumental in forming the Woman's Christian Temperance Union, eventually ascending to its presidency in 1879. Moody had attended some of her sessions with women in Chicago and was deeply impressed. As a result, he invited her to join him at a campaign scheduled for Boston in 1877. Willard eventually agreed, and they conducted several special meetings for women. However, as the campaign progressed, tensions developed between the two because Willard insisted on emphasizing temperance as much as evangelism. This was not acceptable to Moody; he eventually reprimanded Willard for working every spare minute for the cause of temperance, to the neglect, he thought, of her evangelistic duties.[14] Unable to reconcile their differences by the end of the campaign, the two parted.[15]

This episode illustrates Moody's belief in conversion as the foundation for all other lifestyle changes. Perhaps Moody's words best summed up his position: "To drinking men, as to everyone else, [I say] believe on the Lord Jesus Christ."[16] His theological commitments drove his approach to social action. For Moody, pledges of total abstinence should never replace promises to Jesus, and this was precisely where Moody believed Willard had erred.

MOODY THE EDUCATOR

The sight of poor boys and girls deprived of the means of education would not let him rest until he had provided some method by which their lives should be enriched and made more in accordance with Heaven's designs for them. He dotted this fair plain with houses that young men and young women should have the means of so enlarging their lives that they might be useful to their fellows. His work was in the line of Christ's miracles, which never enriched the object with bounties of land or money or resources, but always gave power to life, making the dead eye to see, touching the dead tongue, the dead ear, the dead limb, and in His highest miracles bringing the dead to life.[17]

—PRESIDENT H. G. WESTON,

OF THE CROZER THEOLOGICAL SEMINARY

These are the best pieces of work I have ever done. I have been able to set in motion streams which will continue long after I am gone.[18]

—DWIGHT MOODY,

ABOUT THE NORTHFIELD AND MOUNT HERMON SCHOOLS

Even to those closest to Moody, his immersion into education initially seemed odd. Henry Drummond expressed amazement that "the greatest evangelist of his day, not when his powers were failing but in the prime of his life and in the zenith of his success, should divert so great a measure of his strength into educational channels."[19] Furthermore, since Moody's education was severely limited, he hardly seemed a candidate for building schools.

However, it was precisely Moody's lack of education that drove him to promote the cause. On one of his trips to Scotland, Moody quaintly observed that he "regretted exceedingly he had never had a college education himself; but he did not get it, and he was doing the best he could without it."[20]

Moody also had seen the impact of the lack of education on others. The Chicago Sunday school had taught him this truth well. Moody told the story of one of the little boys at the school coming one Sunday barefoot during a snowstorm. Moody immediately went out and purchased the young lad shoes. However, the following Sunday, the boy returned barefoot. When Moody inquired about his shoes, the boy told him his parents had sold them for liquor. Moody began to grasp the limited impact of some single acts of charity and the limitations of the Sunday school. A corrupt home could undermine the good of the school. After realizing the Sunday school's limitation, Moody started to dream of a residential school that would provide not only Christian teaching but Christian teaching and a Christian community for the students.[21]

As Moody progressed in his evangelistic ministry, he also began to understand the strategic value of education. For example, the inquiry room was one of the unique characteristics of Moody's revivals. After each message, those interested in Christianity were sent to inquiry rooms where workers were available to answer questions and pray with the inquirers. Moody was in constant need of trained workers for this task. Therefore, he determined that schools that included training in personal work would be a boon for his revival work.[22]

Moody also knew a lack of education often accompanied poverty. By 1876, Moody had purchased a home in Northfield. That summer, while riding in the hills behind his house with his brother Samuel, Moody came upon a small cabin. Two young girls sat in front of the home, with their mother plaiting straw hats. The father, who had a disability, sat watching the women. Moved by what they saw, Dwight and Samuel stopped to talk to the family. The women's plaiting was the only source of income for the family.[23] Although physically limited, the father graduated from Oberlin College; the daughters clearly shared their father's intelligence. As the Moodys left, both felt despondent about the inevitable future for the girls. They knew the closest school provided only rudimentary education and that the nearest high school was thirteen miles away in Greenfield. Even if the girls had a way to travel that distance, they could not leave their family or afford tuition. Consequently Dwight and Samuel began discussing the idea of a school.[24]

By the end of his life, Dwight Moody had founded five different schools: three in Northfield, one in Chicago, and one in Glasgow. All the schools reflected, to varying degrees, Moody's motives for getting involved in education. The schools offered a robust Christian environment and provided an education that was inexpensive, open to all races, and included practical Christian training.

The first, the Northfield Seminary for Women, originated in Dwight and Samuel's experience with the sisters plaiting hats. Dwight and Samuel's desire to see a young cousin named Fannie Holton educated further bolstered the idea of founding a school.[25]

Three men were constructive as Moody sought to establish a women's school: General O. O. Howard, Henry F. Durant, and H. N. F. Marshall.[26] Howard's role in promoting women's education and influence on Moody has already been noted.[27] Henry F. Durant, a Bostonian, was a more immediate and vital source in the founding of Northfield. Moody had been first introduced to Durant in the 1860s. The two shared an interest in women's education, and Moody had visited him at the Mount Holyoke Seminary several times. Durant went on to found Wellesley College (chartered in 1870, opened in 1875), and invited Moody to become a trustee. During Moody's Boston campaign in 1877, he was a guest at Durant's home.[28]

Wellesley College provided a model for Moody. Looking at Wellesley, it is easy to see how Moody was drawn to the school. As Durant conceived it, Wellesley was to have twin emphases: the Bible and advanced education. Further, consistent with the New England work ethic, Durant insisted the students share in the domestic work of the institution.[29] As Moody became convinced of the benefit of Wellesley's approach, he determined to follow it when formulating Northfield.[30]

Marshall met Moody in Boston in 1877. In 1878, he attended a Bible-reading session at Moody's home in Northfield. Both he and Moody were interested in education, and Marshall became one of the school's early benefactors.

The Northfield Seminary for Women was opened in November 1879, and the first twenty-five women students lived in the Moody home while the initial building was being finished. The school reflected Durant's vision for Wellesley, placing a dual emphasis on the Bible and advanced education. As noted earlier, Moody insisted that the Bible be foundational in his schools. In this case, the phrase could be taken literally, as Moody saw that a Bible was placed in the cornerstone of each school building.

The school also expected the women to work. The household duties were divided among them, and chores were designed with two goals. The first of these goals was to inculcate a sense of individual responsibility and the value of labor and money. The second goal was to set students of different racial and religious backgrounds on equal footing. The duties would democratize students, allowing them to find their "prejudices disappearing in the intimate association of a common task." In addition, it was hoped that, through the sharing of household tasks, "mutual sympathy and understanding would be promoted."[31]

The curriculum included two required components, Bible study and music.[32]

The Bible portion was described as including "an unusual amount of instruction in the Bible. The Bible is to have practically, and not only in name, the first place among text-books used, yet not in the interest of any sect."[33] Music consisted of instruction in singing and reading music. Every year of study included music instruction. It was "required of every pupil who is not obviously incapacitated for singing, or who has not already advanced beyond the requirements." The goal was that "all who remain long at the Seminary have the opportunity of learning to read music with freedom, and of considerable voice cultivation."[34] The emphasis on music reflected Moody's belief that music was a critical component in Christian work. Although he was tone deaf, he understood its importance.[35] That initial belief had been verified as he saw the effect of his partner Sankey's singing. Given that Moody hoped the school

would produce a good number of Christian workers among its graduates, it stands to reason they would emphasize music.

Beyond the two core components, three courses of study were offered. The college preparatory track was designed to prepare those so
gifted to enroll in college after their time at Northfield. It included a
broad liberal arts curriculum and Latin. The second track, referred to
as the "general course," also had Latin but provided more electives. The
final, "English track," replaced Latin with additional work in sciences,
history, and literature.[36]

Reflecting Moody's burden for the poor, the schools were "restricted
to those who have small means and high aims." They particularly encouraged "the attendance of those who from the necessity of self support or
otherwise, have been providentially hindered in getting the desired education, but who would be determined to make the most of an opportunity
here."[37] In fact, Moody went so far as to say that he had no right to raise
funds for those who could afford more expensive schools.[38]

Moody was particularly concerned about Native American and African American girls.[39] Regarding Native American girls, Moody reasoned,
"Our Government has misused the Indians, and this is one way we can
make reparation to them."[40] Thus, in its first year of operation, Moody
sent one of the principals, Harriett W. Tuttle, a Wellesley graduate, out
to the Indian reservations in the western United States to "learn what
Indian girls were to be found prepared to enter the Seminary, who
might be trained to become teachers among their own people." Moody
proposed entirely funding twelve such students. However, when Miss
Tuttle identified sixteen, Moody quickly agreed to raise funds for the
additional four.[41] In addition to the Native American students, several
African Americans made up the student body.[42]

The school's 1899 handbook explained Moody's understanding of
the acute need for a school for girls.

The girls in disproportionate numbers stay at home, attend district schools for a few terms, and often live with but little society and meager opportunities fitted to stimulate their minds in healthful directions, or properly develop their resources. . . . This is the class of girls for whom the Northfield Seminary exists: to help and encourage them, to fit them in the best way for a happy and useful life.[43]

Thus, while the school served to prepare women for Christian service, Moody was interested in seeing women develop as people.

In 1890, Moody opened another school for women, the Northfield Bible Training School for Women. Moody had become convinced women were particularly adept at working with the poor. At the same time, he believed most women were not adequately trained for such work. Therefore, this school was founded to fill that gap.[44]

In addition to a heavy dose of training in the English Bible, the school included instruction in domestic chores. Specifically, "the pupils are taught those branches of domestic economy which are most likely to be useful in their work among the homes of the poor. Much stress is laid upon cooking, especially the preparation of foods for the sick, and a distinct department is also devoted to dressmaking."[45]

Between the founding of the two women's schools, Moody founded two other schools: the Mount Hermon Boys' School in 1881 and what would become the Moody Bible Institute in 1886.

Although Moody's first school was for women only, he was hopeful of having a school for boys as well. So, at the dedication of the East Hall at the Northfield School, Moody said in his remarks:

You know that the Lord laid it upon my heart some time ago
to organize a school for young women in humbler walks of life,
who would never get a Christian education but for a school like

this. I talked about this plan of mine to friends, until a number of them gave money to start the school. Some thought I ought to make it for boys and girls, but I thought that if I wished to send my daughter away to school I should prefer to send her to an institution for girls only. I had hoped that money might be given for a boys' school, and now a gentleman who has been here for the last ten days has become interested in my plans, and has given twenty-five thousand dollars toward a school for boys.[46]

The Mount Hermon Boys' School was located on the other side of the river from the Northfield schools. It was a copy of the Northfield School in most ways, as it was also devoted to providing educational opportunities for the poor and orphaned.[47] Like Northfield, the students came from diverse ethnic and religious backgrounds.[48] Racial diversity was demonstrated during the first graduation ceremony at Mount Hermon. As the program put it, "William Moody, who goes on to Yale College, spoke for Americans; Louis Johnson, a full-blooded Choctaw, spoke in his own language for the various Indian tribes represented in the school; Chin Loon, in full Chinese dress, spoke for his nationality, which has several representatives at Mount Hermon; Thomas N. Baker, a full-blooded Negro and a general favorite in the school, spoke for his race."[49]

The early years at Mount Hermon were a bit chaotic. The school's history described the first three years euphemistically as "in a sense experimental."[50] No transparent administrative model was established, and the curriculum seemed a bit fluid. Nonetheless, twenty-six boys arrived for the first year of classes. Only boys under the age of sixteen were admitted.[51]

Soon after the "experimental years," the school began to take shape. A basic curriculum emerged that followed Northfield's with slight variations. For example, in addition to Northfield's core of Bible and music, an "industrial" set of courses were added.[52] By 1899, it had grown to over three hundred students, and the age limit had changed so that the school admitted only boys over sixteen.[53] The industrial core reflected Moody's commitment to the value of hard work. The core consisted of two parts. The first part involved work around the school, including tending to crops and the garden, attending to the dairy, maintaining the grounds, cutting wood and ice, snow plowing, teaming, carting refuse, carrying the mail, and general cleaning. Each boy was assigned one of these tasks on a rotating basis. Second, the boys were taught a trade. Among the trades practiced were carpentry, house-painting, barbering, sailing, carriage-painting, glass-painting, blacksmithing, clock working, printing, harness-working, and telegraphing.[54]

Mount Hermon offered only two tracks instead of Northfield's three. They were the English division and the Classical division. The English division was designed for "(1) The majority of those who do not look forward to attending other schools upon quitting this. (2) Those who have no aptitude for classical study, and do not aim at a literary training. (3) Those who wish to pass directly from Mount Hermon into strictly scientific and technical schools for a professional course." By comparison, the Classical division was for "those who are ambitious to obtain a liberal education; whose age and love of learning favor it, and who live in hope of taking the full collegiate course."[55] The number of students enrolled in each track is unknown. This is probably because admission was fluid. This policy made the school unique among American schools of that era. Boys could attend for a year, drop out, and then return. They were free to do this until they graduated. Some only went for two or three years, never graduating, while others took as long as eight years to graduate.[56]

The fourth school was in Chicago, Illinois, founded by D. L. Moody in 1886. The school's origins lay in the work of Miss Emma Dryer, a principal and teacher at Illinois State Normal University. Moody noticed her work with poor urban women in the summer of 1870. A year later while ministering to homeless victims of the Chicago Fire, Dryer developed a Bible study and home visitation program for young women.[57]

Following the example he had seen with Pennefather's Anglican order of deaconesses, Moody encouraged her in this work and arranged for it to be done under the auspices of his church. Eventually Dryer expanded the ministry into a training institute for women. In addition to training in the English Bible, the women were taught practical skills like dressmaking and cooking in order to aid the poor women they served. As the work developed, Dryer began to encourage Moody to help her establish an institute for both men and women.[58]

By 1883, Dryer had been joined by other Chicagoans in a concerted prayer effort to get Moody to return to Chicago to build a school.[59] Moody's brother-in-law, Fleming H. Revell, in a religious journal he owned, began to drop hints about Moody's need to return to Chicago to help with a school.[60] In an editorial, Revell summarized Moody's thinking in the following manner.

> When we remember that the United States leads all countries in the commission of crime, we have reason to look about us for the means to remedy this terrible evil. The increase in crime over the last twenty years has been appalling, and there is everywhere a feeling of uneasiness manifest as to the future of the country, with such a state of things growing upon us. If we could have a school that should have for its one aim to train men and women to work successfully among the people, a vast good would be done. Not a school so much to learn to study—that we have— but to learn to direct Christian work—applied Christianity. We have come upon times that demand the services of scores and hundreds of such workers and the nation calls for them but there is no school to train them in.

There are men and women too who could . . . preach Christ to all the unevangelized in the centers of America, if not the world. While Church Congresses are being called to consider the condition of the cities, and what shall be done, an institution could be established now and set in operation to teach men and women how to do this most difficult work now—not necessarily for ministers and missionaries only, but for men and women who will not leave their business or home, but will be lay workers all their lives. What a help such a training would be to all our churches![61]

He ended the piece by reiterating Moody's call for $250,000 to start the school.

The conditions in Chicago can at least partly explain Moody's burden to form a school. In 1881, fully half of the infants born in Chicago died before reaching the age of five. In addition, the children of the slums, the target of Moody's first ministry effort, suffered inordinately. An 1882 study by the Department of Health reported that the deaths in the slums outnumbered those in other city wards by roughly three to one.[62] In 1879 and again in 1885, the city experienced torrential rains that resulted in overflows of the sewer system. The impact on the general populace was catastrophic. After the 1885 rains, the city was wracked by typhoid, cholera, dysentery, and other diseases that killed about 12 percent of the city's population. As the nineteenth century ended, Chicago became known for having some of the worst slums in the civilized world.[63]

From Moody's perspective, these appalling conditions, combined with the Haymarket riot and a litany of other urban ills, simply reinforced the urgent need for the Chicago school. In a fundraising letter written in 1887, Moody articulated his concerns. He wrote, "Of the 800,000 people of Chicago, probably not more than one-fourth attend regularly some church, Catholic or Protestant, and are directly in sympathy with any movement which upholds law and order, and elevates humanity." He continued, "The formation of societies and organizations not in sympathy with religious work have made rapid increase during the last twenty years. Laws related to Sabbath desecration are unheeded, and intemperance, laziness, and crime, largely resultant there from, are rapidly demoralizing the youth of the city."[64]

Apparently, Moody connected the disintegration in living conditions with what he perceived as moral disintegration. As previously demonstrated, Moody believed conversions provided the best antidote to poverty. Thus, his solution was to raise a legion of trained workers to labor among the masses.

The Chicago school was to raise just such a legion of volunteers to act between the preachers and the people to get the gospel directly to the working class. Moody's vision was to fill communities with young people who had been taught to accept the obligations of living the Christian life so that their example of Christ might pervade their society and make revivals no longer necessary.[65] His purpose was clear.

> Some of you may think I oppose theological seminaries. I want to say I believe we want thoroughly trained men. I don't think we have enough trained men. At the same time, we want some men to stand between the laity and the ministers—I don't know what you would call them—gap men. We want men to stand in the gap. There is such a thing as educating a man away from the rank and file. There is a class of men, I believe, that have got to be raised up to do what we used to call in the war bushwhacking. We want irregulars—men that will go out and do work that the educated ministers can't do: get in among the people, and identify themselves with the people.[66]

Moody believed the working masses needed to be converted and created the Chicago school to educate and train people to meet that challenge.

Moody's educational work was not limited to the United States. He was instrumental in forming the Glasgow Bible Institute in Scotland in 1892.[67] In a story similar to the one in Chicago, Moody came alongside someone to shape and give life to that man's vision. This time the initial visionary was J. Campbell White. White, the future Lord Overtoun, was a chemical manufacturer who was active in the Free Church and later the United Free Church. White and his wife had come under the influence of Moody during Moody's first campaign in Scotland in 1874. After the campaign, the organizing committee transformed itself into the Glasgow United Evangelistic Association, of which White became president. In the first thirty years of its existence, the Association raised, apart from gifts in kind, a sum of over £380,000. Out of this sum, a building was erected on Bothwell Street at the cost of over £100,000. The building housed the Bible Training Institute, the Young Men's Christian Association, Young Men's Christian Club, and other institutions.[68]

Like the institute in Chicago, the Glasgow Bible Institute emphasized the Bible and practical training. The school was designed to train workers to go among the poor of Glasgow, doing evangelism and providing practical help.[69] Throughout the school's founding, Moody was active in raising funds, providing advice, encouraging White, and rallying the evangelical community in Glasgow. Moody suggested the name of the school's first principal.[70]

When one surveys Moody's educational work, several things become apparent. First, the influence of O. O. Howard, Müller, Spurgeon, and Pennefather is evident. Howard helped form Moody's vision for education. Müller's Scriptural Knowledge Institution for Home and Abroad and Spurgeon's Pastor's College provided models for Moody to copy. Müller's school targeted women, and both schools were racially mixed. We have already noted Pennefather's deaconess movement's role in what would become the Northfield Bible Training School and the Moody Bible Institute. The impact these four men had on Moody is clear.

Second, Moody's schools were all geared toward the poor. Although his effectiveness might be debated, there is no doubt that he consistently tried to minister to the poor. His schools sought not only to provide educational opportunities for the poor; they also often included practical instructions on how to help the poor. The schools were subsidized to keep costs low, so the poor could attend. Moreover, all the schools required students to work around campus and taught basic trades and skills necessary for self-help and helping others.

Third, all of Moody's schools reflected his commitment to evangelism and the power of regeneration. Moody's goal was that all his schools would produce Christian workers. He certainly was aware that both the Northfield schools would make men and women who would go into other fields, something of which he obviously approved; nevertheless, even at those two schools, it is evident he hoped they would produce their fair share of Christian workers.

Finally, Moody's educational endeavors were progressive. Specifically, Moody's schools for women were innovative in the field of women's education. Furthermore, all his schools were racially, socially, and religiously diverse.

Moody's work for women's education was consistent with his view of women generally. Although not a feminist, Moody's position on women was quite progressive for his time.[71] Women like Frances Willard criticized Moody for not being aggressive enough regarding women's roles.[72] However, Moody committed early in his career to a principle he learned from the revival of 1857: avoid controversial issues. Because of that, he

remained silent on questions like the ordination of women.[73] Nevertheless, he gave women significant responsibilities and opportunities.

In addition, he was sometimes willing to undergo criticism to bring
women to the fore. Therefore, while he may not have permitted women
to preside at mixed-gender meetings, he did encourage women to pray
publicly at such meetings.[74] When he introduced this public prayer by
women for the first time in Edinburgh, it created some controversy;
Moody continued the practice nonetheless and encouraged the women
in their public prayer. He supported women Bible teachers and even
argued that women graduates of the Northfield Bible Training School
could "stand in the gap" in rural churches. Moody believed those women
could lead Bible readings and preach in small churches as needed.[75]
Moody could support these activities without risking the bulk of his
support for his ministry.

MOODY'S OTHER SOCIAL WORK

*Reading the Bible and remembering the poor—a combination of faith and
works—will always bring joy.*

—D. L. MOODY[76]

In addition to his work as an educator, Moody engaged in numerous
acts of personal charity as prompted by his theology and his zeal for
evangelism. Because of his commitment to charitable action, Moody
earned a reputation as a man of incredible generosity.[77]

His son William recounted a story of Moody's encounter with a
beggar after a cab ride. Recognizing Moody, the man approached him
and asked for money for food. Moody had just paid the cab fare and
was entirely out of cash. Moved by the man's plight, he returned to the
cabbie and asked to borrow money to give to the beggar.[78]

Moody's sermons often contained stories of poor mothers whose
children died from accident or disease and whose fathers had left them

destitute because of alcoholism. When Moody encountered such circumstances, he would personally pay for the burial of the child and preach at the funeral.[79] These types of stories are repeated numerous times in the various biographies of Moody.

As we have seen, Moody served in the United States Christian Commission during the American Civil War. Moody was instrumental in establishing an employment bureau as part of that work. The bureau was created to help wounded soldiers find employment. In 1865, the bureau found work for 1,435 men, 124 boys, and 718 girls. Between 1867 and 1868, it secured another 3,411 jobs and found employment for nearly 9,000 people from 1869 to 1871. In addition, the bureau provided temporary work for scores of others.[80]

We have already seen how Moody provided for the physical needs of families in his early days at the YMCA and the Sunday school. He continued to meet the physical needs of others throughout his career with these institutions.[81] This commitment was in evidence after the Chicago Fire. Almost immediately after the fire, Moody, in connection with the Sunday school and Illinois Street Church, had a large structure erected to provide temporary shelter for displaced people. Moody raised funds for the building and helped recruit the staff for the enterprise. Food was prepared and served daily. Religious counsel and instruction were also provided.[82]

The Illinois Street Church, later named Moody Church, was designed mainly for the poor. It was located in the center of Chicago's impoverished North Side near the corner of Illinois and Wells Streets. The design was simple, so simple that one observer remarked, "It looks as if pains had been taken to make it as plain as possible so that no one, however poor, might be driven away by any outward display."[83] The plain sign outside the building that read, "Ever welcome to this house of God are strangers and the poor," reinforced the architecture.[84]

The Bible Institute Colportage Association represented another of Moody's efforts to minister to the poor. Founded in 1894, the association grew out of Moody's frustrated efforts to locate inexpensive Christian literature at a bookstore in Wisconsin. Unable to find literature at a low cost, he established his own publishing service. A brief description in the back of one of its 1908 books summarized its work: "This Association has continued to deliver, through means of the printed page, messages that convict of sin, quicken the devotional life, arouse to evangelistic effort and missionary activity. It has carried the gospel where church privileges were wanting, or not embraced."[85]

The Colportage Association aided the poor in multiple ways. First, it addressed what Moody considered their greatest need—conversion. The literature's low prices made the materials available to the working poor. Second, it provided an employment opportunity. The 1908 book cited above included a call for colportage workers. It pointed out that "employment is presented you at the smallest outlay of money and the least possible risk of failure or loss. The remuneration is in accordance with interest, time and energy expended. . . . The plan is workable and thoroughly tried as one of the great avenues through which the non-church goer can be reached. It is applicable in YOUR community, whether village, town or city."[86] After its founding, many of the students at the Mount Hermon school worked as colportage agents to help pay for their schooling. Finally, Moody used the Association to provide for such undertakings as free libraries for prisons and houses for the poor.[87]

In addition to his efforts, Moody's message and work spawned other charitable acts for the poor. The effects of Moody's campaign in Glasgow provide an excellent illustration of this fact. Lord Overtoun, J. Campbell White, identified Moody as the crucial figure in forming his activist spirit. He became the key figure in various charitable enterprises that developed from Moody's labors. Historian David Bebbington has described the various charitable enterprises that sprang from Moody's work in Glasgow. One of the most prominent was the Glasgow Tent Hall. The Tent Hall was built in 1876 for the United Evangelical Association, which had been meeting since 1874 in a mission tent on Glasgow Green. The Association was heavily involved in the temperance movement. On Saturday evenings, the Association in the Tent Hall offered the alternative entertainment of lantern slide shows that illustrated the evils of alcohol. The Tent Hall also hosted the Sabbath Morning Free Breakfast and the Glasgow Poor Children's Sabbath Dinner. Some of Moody's other legacies in Glasgow, as noted by Bebbington, included the Poor Children's Day Refuges, where children were cared for while their parents were at work, and the Crippled Children's League of Kindness, in which West End children were individually linked with East End children with disabilities. There were also the Weary Workers' Rest at Dunoon, the Homes for Destitute Children at Saltcoats, a Rescue Home for girls in danger of going astray, the Poor Children's Fresh-Air Fortnight Homes, and William Quarrier's Orphan Homes of Scotland.[88] In 1898, after surveying the impact of Moody's work in Glasgow, Sir George Adam Smith concluded that Moody's efforts had been a significant force for civic righteousness in Glasgow.[89]

Although it predated him, another institution experienced a boon due to Moody's work in Scotland. Carruber's Close Mission in Edinburgh was established in 1858 to provide a Sunday school for city children. The work quickly expanded to include "almost every form of Christian enterprise and philanthropy. Every age and class were embraced in their mission."[90] When Moody was in Edinburgh in 1883, he became acquainted with the mission and embraced their ministry. Struck by their lack of space, Moody embarked on a fundraising effort on their behalf. Before leaving Edinburgh, he had raised £10,000 and had preached as the cornerstone for their new building was laid.[91] By the time of his death, Moody was responsible for many such mission halls throughout the British Isles.[92]

In Liverpool, Moody worked to establish the British Workingman Company Limited. The company developed a series of houses of refreshments designed to provide inexpensive meals for workers as an alternative to the saloon. While conducting a campaign in the city, Moody invited Reverend Charles Garrett to speak for ten minutes. Garrett presented his belief that the masses needed an alternative to the saloon and suggested a series of cheap eating establishments. Moody began whispering to a number of the men on the platform while Garrett finished his talk. When Garrett finished, Moody sprang to his feet and announced the formation of the British Workingman Company, an organization designed to meet Garrett's challenge. The project prospered and was copied by innumerable towns and cities throughout Great Britain.[93]

CONCLUSION

Dwight Moody believed that urban social issues were the product of human sinfulness. Therefore, the only ultimate solution was personal conversion. Nevertheless, he was committed to working in various ways to alleviate human suffering. Because of his high regard for the Bible, Moody supported charitable work, especially emphasizing education for the poor during the latter phases of his career. The schools he founded were significant because they showed the value he placed on education to improve the lot of the poor. In addition, Moody believed that the Bible taught love for others, especially the poor. Therefore charity, primarily directed toward the poor, was appropriate if also subject to the Bible's teaching about laziness.

Consequently charity was never to be practiced to promote sloth. Further, because of his understanding of sin and his premillennialism, Moody had no confidence in solutions to social ills that were not rooted in conversion. Moody's theological conviction was that individual humans could not ultimately solve their sin problem and the trajectory of human civilization was inevitability downward. These theological ideas provided the primary framework for Moody's social vision and social work.

6

MOODY'S SOCIAL ACTION

Learning from His Failures

But now apart from the law the righteousness of God has been made known, to which the Law and the Prophets testify. This righteousness is given through faith in Jesus Christ to all who believe. There is no difference between Jew and Gentile, for all have sinned and fall short of the glory of God, and all are justified freely by his grace through the redemption that came by Christ Jesus.

—ROMANS 3:21–24

For the creation was subjected to frustration, not by its own choice, but by the will of the one who subjected it, in hope that the creation itself will be liberated from its bondage to decay and brought into the freedom and glory of the children of God. We know that the whole creation has been groaning as in the pains of childbirth right up to the present time. Not only so, but we ourselves, who have the first fruits of the Spirit, groan inwardly as we wait eagerly for our adoption to sonship, the redemption of our bodies.

—ROMANS 8:20–23

Dwight Moody was a remarkable human whom God used in profound ways. It would be easy to present a two-dimensional Moody as a towering hero of the faith or alternately as a person so tainted his work should be dismissed. However, neither would be valid or fair. Moody was a human, and he, like all humans, was flawed. Even he would describe himself as merely a sinner saved by grace. As such, we should expect to find both the impact of God's grace and signs of sinfulness in his life.

In this chapter, we explore one of Moody's flaws, specifically, his handling of racial issues. From our vantage point today, Moody's responses are both perplexing and complicated. Taken as a whole, they show both strengths and weaknesses. While providing insight into Moody's theological commitments, these events also demonstrate that a stalwart person can flinch in the face of pressure.

Some may object that it is not necessary or even appropriate to criticize a man like Moody. However, Christians are to be truth tellers. The Scriptures themselves present humans as both marvelous and flawed. While many elements of Mr. Moody's life are laudable, he is also flawed. It would be less than honest to ignore his flaws.

Scripture records the full truth about Bible characters we regard as heroes: Abraham passed off Sarah as his sister, Moses murdered a man, Jacob deceived his father, David committed adultery (if not rape) and murdered to cover it up. Thomas doubted; Peter denied Jesus, and was later rebuked by Paul because of his attitude toward Gentiles; Paul wrote off Mark; and Lot, whom Peter declared "righteous" in 2 Peter 2, offered his daughters to the men of Sodom. This theme continues throughout church history. Admirable figures like Augustine, Peter Abelard, Martin Luther, Jonathan Edwards, and Billy Sunday (to name a few) are found wanting after close investigation.

Mr. Moody was committed to the Bible. He believed the Scriptures should frame one's understanding of their life and world. He urged his followers to be so saturated with the Bible that it would be reflected in all areas of their existence. Consequently, it seems appropriate to consider the texts at the start of this chapter as the framework to evaluate Moody's life: Romans 3:21–24 and Romans 8:20–21. These Scriptures teach us that sin is insidious and pervasive. It affects every individual, culture, institution, and the entire created order—it corrupts, destroys, and brings death.

Moody believed Christ paid for our sins with His blood. He believed Jesus defeated death when He rose from the dead. He believed Jesus promised to free His creation from its bondage to corruption. However, while the ultimate end of sin and death is guaranteed, it is not yet fully seen. So, Moody lived in that hope, confident of the final victory of Christ. In this life, Moody maintained that we see signs of both the power of sin and the power of God. Consequently, human lives, cultures, societies, and institutions testify to both the continuing strength of sin and the sovereign power of God.

Moody was shaped by his era, and in some ways transcended his world. If judged by the standards of the time, Moody's approach to race was quite progressive in some ways and quite conforming in others. But our role as truth tellers pushes us to dive more deeply into these accounts. We must look past "the standards of the time" and instead compare his actions to the expectations of the Bible. The purpose of this chapter is not to discredit Moody. Instead, it shows that his life displayed what he believed in and proclaimed. Specifically, all human beings come up short when examined in light of the commands of the Bible.

Finally, our honest reckoning of Moody's life is consistent with one of his noted character qualities, his essential humility. Throughout his career, Moody was adamant about making sure he was not the focus of his work. He refused to attach his name to any of the institutions he founded, though others did this after he died. "Moody's willingness to receive criticism and to confess faults revealed genuine greatness of soul," a coworker said after his death.[1]

Dwight Moody was obsessed with a focus on Jesus and the gospel. Jesus was his brand. Consequently, constructing a two-dimensional portrait of a perfect Moody would hardly fit with his desire to keep the focus off him. With these provisos in place, let us turn to Moody and his approach to racial issues.

MOODY'S RACIAL COOPERATION

When Dwight Moody preached to Northern audiences, they reflected his admirable passion for reaching all people. In 1893, a reporter at the World's Columbian Exposition gave this account of his sermons: "Side by side stood rough men and fashionably dressed ladies, negroes and working women and gentlemen, all anxiously pressing forward."[2] And as was noted, Moody aggressively recruited students from diverse backgrounds—men, women, many ethnic groups, and especially immigrants—something unusual for his era. His schools were never segregated racially.

He sometimes used African Americans in his revival work. For example, during his first campaign in the United Kingdom, Moody partnered with the Fisk Jubilee Singers, an all-black choir from Fisk University in Nashville, Tennessee. First used at Edinburgh in 1874, the choir traveled on and off with Moody for the rest of his tour, concluding with extended appearances in London.

Moody met the choir in Newcastle when they attended one of his meetings. As he described it, "There were about three million of that race just coming out of the state of slavery, and the Jubilee Singers were traveling through Christendom, and laboring hard to collect funds, to lift up their brethren from the depths of ignorance in which they lived." When someone suggested that Moody include them in his meetings, he questioned their spiritual commitment, saying, "I suppose they are just merely public singers." However, upon learning of their Christian faith, he became an immediate supporter and invited their participation in the meetings. It was an unusual move that met some initial resistance. However, Moody continued to include the choir, and soon the naysayers were won over.[3]

Moody demonstrated his appreciation of their ministry by calling on them again during the London phase of his 1875 campaign. As a Fisk University historian described it, shortly after the choir arrived in London, Moody contacted them and bid them to sing that afternoon as part of his London meetings. The choir responded by "temporarily turning from their concerts to help win souls. The company secured quarters in London and labored with Moody for a month singing to approximately 10,000 to 12,000 people daily."[4] After the London campaign, Moody and the Fisk singers continued their busy schedules, which apparently did not intersect again during his lifetime.[5]

MOODY'S ENCOUNTERS WITH SEGREGATION

After returning to America, Moody made an unplanned trip to Augusta, Georgia, in 1875. This trip demonstrated the limits of his commitment to integration. Moody's foray into the American South was novel. Although the earlier revivalist of the First Great Awakening, George Whitefield, had worked extensively in the South, the champion of the Second Great Awakening, Charles Finney, never ventured into the Southern states and was never confronted with the issue of segregated meetings. By going to Georgia, Moody would run headlong into this controversy. These meetings would put Moody to the test.

When Moody arrived in Georgia, he was astonished that the meetings were segregated. Earlier that same year, the congregation at one of his New York meetings had been described as "a mixed assemblage of all classes; some very poor, a few not very clean. Many black faces dot the congregation."[6]

His initial response to what he saw in Georgia was moral indignation. Moody declared that some Southern whites "might possibly be astonished some day to see these blacks marching into the kingdom of heaven while they themselves were shut out."[7] The response from the white community in the South was swift and ferocious. "If Moody has come south for the purpose of endeavoring to change the relation of the black and white races," a news reporter wrote, he would face the "contempt and abhorrence of our entire people."[8]

One of Moody's close friends and traveling companions, Major Daniel W. Whittle, intervened at this point. Whittle understood Moody's anger. However, Whittle told Moody that if they insisted on integrating the meetings, the white population of Georgia would not attend. Whittle defended the segregated plan in his diary, writing that "not to have done it would have kept the white people away." Whittle believed there was "no way we could carry on the meetings" without acquiescing to the segregated plan.[9] In the end, Moody followed Whittle's advice.

After the 1876 controversy in Augusta, Moody did not plan any extended campaigns in the South for several years. In 1885, he held campaigns in Richmond, Virginia, and Washington, DC, both of which garnered significant criticism, discussed below. In 1886, Moody held fifteen campaigns in Southern states, all of which had segregated seating or separate services for blacks and whites.[10] In later years he returned to the South and continued segregated meetings, some as late as 1894 in Richmond, Virginia.[11]

However, it was clear Moody was not comfortable with his decision and tried to hold separate meetings for blacks in the South. In the 1880s, he offered to go to Louisville, Kentucky, for a series of meetings designed exclusively for blacks. He seemed to be searching for a way to reach blacks in the South while maintaining a white audience.[12]

Moody's segregated meetings are both puzzling and troubling. As noted in chapter 4, he was a committed abolitionist and an avid supporter of the Union. As a young man, he listened to the influential abolitionist speeches of William Lloyd Garrison, Elijah P. Lovejoy, and Wendell Philips. While in Boston, he was involved in the antislavery demonstrations at Faneuil Hall. Moody hated slavery; he saw it as a sin against God. As he put it, "Nations are only collections of individuals, and what is true of the part in regard to character is always true in regard to the whole. In this country our forefathers planted slavery and an open bible together, and didn't we have to reap? Didn't God make this nation weep in the hour of gathering the harvest, when we had to give up our young men, both North and South, to death, and every household almost had an empty chair, and blood, blood, blood, flowed like water for four long years? Ah, our nation sowed, and in tears and groans she had to reap!"[13]

Later the *New York Times* would report Moody objected to the application of the term "heathen" to the people of Asia. Mr. Moody stated, "America has far more sins to answer for than have China, and India is in accordance with the facts. It is only in this generation we have succeeded in abolishing slavery, more inhuman than any institution known in 'heathen' lands." He continued by claiming "the legislation of our country is vulgar and cynical" and a "violation of the first principles of the ethics of Christianity." The paper stated, "Mr. Moody's influence will advance the improvement in manners as well as the morals of professed Christians."[14]

By the 1890s, Moody could no longer accept the Southern segregated meetings. At a series of meetings in Texas in 1895, Moody began defying Jim Crow laws and segregation. On entering the site of the planned revival, Moody became enraged when he saw a fence designed to separate blacks from whites. He was so angry that he tried physically to tear the rail down. Although the rail withstood this initial assault, workers had torn it down by the time of the meetings.[15]

From this point on, Moody's meetings in public venues were likely integrated. The historical record is not always clear—contemporary accounts do not always give exact details of the seating for his citywide conventions. Later in his ministry, Moody was more willing to visit several churches in the same city, rather than speaking in a large public hall. In such cases where Moody was invited to speak to both black and white congregations, it is difficult to draw direct conclusions.[16] Whenever the practice stopped, the damage had been done.

AFRICAN AMERICAN RESPONSES

In addition to violating his conscience, Moody's segregated meetings had a long-term impact. Outraged by Moody's decision to segregate the meetings in Georgia, one black pastor declared that he would not allow Moody to preach in a barroom, let alone a church.[17] Ida B. Wells commented, "I remember very clearly that when Mr. Moody had come to the South with his revival sermons the notices printed said that the Negroes who wished to attend his meetings would have to go into the gallery or that a special service would be set aside for colored people only."[18] Wells found this to be despicable, but after attending meetings, she also expressed admiration for Moody: "His style is so simple, plain and natural that he does not preach a faraway God—a hard to be reconciled Saviour," she said, adding that he proclaimed "the simple truth that Christ Jesus came on earth to seek & save that which was lost. Mr. Sankey's singing is a sermon in itself."[19]

Perhaps the most prominent African American of the era, Frederick Douglass, issued stinging criticism during a Moody visit to Philadelphia. "Of all the forms of negro hate in this world," Douglas proclaimed, "save me from that one which clothes itself with the name of the loving Jesus." To Douglass, the hypocrisy of Moody's revivals was galling: "The negro can go into the circus, the theatre, and can be admitted to the lectures of

Mr. Ingersoll, but he cannot go into an evangelical Christian meeting."[20]

The heaviest criticism came from African American pastor Francis Grimké, a cofounder of the NAACP whose theology and ministry philosophy was close to Moody's. At one point Grimké expressed glowing admiration for Moody, describing him as "a soulwinner. He was ever looking out for opportunities to point men to Jesus, the Lamb of God, whose blood cleanses from all sin. That was his business; he had no other, lived for no other purpose. And hence the tremendous work which he did, and the wonderful success which attended his efforts."[21]

Then came Moody's fifteen-city Southern tour, with a stop in Jacksonville, Florida, where Grimké pastored a church. As was Moody's practice during this time, the meetings were segregated.[22] A few days earlier, the local newspaper had thanked Moody for avoiding "the extremists, the cranks, and those who delight in strife" who wanted "no distinction between blacks and whites at his meetings.[23] Moody had excused segregated seating by saying, "No, I will not touch the race issue. Let the local committees deal with it, so far as my meetings are concerned, as they may think best. They know more about it than I do, and doubtless will avoid the mistakes that I would be liable to make."[24] The editorial blamed Northern "agitators," claiming the problem was "not one that can be settled in a day or a year . . . it can only be settled by time—that is, it will eventually work out its own settlement."[25]

But Francis Grimké believed the issue had been settled by emancipation—which didn't call for a waiting period. He wrote "Mr. Moody and the Color Question in the South" for the *New York Independent*, delivering a withering critique of Moody:

> This discrimination against the Negro was not at all necessary
> to the success of his meetings. So great is his reputation as an
> evangelist, that his appearance would have secured crowds
> of willing listeners anywhere. There would not have been the

slightest difficulty in securing a mixed audience of both races. No amount of blackness and ignorance would have been sufficient to have kept the white people away from these meetings.[26]

Grimké pointed out that many whites had attended Jacksonville's "blacks only" meetings and had enjoyed the experience, further proving that the policy wasn't necessary. He further asked if Moody, "occupying the position that he does, as an ambassador of Christ, had a right to hide behind a local committee and become a nonentity in the presence of this great evil."[27] He viewed Moody with "mingled feelings of pity and disgust, " and suggested that "perhaps in the future Mr. Moody may learn that God is no respecter of persons; that of one blood he has made all races of men; that Christ died for all alike, and that the soul of the Negro is as precious in his sight as that of the white man."[28]

Returning home after the Southern tour, Moody also received criticism from the New York Annual Conference of the African Methodist Episcopal Church. One conference delegate called for the assembly to condemn the conduct of Mr. Moody.

> I would not have "Evangelist" Moody preach in a barroom
> of mine if I owned it, much less in a church. His conduct in
> his Southern tour has been shameful towards the negroes of
> the South, and in Charleston, when I was there, he positively
> refused to allow representation in his evangelical meetings from
> among the colored churches of the city, placing caste above
> Christianity and his patented system of salvation, by which the
> whites could be saved and the blacks lost, above the glorious
> Gospel of Jesus Christ, which offers salvation to every sinner. [29]

Another delegate asserted, "We are more cordially received in haunts of vice than in the alleged temples of Christ. Mr. Moody shows his narrow nature by his appeal to caste in the South, and dragged his meetings to the level of a circus, in which he plays the clown."[30]

During the AME meetings, a representative from the Northfield Conference rose to defend Moody—only to be shouted down by the delegates. "He was made to learn that he had mistaken the body of men he was talking to," the *Christian Reporter* said. "They were not the men to be hoodwinked to hide Mr. Moody's prejudice."[31]

Moody also received criticism from African American newspapers such as the *Washington Bee*. The paper's characterization of Moody's work is telling. "White people have a separate religion. Moody and Sankey might be serving God, but no Negro need apply. It was a white man's meeting."[32] A month later it covered an address by C. H. J. Taylor, a black newspaper editor and former ambassador to Liberia. "Whatever wrong the colored people suffered and whatever sores they have, the Church alone can relieve. Since God has no preference, His children should show none in their treatment of one another." Taylor directly blamed "Moody and Sankey, Sam Jones and Sam Small and all of their ilk for their conduct toward the Negro."[33]

On the other hand, some blacks were more circumspect with their comments. For example, Booker T. Washington spoke at the 1895 Northfield conference and considered Moody a friend. Moody in turn promoted the Tuskegee Institute and encouraged support from Northern donors.[34] A month later, Moody was in Atlanta when Washington delivered an address at the Atlanta Cotton States and International Exposition. By this point, Washington was attracting his own criticism from younger blacks who felt he was too accommodating—they dubbed his speech "The Atlanta Compromise," and the name stuck.[35] Later, when Moody was near death, Washington sent a warm note to Emma Moody, thanking him for work that "benefited people of all races."[36]

A letter from pastor L. H. Smith of an AME church in Savannah,

Georgia, began, "We, the Negroes of Savannah, thank you more than language can express . . . for the services you gave us at our churches." The letter describes the "good and lasting results of your brotherly and divinely directed labors among us." Smith commented that the local paper, the *Morning News*, had done well when it described Moody's work among the Negroes during the Civil War. However, it would have done "itself, the South, the Colored people, yourself and the Master a lasting service had it reported your service with us, some of the many good things you said to us." The letter concluded with Smith noting he and another pastor had collected $15.03 to support Moody's effort to place literature in prisons and poorhouses.[37] While Moody had critics among the black churches in the South, he also had some supporters.

RESPONSE TO LYNCHING

While the controversy over segregated meetings continued, Booker T. Washington's Tuskegee Institute began documenting a significant tragedy—the alarming rise in lynching attacks of African Americans.[38] By this point the Southern states had all passed legislation to codify Jim Crow practices and disenfranchise black voters. When lynchings reached their peak in 1892, white religious leaders were oddly silent.

"The attitude of the Anglo-American pulpit in relation to Southern outrages is one of the most discouraging features of the so-called Negro problem," Francis Grimké said in another article for the *Independent*.[39] He noted how white preachers were more than willing to denounce sins such as the liquor traffic, gambling, Sabbath desecration, and polygamy in Utah. "But not even a whisper has been heard on Southern outrages."[40]

In the same way, Ida B. Wells was particularly vociferous in her criticism:

"There was no movement being made by American white Christians toward aiding public sentiment against lynch law in the United States." Moreover, "Not only was this true, but the actions and utterances of certain well-known Christian workers had served to give encouragement to the practices of the southern states of America toward the Negro." "I mention," she says, "both the Rev. Dwight L. Moody and Miss Frances E. Willard in this country."[41]

On another occasion, Wells reported her conversations with believers in the United Kingdom. When she explained that most Christians in the United States remained silent in the face of segregation and lynching, she was asked about Moody and Francis Willard. They assumed these two had indeed spoken up. Wells went on to say,

> My answer to these queries was that neither of those great exponents of Christianity in our country had ever spoken out in condemnation of lynching but seemed, on the contrary, disposed to overlook that fashionable pastime of the South.

> Whatever the cause, no Negroes had ever heard of Rev. Moody's refusal to accept these Jim Crow arrangements or knew of any protest of his against lynchings.[42]

In fact, Moody did address lynching shortly before his death. Specifically, in 1899 just months before his death, Moody identifies lynching as a sign of the sinfulness of America.[43]

THE LASTING EFFECTS OF SILENCE

Moody's tolerance of segregation and prolonged silence on lynching would lead to long-term consequences shaping the country and extending racism in America. While this was not Moody's intent, there is evidence to support this claim. As early as 1893, Francis Grimké had been predicting the lasting effects. Noting the potential influence of white clergy, a group comprising more than 75,000 nationally, Grimké asked why they remained silent on racism. "If these seventy-five thousand men had done their duty, had taken the pains to set clearly before their people their duty in this matter in view of the requirements of God's Word and the principles of justice and right, which require us to render to every man his due, to do by others as we would be done by and to love our neighbor as ourselves, the outlook for the Negro would be very much more promising than it is today."[44]

Edward J. Blum's *Reforging the White Republic* (2005) argued that Moody's message was instrumental in rebuilding the White Republic by emphasizing reconciliation among Northern and Southern whites at the expense of African Americans. During Reconstruction, abolitionists in the North had a golden opportunity to pursue true racial justice and permanent reform in America. Why did the moment slip away, leaving many whites more racist than before? As Grimké had suggested a century earlier, Blum charges Moody with promoting white religious unity by keeping quiet in the face of racial prejudice.[45]

I believe Blum is correct in his assertion concerning the role of religion following the Civil War. The Civil War was, in many ways, a religious war.[46] It is easier to understand the war's immense carnage by looking at religious dynamics on both sides, a primary motivating factor for soldiers—as well as the women and children away from the battlefield.[47]

"The United States in 1860 was not uniquely religious," Mark Noll observes, "but it was nonetheless, and by almost any standard of comparison, a remarkably religious society."[48] Noll cites statistics from 1860, when between a third and two-fifths of Americans were formal members of churches. Further, the rate of adherence (people who regularly participated in church life) was probably double the rate of membership. "Religion was then much more important than any other center of value at work in the country," Noll concludes.[49]

During this era the church faced much less competition in its attempts to shape society's hearts and minds. Imagine a world free of cellphones, televisions, computers, and social media. The preacher during the Civil War era never faced the onslaught of voices today's preachers face contending for the minds and hearts of their congregations.

Consequently, it is necessary to remind the modern reader of religion's role in nineteenth-century America. Although the country had experienced waves of immigration that heightened the influence of Roman Catholicism and Judaism, it remained predominantly Protestant.[50] Indeed, in his work "Evangelicals and Politics in Antebellum America," historian Richard Carwardine noted that about 40 percent of the population identified with evangelical Protestantism and thus was the "largest, and most formidable, subculture in American society."[51]

Considering these realities, two ideas significantly influenced most Americans' minds. First, the Bible played a decisive role for many in forming private and public morality. Second, there was an overarching belief that America had a special relationship with God and had a unique position in human history. Antebellum debates about the institution of slavery raged within this framework, and it helps us better understand the increasing ferocity of the exchanges.

Because of the populace's broad regard for the Bible, the decades leading up to the Civil War featured preachers in both the North and South constantly appealing to scriptural texts to support their beliefs. Thousands of sermons proclaimed with absolute certainty the righteousness of both positions while denouncing the other side. Two examples show the contrast.

Robert Lewis Dabney, a Southern Presbyterian and slavery advocate, believed that "we must go before the nation with the Bible as the text, and 'Thus saith the Lord' as the answer . . . then the whole body of sincere believers at the North will have to array themselves, though unwillingly, on our side. They will prefer the Bible to abolitionism."[52]

Jonathan Blanchard, the first president of Wheaton College and an ardent abolitionist, believed the Bible taught the opposite: "Abolitionists take their stand upon the New Testament doctrine of the natural equity of man. The one-bloodism of humankind, and upon those great principles of human rights, drawn from the New Testament, and announced in the American Declaration of Independence, declaring that all men have natural and inalienable rights."[53]

Overarching both of these views was an assumption, shared in the North and the South, that America had a unique relationship with God. There was a shared sense that this country had a special role in God's economy. We were an exemplar to the rest of the world, the chosen of God to demonstrate actual Christian society. As a result, any deviation from the laws of God would bring God's wrath to bear on the land.

Lincoln's second inaugural address described the two sides this way:

> Both read the same Bible and pray to the same God and each invokes His aid against the other. It may seem strange that any man should dare to ask a just God's assistance in wringing their bread from the sweat of other men's faces but let us judge not that we be not judged. . . . The Almighty has His own purposes. . . . If we shall suppose that American slavery is one of those offenses which in the providence of God must needs come, but which having continued through His appointed time He now wills to remove, and that He gives to both North and South this terrible war as the woe due to those by whom the offense came, shall we discern therein any departure from those divine attributes which the believers in a living God always ascribe to Him?[54]

Given the power of religion in the Civil War era, the Grimké and Blum argument is compelling. Protestant churches were in a position to forcefully address issues of race after the war. As Mark Noll notes, "The evangelical Protestant traditions that had done so much to shape society before the war did possess the theological resources to address both America's deeply ingrained racism and its burgeoning industrial revolution." He contends the Civil War essentially "took the steam out of Protestants' moral energy." Thus, the Protestant Church remained "divided, North and South" and "even more divided along racial lines."[55]

Moody cast a long shadow over Protestant Christianity in the United States and the United Kingdom. He was in a position to challenge segregation. Because of his prominence, Moody's decision to tolerate segregation made a significant statement. The numerous complaints made by contemporaries, particularly African American Protestant evangelicals, are echoed by historians who argue that Moody's determination played a role in perpetuating discrimination. Moody's silence had a devastating effect on African Americans. While this was not Moody's intent, it nevertheless is troubling and must be acknowledged.

ANTISEMITISM AND JEWISH STEREOTYPES

The story of Moody's relationship with the Jewish people is also one of contradictions. On the one hand, Moody reinforced the stereotypes of the day. In one of his published sermons, he stated, "You know a Jew must have a very poor opinion of a man if he will not do business with him when there is a prospect of making something out of him."[56] On the other hand, Moody spoke against prejudice against the Jewish people. Commenting on the notorious Dreyfus Trial in France, Moody remarked, "I pity the man or a nation that allows prejudice to enter the heart against God's chosen people."[57]

One troubling episode comes from Moody's work at the World's Fair in Chicago in 1893. Moody had invited pastors and evangelists from nearly every European country to speak to various immigrant groups at the fair, including Adolf Stoecker (1835–1909).[58] A Lutheran theologian and a former court chaplain to Kaiser Wilhelm II, Adolf Stoecker was also well-known for his antisemitic rhetoric. Two days before Stoecker preached, the *Chicago Tribune* published a biographical essay noting that "his anti-Semitic speeches made him world renowned. He claimed that the Jews were clannish and that they formed a state within a state. He advocated laws disbarring Jews from official positions, such as lawyers, judges, and officers in the army."[59]

A day later, speaking to reporters through an interpreter, Stoecker did not deny the accusations, but "emphasized the fact that he had come to Chicago to preach the gospel and not attack the Jews."[60]

Moody rejected the published accusations and gave Stoecker a glowing introduction: "We give you a warm welcome. God bless you. We don't believe the newspapers. We believe in the Bible. We have confidence in you. We love you."[61] In a later Stoecker meeting, Moody pointed out another platform guest, Rabbi Joseph Rabinowicz, a convert to Christianity who led a Christian synagogue in Kishinef, Russia. Moody evidently believed that if a rabbi was not offended by Stoecker, other Jews should not be either.[62]

Moody apparently did not bother to check the accusations against Stoecker. Perhaps Moody believed in good faith that Stoecker was innocent and that the allegations against him were part of a campaign to undermine the German preacher's work. He saw him as a fellow evangelist who was doing in Germany the same kind of work as he was doing in America and therefore trusted him. Jews viewed the matter differently. For them, Moody's welcome to Stoecker meant an endorsement, and they developed a suspicious and contemptuous attitude toward Moody. Moody was a man with a passion for the gospel and his desire to see all people saved, including those of the Jewish people. However, many Jews associated Moody with missionary enterprises attempting their conversion. For them, such attempts were insults to their religious heritage and a threat to Jewish survival.[63]

This comment by Yaakov Ariel probably best summarizes Moody: "[His] attitudes toward the Jews were marked by ambivalence which reflected both deep-rooted prejudices against them as well as appreciation and hope for that people's glorious future. While Moody's prejudices were influenced by his cultural background, his hopes for the Jewish People resulted from his premillennialist eschatological belief."[64]

EVALUATION FROM SCRIPTURE

Moody's response was consistent with his commitment to evangelism. As we have seen, Moody believed conversion was the ultimate remedy for social ills. Though he did not express this in so many words, it seems reasonable to assume he felt the same way about racism. His goal was to ensure the presentation of the gospel to the largest number of people. If that meant tolerating segregated meetings for a period, then Moody was prepared to deal with that distasteful reality.

Regardless, Moody's decisions on these questions fall far short of the expectations laid out in Scripture. While it may be argued Moody reflected his times, we will not be judged on those standards. As Paul enjoined in Romans 12:2, we are not to conform to the pattern of this world, but be transformed by the renewing of our minds. It seems apparent that while Moody was not personally a racist, he chose at times to conform to the pattern of this world's racial ideology. I would like to suggest three plausible explanations for Moody's failure.

Moody believed in the gospel's ability to transform humans. The New Testament testifies to the power of human prejudice. In Acts 6:1 and 2, tensions arise in the early church about the unequal treatment of widows based on ethnicity. Galatians 2 records Paul confronting Peter about not eating with Gentiles. Sadly, bigotry in the church was hardly new. In addition to the biblical accounts, Moody had plenty of personal experiences to show that some Christians remained bigots. Further, it seems theologically naïve to believe conversion would immediately eradicate the sin of bigotry in all believers. Moody knew the way people of opposing viewpoints used the Bible leading up to the Civil War.

Moody believed in the power of the gospel to heal all wounds. Earlier we noted Protestant churches split before the country split.[65] It is conceivable Moody reasoned that if religion played such a critical role in causing the war, it must play a crucial role in healing the wounds. Consequently, he engaged in "ends justify means" reasoning, believing that an acquiescence to the Southern attitude on race would produce massive conversions among whites and lead to the dismantling of segregation. However, as we noted above, this seems naïve.

Moody's childhood included significant trauma. Moody lost his father as a little boy. Not only was the death shocking to the child, but it also pushed the family into poverty. Moody was forced to live with other families to help make ends meet. Education was a luxury the family could hardly afford, and Moody would bemoan his lack of education throughout his life. It is not hard to imagine the insecurities and abandonment issues these events would create within the maturing Moody.

What is clear is that throughout Mr. Moody's life, there is a consistent pattern of conflict avoidance.[66] It is not insignificant that his approach to racial concerns paralleled his responses to other major issues of the day. We have seen how Moody often brushed away serious theological issues and championed nonsectarianism in his schools, meetings, and church. The episode Washington Gladden described bears repeating. He reported that a dispute had broken out at Northfield between an evangelist and a higher critic. After listening, Moody simply prayed, "God bless our brother higher Biblical critic and qualify him for his great work. God bless our brother listener and strengthen him for the load that has been laid upon him. God bless our brother accuser and give him more love. Amen." Gladden concluded, "That was the end of the matter."[67] As Dorsett noted, "Moody certainly witnessed these great divisions inside conservative Christian circles, but he was unable or unwilling to do much about them in the place where he had the most influence—Northfield, Massachusetts."[68] Later, Dorsett concludes that "Moody's propensity to want to hide from problems often led to results that were destructive to the very goals he so diligently sought to accomplish."[69] That is clearly the case with his handling of racial questions after the Civil War.

Moody's propensity to avoid conflict was likely intensified by the Civil War. As was noted in chapter 2, the amount of death and destruction caused by the war is astonishing. During the war, Moody went to the front on nine different occasions. He saw the carnage firsthand. One of his first experiences was at the Battle of Shiloh in 1862. After the battle, he writes to his mother, describing seeing dead soldiers strewn all over the battlefield with no one to bury them. In addition, he writes of the rough treatment of the wounded.[70] Moody may have been concerned about reigniting armed conflict. Given what he saw, a desire to avoid more violence is understandable. Whatever the reason, Moody failed. Even a person as zealous for the Scriptures as Moody flinched when faced with this sin. It would be easy to denounce Moody as a man lacking moral courage, but that is far too easy. We humans are frail, and often our faith is weak. That is not to excuse Moody but to remind us of Paul's injunction in 1 Corinthians 10:12, "So, if you think you are standing firm, be careful that you don't fall!"

From one angle, Dwight Moody towers as a man of great faith. He was a person with fundamental limitations who gave himself entirely to

God. What God chose to do through Moody was astonishing. However, from another angle, this giant had clay feet. When faced with the besetting sin of his country, he backed down. In many ways, Moody's failure should not be surprising; as we noted at the beginning of the chapter, the Bible is full of stories of godly men and women who failed in times of testing.

Ultimately Moody's life demonstrates the gospel. In Moody, we see a man gripped by the Holy Spirit, driven to bring people to Christ. We see a man devoted to Scripture and prayer who genuinely loved children and the poor. We see a genuinely humble man who forgoes personal fame. And yet, when presented with opportunities to stand against the sin of racism, Moody remained silent.

Nevertheless, what we see in this moment of failure is the truth of the gospel. While we may be inspired by the past lives of men and women of faith, we must ultimately look solely to Christ, our faith's author and finisher. Christ alone does for us what no human could ever accomplish. He alone brings spiritual life, forgiveness for sin, right standing before God, and victory over death. That is a sentiment with which Dwight Moody would heartily agree.

7

CONCLUSION

Lessons from Moody's Work

Dwight Moody was supremely practical. He was not a detached idealist; he was a man who rolled up his sleeves and dug into work. He developed his ministry methods by doing ministry rather than theorizing. It is hardly surprising one of Moody's most famous books is titled *To the Work! To the Work! Exhortations to Christians.* Consequently, ending without something practical would be a disservice to him.

While the focus of this book has been to create a more accurate assessment of his work, as I noted in the introduction, I hoped to write something Christians would find helpful. Because of the extensive nature of Moody's life and work, there is much to be learned, both positive and negative. I hope we can learn from his triumphs and avoid repeating his mistakes as we seek to live out the gospel in our time. Consequently, what follows is an attempt to draw practical lessons from Moody's work. To that end, here are six lessons I believe apply to us in our time.

1. GOD USES THE ORDINARY TO ACCOMPLISH THE EXTRAORDINARY

Elijah was a human being, even as we are. He prayed earnestly that it would not rain, and it did not rain on the land for three and a half years.

—JAMES 5:17

At first glance, Dwight Moody seems an unlikely instrument for God's work. Raised by a single mother in poverty, Moody was uneducated and unpolished, hardly a candidate for a world changer.

Moody's preaching illustrated this reality. As might be expected, it also reflected his somewhat unique approach to grammar by including phrases like "The Spirit done it," "tain't no use," and "git right up."[1] One observer in England wrote: "Oh, the way that man does mangle the English tongue! The daily slaughter of syntax at the Tabernacle is dreadful. His enunciation may be pious, but his pronunciations are decidedly off-color. It is enough to make Noah Webster turn over in his grave and weep to think that he lived in vain."[2]

His sermons were all delivered at an alarming rate of speed. As one observer put it, "Moody seemed to seize the idea that his messages were to be delivered over wires kept hot and that there was neither time nor money to be wasted in their delivery."[3] The observer continued noting that, in passages of intense excitement, the sentences possessed an explosive quality suggesting a pack of firecrackers set off by accident.[4] Another described his sermons' endings as having the feel of a calvary charge, saying one either went with it or got out of the way.[5] His delivery speed and limited vocabulary meant he rarely used words with three or four syllables. When he dared use them, they often emerged in a tortured fashion.[6]

Given this description of his preaching, his popularity is astonishing. Moody crossed class lines, preaching to poor children and urban immigrants as well as the aristocracy in the United Kingdom. What

Moody lacked in education and polish, his earnestness and the power of God more than made up for. One observer recounted a conversation with Moody after observing the young Moody's inadequacies at a meeting. Flabbergasted by Moody's limitations, he approached him. Aware of his inadequacies, Moody told the man, "I have got only one talent; I have no education, but I love the Lord Jesus Christ, and I want to do something for him: I want you to pray for me."[7] Moody was committed to God, and his life demonstrates God's willingness to use those earnestly committed to Him. Moody's life reflects his plea to others, "Give your life to God; he can do more with it than you can!"[8]

2. HUMILITY IS ESSENTIAL TO CHRISTIAN SERVICE

If we only get down low enough, my friends, God will use every one of us to His glory.[9]

—DWIGHT MOODY

If a man is proud and lifted up, rivers of grace may flow over him and yet leave him barren and unfruitful, while they bring blessing to the man who has been brought low by the grace of God.[10]

—DWIGHT MOODY

As I have been studying some Bible characters that illustrate humility, I have been ashamed of myself. If you have any regard for me, pray that I may have humility.[11]

—DWIGHT MOODY

In recent years we have seen ministries and megachurches spectacularly implode. Time after time, as the wreckage is cleared, we hear a tale of power, control, and ego.

It would be easy to listen and be angry at "them," but the reality is we are them. As Walt Kelly put it in his comic strip *Pogo*, "We have met the enemy, and he is us." We love celebrities who glitter in the light.

We are drawn to their charisma and grant them power because of their skills. We fawn over them, feeding their egos, attending seminars, and buying books. Perhaps even more troublesome, we crave to be them in our souls. We dream of being the godly man or woman leading a massive ministry admired by others. Unfortunately, marketing schemes have replaced prayer meetings in too many of our churches.

Throughout the history of the church, God has brought forth men and women who stand as examples for us. Moody is one of those people. As we have seen, some things could be improved in Moody's work; he sometimes failed. Despite these failings, Moody's ability to avoid the trap of ego and power is instructive. We are a power-, personality-driven culture. As the old Canon camera commercial said, "Image is everything." For Moody, Jesus and the gospel were everything.

As I have studied the life of Moody, I have been struck by Moody's adamant refusal to attach his name to anything. Moody Bible Institute was not named after Moody until he died. The same is true with Moody Memorial Church. I have been increasingly impressed with the wisdom Moody showed in this choice. How many of us could remain grounded if surrounded by a group of people committed to making our name a household word? Moody knew this and aggressively sought to protect himself from this temptation.

Moody was also aggressive about sharing his meetings. Others preached at his events. There are stories of Moody walking into meetings and announcing to a colleague he was speaking as he entered the building. He sometimes even waited until he was on the platform before informing a colleague he was preaching. Moody wanted his campaigns to be focused on someone other than him.

There was a humility to Moody. He knew his limitations and was not afraid to acknowledge them. He was especially vocal about his lack of education. Throughout his life, Moody regularly deferred to educated Bible teachers. He would sit with gifted scholars and spend hours peppering them with questions. His formation of the Northfield Bible Conference was partly driven by his desire to sit under the teaching of quality Bible teachers. He would always begin by reading Charles Surgeon's notes on his selective text when preparing sermons. Moody insisted he be called "Mr. Moody, not Rev. Moody." On more than one occasion, when he was introduced as "Rev. Moody," he would spring to his feet and quickly correct the speaker, insisting he was plain old Mr. Moody, a lay Sunday school teacher.

I remember being impressed the first time I heard about Moody's reluctance to have his picture taken. He was transparent about his reasoning; he never wanted it to be about him. However, newspapers flocked to him for interviews when he became well-known. During the interview, he would spend much of the discussion quoting Scripture because he wanted to make it about God. This is at the heart of Moody's approach to ministry. Dwight Moody was obsessed with making it about Jesus and the gospel. Jesus was his brand.

I was raised in evangelical churches. My parents served with an evangelical foreign mission most of my life. I attended Christian colleges. I have served on church and mission boards and worked in Christian higher education my entire career. Evangelical institutions have shaped me. Reflecting on my life, I see a broad continuum between those churches and institutions. I have seen some institutions elevate brand over mission, valuing loyalty to brand over truth. Leaders isolate themselves, muzzling questions and eliminating accountability to those they serve. I have also seen real servant leaders who kept their institution focused on Jesus and pursued accountability and input from others.

The Lord is calling us to look at ourselves and our institutions. First Samuel 8 tells the tragic story of Israel demanding a king. God had warned them they were different; God was their King. But they insisted they needed to be like everybody else. The results were catastrophic. We court disaster when we build around charismatic, gifted people and grant them almost unlimited power. When we look to God and value spiritual growth over numbers, we are in a place to see God work. There is nothing wrong with being gifted and charismatic, but we owe it to those folks to remember it is always only about Jesus. I think that is something Mr. Moody understood, and we should also.

3. DO THE THINGS THAT NEED TO BE DONE THAT NOBODY ELSE IS DOING

There are many of us that are willing to do great things for the Lord, but few of us are willing to do little things.[12]

—DWIGHT MOODY

Dwight Moody was an innovator but not a copycat. I remember a Christian leader saying, "There are many regiments in God's Army, and we will trust God to use them and concentrate on our mission. We will support and respect the work of other schools and ministries." That statement captured Mr. Moody's approach to ministry. Dwight Moody never competed with other ministries. He trusted God to use others and looked instead for places without Christian work. When Moody ran city revivals, he aggressively sought collaboration with the local churches. Moody repeatedly described his goal as serving the church, not replacing it. This attitude explains why many churches and Christian leaders so widely admired Moody.

The two best examples from Moody's life were his Sunday school and his foray into publishing. When Moody was "encouraged" to rethink his practice of bringing street kids to church, he innovated. He reasoned no one was willing to enter their neighborhoods; no Christian work existed. So, he went to a place of great need without any workers. The same can be said of his publishing venture. Moody got into publishing because he saw a need that no one addressed. He was motivated by ministry needs, not money or fame.

I have often wondered how much evangelicals have spent on redundant ministries. Too often, we are unwilling to trust God to work through others, as if only our group can do it right. How much more ministry could we accomplish if we cooperated rather than competed? Moody is an example of how much more can be done by focusing on cooperation and finding areas without Christian work, even if they are not glamorous.

4. EVANGELISM AND SOCIAL WORK ARE NOT MUTUALLY EXCLUSIVE

Do all the good you can, to all the people you can, in all the ways you can, and as long as ever you can.

—MOTTO IN MR. MOODY'S BIBLE

Reading the Bible and remembering the poor—a combination of faith and works—will always bring joy.[13]

—DWIGHT MOODY

If you have done much reading about Moody before this book, you certainly came across the claim that Moody turned evangelicalism away from social engagement to exclusively evangelism. By now, you can see the falseness of that claim. While Moody prioritized evangelism, he never excluded addressing social concerns.

What is crystal clear from surveying Moody's work is that he cared deeply about outcasts and about people experiencing poverty. Much of his work was directed toward alleviating their suffering. In short, Moody was an example of the necessity of doing both evangelism and engaging social ills. It is certainly fair to question Moody's methods but not his intentions. Poverty, discrimination, and evil social structures are complex issues with a variety of opinions on how best to address them. Reasonable people can disagree sharply about methods of dealing with these problems; however, Moody would say no Christian has the right to ignore them. According to Moody, the Bible is clear: Christians care about the plight of the widows, the poor, and the orphans. Any Christian who fails to address social problems is not following the example of Dwight Moody. Indeed, Moody is an enduring testimony to the truthfulness of the necessity of doing both.

5. WE MUST STAND AGAINST THE CULTURAL SINS OF OUR DAY

Do not conform to the pattern of this world, but be transformed by the renewing of your mind.

—ROMANS 12:2A

In the verse above, Paul encourages the Christians in Rome not to conform to their world's values and behaviors but to have their minds renewed, changing their thoughts. Christians are to think about things differently. This means we are to respond to the beliefs and practices of the world considering the teachings of the Bible.

In the previous chapter, we explored one of Moody's failures. On issues regarding race, Moody conformed to the values of his age. Very few people knew their Bible like Moody; consequently, in his case, this was not a matter of ignorance of the teachings of the Bible.

It would be easy to condemn Moody, but the purpose of this chapter is to learn not to pass judgment. Moody, like all of us, was shaped by his times. We know it is easy and safe to conform. It is also easy to rationalize compromise, particularly to achieve a perceived greater good. In Moody's case, he seems to have believed that preaching the gospel trumped speaking against things he knew were wrong. But ends do not justify means.

There is a fine but important distinction between being sensitive to our culture and paying no heed to sin. Indeed, we are not to cause undue offense, but the Scriptures do not allow us to ignore personal or cultural sin. Christians and the church are to be salt and light. We may disagree about how to respond to the sins of our times, but acquiescence is not an option.

The challenge we face is threefold. First is the temptation to choose to remain quiet. Moody demonstrates what happens when Christians and the church decide to stay silent. We must speak out against evil. This is a lesson we must take to heart. Second, we must avoid choosing what sins to address and what ones to ignore. We must read Scripture carefully and follow all its precepts. When Christians oppose abortion while ignoring things like hunger, mental illness, and domestic abuse, they are not biblical. This is not to say all sins are equal; however, we must follow the whole counsel of God. Third, we must constantly check to see how much we are driven by culture rather than Scripture. All Christians would acknowledge every culture contains beliefs that are incompatible with Scripture. But in today's media-driven society, becoming immune or blinded to our flaws is easy. Ask yourself, how have your values changed over the last decade? Are the changes a result of a deeper understanding of Scripture or the impact of media? Make no mistake, this is hard work but essential work. That is why we must be seeking, as Paul puts it, to renew our minds constantly.

6. WE MUST HAVE A PROFOUND COMMITMENT TO GOD

Moody gave his life to God. Perhaps the best way to end this book is to remind ourselves of the challenge that drove Dwight Moody. While visiting Bristol, England, in 1867, he heard evangelist Henry Varley say, "The world has yet to see what God will do with and for and through and in and by the man who is fully and wholly consecrated to Him."[14] Moody took the words as a challenge and responded, "I will try my utmost to be that man."[15] May the same be true of us.

ACKNOWLEDGMENTS

It has been said it takes a village to raise a child. In this case, it took a village to write this book. An acknowledgment hardly seems sufficient; nonetheless, it must suffice.

I have had the privilege of working under many gifted scholars. I am particularly grateful to Mark Noll and Patrick Carey for their patience, guidance, and encouragement during my graduate classroom years. They modeled expertise in scholarship and provided a superb classroom experience. John Wolffe and the late Edith Blumhofer coaxed, encouraged, and corrected through the writing of my thesis, from which this is primarily drawn. Without their steady hand, none of this would have happened. Any weakness in this effort is the product of my limitations, not their tutelage.

As is always the case with all researchers, I am dependent on the work and input of others. I would like to particularly thank the work of Lyle Dorsett, Mark Noll, David Bebbington, Stanley Gundry, and James Findlay. Their work was foundational for this effort. James Spencer has served as an essential dialogue partner during the process. Finally, no one played a more pivotal role than my friend and former colleague Michael McDuffee. Mike provided feedback, insight, direction, and encouragement throughout the entirety of this program. I am deeply grateful.

Over the years, several librarians and archivists have provided invaluable support. The archivists and librarians at Moody Bible Institute over the last decade were kind and helpful. I am grateful to you all. Peter Weiss, the archivist at Northfield Mount Hermon School, has been exceptionally helpful. As a Red Sox fan, Peter shares the angst that often accompanies being a Cubs fan. We have commiserated together too many times. David Malone, dean of the library at Calvin University, provided help and encouragement when he served in the archives at the Billy Graham Center at Wheaton College. David was not only a help; he and his wife, Kelly, have been steadfast friends for over three decades.

A little over ten years ago, David Powell and his son, Timothy Powell, stopped by Moody Bible Institute. David was Mr. Moody's great-grandson. He and Tim were keen to preserve and promote Mr. Moody's legacy. Although both have passed, they provided energy and insight throughout my research.

The staff of Moody Publishers has supported this project and helped with access to sources. This is a better book because of their work. I am also indebted to Andrew Hagen for his research on my behalf.

I have recently stepped away after thirty-six years on the faculty at Moody Bible Institute. I would be remiss not to acknowledge the critical role faculty colleagues and scores of students have played in my teaching career. I am in all your debt. You will never know the role you have played in my life.

A group of steadfast friends provided support throughout. Peter Walters, Brian Hillstrom, Jon Laansma, John Goodrich, Eric Redmond, David Pappendorf, David Fetzer, and Ashish Varma have remained like "David's mighty men"—consistently loyal and supportive. They have made me a better man.

Of course, foundational to all this is my family. My mother and father, both with the Lord, supported me consistently. They were children of the Depression, when the thought of attending college, let alone earning a doctorate, was impossible. What was impossible for them, they made a reality for me. Besides encouragement and financial support, they prayed for me and my family daily. My children tolerated my absence, both physically and, at times, mentally, as I worked through this project. At times, balance was elusive; thank you, William and Emily, for your patience. The burden often fell hardest on my wife, Mary. She stepped in during my absence and encouraged me through dark times. I cannot express how much you made this possible. Thank you!

At the core of all of this is the Lord. Why He has been kind to me is inscrutable. I echo the sentiments Paul expressed in his letter to the Romans: "For from him and through him and for him are all things. To him be the glory forever! Amen" (Romans 11:36).

NOTES

Introduction

1. William H. Daniels, *Moody: His Words, Work, and Workers* (New York: Nelson & Phillips, 1877), 431–32.

2. D. L. Moody, *Men of the Bible* (Chicago: Bible Institute Colportage Association, 1898), 67.

3. John McDowell and Others, *What D. L. Moody Means to Me: An Anthology of Appreciations and Appraisals of the Beloved Founder of the Northfield Schools* (East Northfield, MA: Northfield Schools, 1937), 8.

4. *Boston Journal*, December 27, 1899, 3. Quoted in Evensen, *God's Man for the Gilded Age*, 9.

5. David Bebbington, *The Dominance of Evangelicalism: The Age of Spurgeon and Moody*, vol. 3 in *A History of Evangelicalism: People, Movements and Ideas in the English-Speaking World* (Downers Grove, IL; InterVarsity, 2005).

6. Martin Marty, "Introduction" in *Dwight L. Moody: American Evangelist 1837–1899*, James F. Findlay (Chicago: University of Chicago Press, 1969), 1.

7. Dorsett, *A Passion for Souls*, 21.

8. George, *Mr. Moody and the Evangelical Tradition*, 1.

9. George Marsden, *Fundamentalism and American Culture* (New York: Oxford University Press, 1980), 33.

10. Dorsett, *Passion*, 206. The 2.5 million figure is a total number of attendees and does not allow for people who attended more than once.

11. Evensen, *God's Man*, 44. Evensen cites material in the D. L. Moody Collection, MBI Archives.

12. George, *Mr. Moody*, 113.

13. Bebbington, *The Dominance of Evangelicalism*, 40–50.

14. Billy Graham to Emma Moody, date unknown, https://moodycenter.org/d-l-moody-digital-archives.

15. Presbyterians in 1838, the Methodists in 1844, and the Baptists in 1845.

16. Bebbington, *The Dominance of Evangelicalism*, 12–20; and Stanley Gundry, *Love Them In: The Life and Theology of Dwight Moody* (Grand Rapids, MI: Baker Books, 1976), 58–68.

17. According to the 1890 *Census Bulletin*, the average annual wage per industrial worker (including men, women, and children) rose from $380 in 1880 to $564 in 1890, a gain of 48 percent.
18. Davidoff and Hall, *Family Fortunes: Men and Women of the English Middle Class*, 71–148.
19. Here are just a few examples: the General Association of Regular Baptist Churches (1932), Orthodox Presbyterian Church (1936), Conservative Baptist Association (1947), Association of Baptists for World Evangelization (1937), Independent Board for Presbyterian Foreign Missions (1933), Westminster Seminary (1929), Denver Seminary (1950), Baptist Bible College Clarks Summit (now Clarks Summit University), Bible Institute of Pennsylvania (1913).
20. Kathryn T. Long, *The Revival of 1857–1858* (New York: Oxford University Press, 1998), 124–25; and George Marsden, *Fundamentalism and American Culture* (New York: Oxford University Press, 1980), 85–93.

1. The Journey to Christ: His Boyhood and Adolescence

1. William R. Moody, *The Life of D. L. Moody*, 376.
2. In this section, I do not intend to provide a biography of Moody; instead, I will sketch an outline of his life and ministry.
3. Findlay, *American Evangelist*, 25–42; and Dorsett, *Passion*, 28–30.
4. William R. Moody, *The Life of D. L. Moody*, 20.
5. Narrative details and quotations in this section are from *The Life of D. L. Moody*, 20–30.
6. See Daniels, *Moody: His Words*, 12. "This man was a faithful friend to the widow and her large family of little children. He would visit them betimes, cheer them up with some pleasant words, settle quarrels among the boys, give the little ones a bright piece of silver all around, and bid the mother keep on praying, telling her God would never forget her labor of love. One time he took little Dwight into his family to do errands and go to school—a work of charity, which by all accounts must have sorely tried his patience. The good man was often perplexed what to do with the boy, being forced to laugh at his pranks in spite of himself, when he felt his duty to be stern and severe."
7. William R. Moody, *Life of Moody*, 4–5.
8. Moody admits as much in his sermon on the Prodigal Son: "The first thing I remember was the death of my father. It was a beautiful day in June when he fell suddenly dead. The shock made such an impression on me, young as I was, that I shall never forget it. I remember nothing about the funeral, but his death has made a lasting impression upon me." M. Laird Simons, *Holding the Fort: Sermons and Addresses at the Great Revival Meetings Conducted by Moody and Sankey* (Philadelphia: Porter & Coates, 1877), 198–99.
9. Dorsett, *Passion*, 30–32. Dorsett notes that "Everett's approach starkly contrasted with the Calvinism in which Betsy was reared, especially the Calvinist

doctrine of double predestination. Betsy viewed Everett's emphasis on God's love and compassion as appealing and refreshing. Apparently this also appealed to her son. Throughout his career, Moody remained aloof from some of the articles of Calvinism. For instance, Moody helped develop the doctrinal statement of the Illinois Street Independent Church. The statement parallels the doctrinal statement of the Congregational church, with one significant difference—the Illinois Street church omitted the clause on predestination, primarily at Moody's urging. This does not mean, however, that Moody totally rejected Calvinism, simply that he was not a thorough-going consistent Calvinist like Spurgeon." Also see Fry Jr., *D. L. Moody: The Formative Years 1856–1873*, 13–15.

10. William R. Moody, *Life of Moody*, 4–5, 21. William points out the crucial role Everett played in the life of the Moody family.

11. Dorsett, *Passion*, 27–29; Bebbington, "Moody as Transatlantic Evangelical," in George, *Mr. Moody in the Evangelical Tradition*, xx.

12. Dorsett, *Passion*, 32. It should be noted that Dorsett is wrong in his portrayal of Everett as "old" and "aged."

13. Everett, *Descendants of Richard Everett*, 104.

14. Elmer Powell, "Moody of Northfield," unpublished manuscript in Northfield Mount Herman Archives, n.d., 56.

15. Ibid., 96.

16. William R. Moody, *Life of Moody*, 21.

17. A similar incident from the life of Phillips Brooks supports this interpretation. See Rev. William Lawrence to William Moody, November 22, 1927 (in response to William's question about Phillips Brooks and baptism). Lawrence confirms Brooks was baptized as an infant by a Unitarian in the name of the father, the Son, and the Holy Ghost. Brooks maintained, "In his judgment and knowledge, his baptism was valid." MBI Archives.

18. William R. Moody, *Life of Moody*, 81.

19. Gundry argues, "Certainly to say that his contact with Unitarianism as a youth had any significant impact upon his mature thinking and outlook would be an overstatement." Gundry, 19. In a sense, I do agree with Gundry, but we have noted William R. Moody's and William Daniel's assertion about the vital role Everett played in his father's life. To say the man who became a father figure and who the family credits with being a key figure in holding them together had no impact does not follow. The point is Everett influenced Moody in the realm of practical Christianity rather than his theological convictions.

20. William R. Moody, *Life of Moody*, 21–22.

21. Charles F. Goss, *Echoes from the Pulpit and Platform* (Hartford: A. D. Worthington, 1900), 490–95; and Dorsett, *Passion*, 34.

22. *Third Annual Catalogue of the Instructors and Teachers of Northfield Institute, Northfield, Mass., for the Year Ending November 1853*, Northfield Historical Society, Northfield, MA. The catalog indicates a curriculum consisting of English, Higher English, Latin, Greek, French, Pencil Drawing, Painting, and Piano.

23. *Chicago Tribune*, December 23, 1899; and *New York Times*, December 23, 1899.

24. William R. Moody, *Life of Moody*, 35.

25. Ibid., 23.

26. D. L. Moody, letter to brothers, April 9, 1854, D. L. Moody Papers, Yale Divinity School Library. Another note to his sister speaks of a girl he left behind named Delia. He asks her if she sees Delia to "tell her how much I want to kiss her" and that "there is one or two pretty girls down here but none like Delia and look the world and you will never find the likes of her." D. L. Moody, letter to Sister Lizzie, May 4, 1854, MBI Archives. (To let the reader understand Moody's thoughts and capacities, all unpublished letters are transcribed without corrections.)

27. In a letter to his mother, Moody writes, "I go to meating at Mount Vernon St. Orthodx. I don't know how it is spelt but you know what I mean." Quoted in Pollack, *Moody*, 24.

28. J. Wilbur Chapman, *The Life and Work of D. L. Moody* (Philadelphia: American Bible House, 1900), 76.

29. Edward Kimball, "Mr. Moody's Admission to the Church," *New York Witness Extra*, April 1876.

30. Langdon S. Ward, deacon of the Mount Vernon Church, "Dwight L. Moody's Experience 1855–56," typescript, D. L. Moody Papers, Yale Divinity School Library.

31. William R. Moody, *Life of Moody*, 44.

32. Pollock, *Moody*, 25.

33. Edward N. Kirk, *Lectures on Revivals* (Boston: Congregational Publishing Society, 1875).

34. Quoted in Pollock, *Moody*, 12.

35. Richard Carwardine, *Transatlantic Revivalism: Popular Evangelicalism in Britain and America, 1790–1865* (Westport, CT: Greenwood Press, 1978), 22.

36. Edward Norris Kirk, *A Plea for the Poor: A Sermon Preached in the Old South Church Before the Howard Benevolent Society*, December 23, 1849 (Boston: Tappan & Dennet, 1843), 20, 23, 26, 40.

37. Chapman, *Life and Work,* 81, 82.

38. Edward Beecher, *History of the Formation of the Ladies Society for the Promotion of Education at the West; with Two Addresses, Delivered at Its Organization, by the Reverent Edward Beecher, D. D., and Reverent E. N. Kirk* (Boston: Henry Mason, 1846), 7–10, 17.

39. Smith, *Revivalism and Social Reform*, 168.

40. Pollock, *Moody*, 12–13.

2. The Formation of the Christian Worker

1. Quoted in Donald L. Miller, *City of the Century: The Epic of Chicago and the Making of America* (New York: Simon and Schuster, 1996), 9.

2. Carl Sandburg, *Chicago Poems* (New York: Henry Holt, 1916), 3.

3. Josiah Strong. *Our Country: Its Possible Future and Its Present Crisis,* rev. ed. (New York: Baker and Taylor, 1891), 171.

4. William R. Moody, *Life of Moody*, 263.

5. Dorsett, *Passion*, 260.

6. Howard P. Chudacoff and Judith E. Smith, *The Evolution of American Urban Society*, 5th ed. (Upper Saddle River, NJ: Prentice Hall, 2000), 188. The percentages were determined by taking the number of city inhabitants and dividing them by the total population of the United States. The population figures were taken from the United States census figures of 1860 and 1910, respectively. The numbers from 1860 include the slave population.

7. Alhstrom, *A Religious History of the American People*, 735.

8. Ibid.

9. Chartier, "The Social Views of D. L. Moody," 5.

10. Ibid.

11. Harold U. Faulkner, *American Economic History*, 8th ed. (New York: Harper & Row, 1960), 473–75.

12. Chester Gillis, *Roman Catholicism in America* (New York: Columbia University Press, 1999), 60–61.

13. Alhstrom, *A Religious History*, 555.

14. Chudacoff and Smith, *American Urban Society*, 122.

15. Ibid., 120–21. These pages detail the movement of rural native-born Americans to the new urban centers.

16. Chartier, "The Social Views of D. L. Moody," 5.

17. Edward Beecher, 13–17. Moody never engaged in the rhetoric used by Kirk in the 1846 address previously mentioned.

18. For example, see Lyman Beecher, *A Plea for the West* (1835); and Horace Bushnell, *A Letter to His Holiness Pope Gregory XVI* (1846). He distances himself from his supporters as well. For example, in 1870, William E. Dodge, a staunch Moody supporter, denounced Roman Catholics' attempts to get tax money for their parochial schools. Richard Lowitt, *A Merchant Prince in the Nineteenth Century: William E. Dodge* (New York, 1954), 345.

19. Dorsett, *Passion,* 63–64.

20. D. L. Moody, letter to mother, September 25, 1856, D. L. Moody Papers, Yale Divinity School Library.

21. D. L. Moody, letter to brother, October 19, 1856, D. L. Moody Papers, Yale Divinity School Library.

22. William R. Moody, *Life of Moody*, 53.

23. Ibid.

24. D. L. Moody, letter to mother, February 10, 1860, D. L. Moody Papers, Yale Divinity School Library.

25. D. L. Moody, letter to George, April 26, 1860, D. L. Moody Papers, Yale Divinity School Library. This letter is only available in a transcribed version. Obviously, the transcriber corrected the spelling and grammar.

26. D. L. Moody, letter to Folks, February 12, 1861, D. L. Moody Papers, Yale Divinity School Library.

27. D. L. Moody, letter to mother, June 5, 1861, D. L. Moody Papers, Yale Divinity School Library.

28. D. L. Moody, letter to mother, November 19, 1861, D. L. Moody Papers, Yale Divinity School Library.

29. Long, *The Revival of 1857–1858*, 3–6.

30. Ibid., 3. Long cites James W. Alexander, *The Revival and Its Lessons* (New York: American Tract Society, 1858), 14; Talbot W. Chambers, *The Noon Prayer Meeting of the North Dutch Church* (New York: Board of Publications, Reformed Protestant Dutch Church, 1858), 285; and *Examiner*, March 4, 1858.

31. Ibid.,12–14. The account of the revival found in the following two paragraphs is drawn from these pages.

32. The early phase of the revival in New York actively sought to limit women's involvement. Thus the event is sometimes just referred to as the "Businessmen's Revival." For a detailed discussion, see chapter 4, "Gender Issues and the Masculinization of Urban Piety."

33. Samuel Irenaeus Prime, *The Power of Prayer, Illustrated in the Wonderful Displays of Divine Grace at the Fulton Street and Other Meetings* (New York: Scribner, 1858), 47. Prime is careful to point out the movement also spread to the American South, citing revivals in Richmond, Savannah, Mobile, Vicksburg, New Orleans, and Memphis.

34. Richard Carwardine, "The Second Great Awakening in Comparative Perspective; Revivals and Culture in the United States and Britain," Modern Christian Revivals, eds. Edith L. Blumhofer and Randall Balmer (Urbana: University of Illinois Press, 1993), 88.

35. D. L. Moody, letter to mother, January 6, 1857, MBI Archives.

36. D. L. Moody, letter to brother, March 17, 1857, MBI Archives.

37. D. L. Moody, quoted in Orr, *The Fervent Prayer*, 198.

38. Long, *The Revival of 1857–1858*, figure 4. See the illustrations presented on pages 92 and following. In addition to the slavery question, the other main controverted point was whether women should be permitted to pray aloud in interdenominational prayer meetings.

39. This is not to say Moody's response to this prohibition on discussion of slavery was universal. In fact, many abolitionists attacked the revival. See Harriet Beecher Stowe, "The Revival," *Independent*, March 11, 1858: "Instead of the great revival of 1858, we should be happy to read the great reformation of 1858. . . . A revival of religion that brings no repentance and reformation is false and spurious. . . . We believe in no raptures, in no ecstasies, in no experiences that do not bring the soul into communion with Him who declared He came to set at liberty them that are bound and bruised."

40. James Edwin Orr, "Revival and Evangelism," *World Evangelization Information Bulletin* 38 (March 1985): 6. See also Malcolm McDow and Alvin L. Reid,

Firefall: How God Has Shaped History Through Revivals (Nashville: Broadman & Holman, 1997), 265–67.

41. Orr, *The Fervent Prayer*, 200.
42. Ibid. Italics and capitalization retained from source.
43. See McLoughlin, *Modern Revivalism*; and Marsden, *Fundamentalism*. This is not to say the revival did not reflect those values; instead, Moody took his cues from the revival, not the business community.
44. Long, *The Revival of 1857–1858*, 124–25.
45. Ibid. Long carefully makes this case in chapters 5 and 6. See also Marsden, *Fundamentalism*, 85–93.
46. The definitive study on the American Sunday school movement (including Moody's participation) is Anne M. Boylan, *Sunday School: The Formation of an American Institution, 1790–1880* (New Haven, CT: Yale University Press, 1990.
47. Daniels, *Moody: His Words*, 37.
48. Moody understood this and struggled to overcome the gulf between the evangelical church and the working class. One such attempt, which we shall examine more closely later, is the establishment of Bible training schools designed to produce "gap men," i.e., workers to bridge the gap between the clergy and the masses. For a detailed discussion, see James F. Findlay Jr., "Gapmen and the Gospel: The Early Days of Moody Bible Institute," *Church History* 31 (September 1962): 110.
49. Robert May, *Sunday School Minutebook*, October 20, 1811–January 26, 1812, Presbyterian Historical Society, Philadelphia.
50. Albert Matthews, *Early Sunday Schools in Boston* (Boston: J. Wilson and Son, 1919), 280.
51. Kensington Sunday School Association Minutes, Constitution, 1817, Presbyterian Historical Society, Philadelphia.
52. D. L. Moody, letter to home, February 12, 1861. MBI Archives. In another letter to his mother from June of 1861, D. L. Moody says he has "been to prayer meetings every night but 2 for 8 months."
53. D. L. Moody, letter to mother, June 5, 1861. D. L. Moody Papers, Yale Divinity School Library.
54. *Chicago Tribune*, July 3, 1865.
55. "Watts" letter dated 1908, D. L. Moody Papers, Yale Divinity School Library.
56. Daniels, *Moody: His Words*, 37.
57. Dorsett, *Passion*, 67. Moody also received criticism from the press. For example, see the *Chicago Times*, October 28, 1867.
58. D. L. Moody Papers, Yale Divinity School Library.
59. William R. Moody, *Life of Moody*, 113–14. The author attributed this description to a D. W. McWilliams, about 1861.
60. Daniels, *Moody: His Words,* 36–37.
61. "By Emma Moody Fitt," n. d., D. L. Moody Papers, Yale Divinity School Library.
62. "1858," D. L. Moody Papers, Yale Divinity School Library.

63. D. L. Moody, letter to brother, June 29, 1860, D. L. Moody Papers, Yale Divinity School Library.

64. Dorsett, *Passion*, 73–74.

65. Although this section will center on Moody's work with the Chicago YMCA, Moody's initial contact with the YMCA came in Boston in 1854. In a letter to his brother dated April 19, 1854, he wrote, "I am going to join the Christian Association to-morrow." William R. Moody, *Life of Moody*, 81.

66. Richard C. Morse, *The History of the North American Young Men's Christian Associations* (New York: Association Press, 1918), 122.

67. *Fifty-Five Years: The Young Men's Christian Association of Chicago 1858–1913* (Chicago: The Board of Managers, 1913), 2.

68. Paragraph titled as "Farwell," n. d.,. D. L. Moody Papers, Yale Divinity School Library.

69. Paragraph titled as "Dr. Robert Patterson," n. d., D. L. Moody Papers, Yale Divinity School Library.

70. D. L. Moody, letter to mother, September 24, 1860, D. L. Moody Papers, Yale Divinity School Library. A similar sentiment is seen in another letter to his mother in 1862. Moody writes, "My wife will write to Warren today. We are all praying for him here. I presented him for prayer at the noon meeting yesterday and tell him hundreds of my friends are praying for him out here that he may trust God. Oh my dear mother pray with me that Warren may be converted for without a change of heart no one shall see God." D. L. Moody, letter to mother, September 13, 1862, D. L. Moody Papers, Yale Divinity School Library.

71. Fourth Annual Report, Chicago YMCA, 9; *Advance*, 1 (November 7, 1867): 4.

72. Dedmon, *Great Enterprises: 100 Years of the YMCA of Metropolitan Chicago*. See especially chapters 3 and 4.

73. D. L. Moody, letter to brother Samuel, January 13, 1862, MBI Archives.

74. *Handbook of Texas Online*, s.v. "Farwell, John Villiers," Texas State Historical Association, https://www.tshaonline.org/handbook/entries/farwell-john-villiers. The family also maintained the dry goods business in Chicago until 1926, when it was sold to Carson Pirie & Scott Co. Farwell entered the Texas cattle-ranching scene in 1882, when, as a leading member of the Capitol Syndicate, he helped finance the new Capitol building in Austin. He and his brother Charles were directors of the Capitol Freehold Land and Investment Company, organized in London in 1885 to handle the land that became the XIT Ranch. Two towns in Texas were named for Farwell.

75. "Farwell, John Villiers," Texas State Historical Association. His brother Charles was even more active. He helped form the Republican Party and later served in both houses of Congress.

76. Dedmon, *Great Enterprises*, 54–55.

77. Speaking in Liverpool in 1874, Moody said, "These young men who come to large cities want someone to take an interest in them. I contend no one can do this as well as the Christian Association." William R. Moody, *Life of Moody*, 221.

78. Ibid., 82.
79. John Patrick Daly, *When Slavery Was Called Freedom: Evangelicalism, Proslavery and the Causes of the Civil War* (Lexington: University Press of Kentucky, 2002). This is the best study on this subject of which I am aware. Daly examines the debates concerning slavery that consumed antebellum America. Both sides appealed to the power of God to prove them victorious and, above all, morally superior. See also Harry Stout, *Upon the Altar of the Nation: A Moral History of the Civil War* (New York: Penguin, 2006). Echoing Daly, Stout contends the ferocity and length of the American Civil War can only be explained by both sides claiming that they had God on their side.
80. William R. Moody, *Life of Moody*, 82.
81. For detailed studies of Union and Confederate military casualties, see Thomas L. Livermore, *Numbers and Losses in the Civil War in America 1861–65* (Boston: Houghton, Mifflin and Co., 1901), and William F. Fox, *Regimental Losses in the American Civil War, 1861–1865* (Albany, NY: Albany Publishing Co.,1889).
82. Claudia Goldin and Frank Lewis, "The Economic Costs of the American Civil War: Estimates and Implications," *Journal of Economic History* 35, no.2 (June 1975): 299–326. Various scholars have responded to the Goldin-Lewis estimates; see Roger L. Ransom, "The Economic Consequences of the American Civil War," *The Political Economy of War and Peace*, Murray Wolfson, ed. (Norwell, MA: Kluwer Academic Publishers, 1998).
83. For a complete collection of statistics related to the American Civil War, see Patricia L. Faust and Norman C. Delaney, eds., *Historical Times Encyclopedia of the Civil War* (New York: Harper & Row, 1986).
84. Ahlstrom, *A Religious History*, 659–65.
85. For an excellent analysis of the war's theological underpinnings, see Mark A. Noll, *The Civil War as a Theological Crisis* (Chapel Hill: University of North Carolina Press, 2006).
86. Centennial Brochure, Moody Bible Institute, Chicago, April 7, 2007. Elsewhere the purpose is described as seeking "the spiritual good of the soldiers . . . and incidentally their intellectual improvement and social and physical comfort." Lemuel Moss, *Annals of the United States Christian Commission* (Philadelphia: J. B. Lippincott, 1886), 107.
87. Moss, *Annals*, 81.
88. Centennial Brochure.
89. Moss, "Table V—Summary of Labors and Distributions," *Annals*, 729.
90. Moss, *Annals*, 38.
91. Dorsett, *Passion*, 88–89.
92. For the battle of Shiloh, the final number of dead or missing was 13,000 on the Union side and 10,500 on the Confederate side. The total casualty count of 23,500 was more than the American casualties of the American Revolution, the War of 1812, and the Mexican-American War combined.

93. D. L. Moody, letter to mother, March 4, 1862, D. L. Moody Papers, Yale Divinity School Library.

94. Quoted in Gundry, *Love Them In*, 100. In another letter to his mother, dated February 4, 1863, Moody writes of attending to the sick and wounded of Rosencrans's Union forces, who were defeated at the battles of Murfreesboro and Chickamauga. D. L. Moody, letter to mother, February 4, 1863, D. L. Moody Papers, Yale Divinity School Library.

95. The definitive study on Camp Douglas is George Levy's *To Die in Chicago: Confederate Prisoners at Camp Douglas 1862–65* (Gretna, LA: Pelican Publishing, 1999).

96. Samuel Moody, letter to the folks at Clinton, October 24, 1862, D. L. Moody Papers, Yale Divinity School Library.

97. D. L. Moody, letter home, October 24, 1862, D. L. Moody Papers, Yale Divinity School Library.

98. Levy, *To Die in Chicago*, 334.

99. Details are found throughout Levy's book.

100. William R. Moody, *Life of Moody*, 89–91.

101. See Chapman, *Life and Work*, 189. There is some evidence from later in his life. As the United States moved toward war with Spain, he remarked, "War, awful war! Never has our country had more need of your prayers than at the present time. God keep us from war, if it be possible, and God keep hate of Spain out of our hearts! I have not met a man who served in the last war who wants to see another. God knows that I do not want to see the carnage and destruction that such a war would bring. God pity America and Spain. There are many mothers who will be bereaved, many homes broken up, if we have war. Have you thought of this?"

102. John McDowell and Others, *What D. L. Moody Means to Me: An Anthology of Appreciations and Appraisals of the Beloved Founder of the Northfield Schools* (East Northfield, MA: Northfield Schools, 1937), 24. Here is how Howard described the meeting: "It was the middle of April 1864. I was bringing together my Fourth Army Corps. Two divisions had already arrived and were encamped in and near the village. Moody was then fresh and hearty, full of enthusiasm for the Master's work. Our soldiers were just about to set out on what we all felt promised a hard and bloody campaign, and I think were especially desirous of strong preaching. Crowds and crowds turned out to hear the glad tidings from Moody's lips. He showed them how a soldier would give his heart to God. His preaching was direct and effective, and multitudes responded with a confession and promise to follow Christ."

103. McDowell, *What D. L. Moody Means to Me*, 24.

104. Dorsett, *Passion*, 111–13.

105. Ibid., 111.

106. Anne Richardson, "Oliver Otis Howard—General in the Civil War, Reconstruction, and Indian Wars," The Oregon Cultural Heritage Commission, 2002, http://www.ochcom.org/howard.

107. John A. Carpenter, *The Sword, and the Olive Branch: Oliver Otis Howard* (New York: Fordham University Press, 1999), 288.

108. Richardson, "Oliver Otis Howard."

109. Oliver Otis Howard, *Report of Brevet Major General O. O. Howard, Commissioner Bureau of Refugees, Freedmen, and Abandoned Lands, to the Secretary of War: October 20, 1869* (Washington, DC: Government Printing Office, 1869), 11.

110. Oliver Otis Howard, *Autobiography of Oliver Otis Howard*, Major General, United States Army (New York: Baker and Taylor, 1908), 329.

111. For example, he was one of the founders and served as the first president of Howard University. While the intent of the founders was to uplift African Americans, especially those recently freed from slavery, the university was established on the principle that it would be open to all races and colors, both sexes, and all social classes.

112. Howard, *Report*, 12.

113. Howard, *Autobiography*, 324

114. William R. Moody, *Life of Moody,* 91; and Dorsett, *Passion*, 114.

115. Dorsett, *Passion*, 111.

116. Dorsett, *Passion*, 115.

117. George E. Morgan, *Mighty Days of Revival; R. C. Morgan: His Life and Times* (London: Morgan & Scott, 1922), footnote 2, 70–71.

118. Emma Moody Powell, *Heavenly Destiny: The Life Story of Mrs. D. L. Moody* (Chicago: Moody Press, 1943), 44.

119. Emma Moody, letter to mother, June 18, 1866, D. L. Moody Papers, Yale Divinity School Library.

120. Quoted in Findlay, *American Evangelist*, 132. This portion of Whittle's diary is in the Library of Congress.

121. William R. Moody, *Life of Moody,* 89. Emma's exposure to Civil War battlefields is unclear. As I noted earlier, we know she went with Grant into Richmond. According to *Life of Moody*, Moody talks of taking Emma with him to Tennessee, Kentucky, and Alabama. However, there is no confirmation of this happening. Regardless, the devastation she would have seen in Richmond would have been traumatic enough.

122. Paul Moody, *My Father*, 27.

123. Ibid., 54.

124. Ibid., 55.

125. Ibid., 27.

126. Roger Steer, *George Müller: Delighted in God* (London: Hodder and Stoughton, 1975), 238.

127. George Müller, *The Life of Trust*, 81.

128. Ibid.

129. Ibid., 82.

130. Ibid., 37.

131. Ibid., 43.

132. Ibid.
133. Daniels, *Moody: His Words*, 87.
134. Ibid.
135. Müller, *Life of Trust*, 57.
136. Daniels, *Moody: His Words*, 87.
137. Müller, *Life of Trust*, 39.
138. Daniels, *Moody: His Words*, 88.
139. Müller, *Life of Trust*, 63.
140. Ibid.
141. D. L. Moody, letter to mother, London, England, March 19, 1867, Biographical Files, MBI Archives.
142. D. L. Moody, *Pleasure and Profit in Bible Study* (Chicago: Fleming H. Revell, 1895), 79.
143. Goss, *Echoes from the Pulpit and Platform*, 510.
144. Ibid.
145. The next chapter will include a section on Moody's approach to Bible study. Moody's continued admiration and appreciation for Müller's life and teaching was further evidenced in that Moody brought Müller to America in 1877 and continued to follow his example.
146. Some American scholars use an alternative spelling of Henry's name: *Morehouse* or *Moorehouse*. I will use *Moorhouse*, the spelling employed by British scholars.
147. According to A. P. Fitt, Moorhouse met Moody "in a little meeting hall on a summers' night and DLM preached. Moorhouse saw he was talking outside the Bible. After service he said, Mr. Moody you are deficient in the Word of God. If you'll preach God's word instead of your own, He'll make a great power of you." A. P. Fitt, transcribed comment, n.d., D. L. Moody Papers, Yale Divinity School Library.
148. Steer, *George Müller*, 260–61. A similar account is found in William R. Moody, *Life of Moody*, 138–40.
149. Quoted in Richard E. Day, *Bush Aglow: The Life Story of Dwight Lyman Moody, Commoner of Northfield* (Philadelphia: Judson Press, 1936), 145.
150. Dorsett, *Passion*, 139.
151. The following works show Moorhouse's influence on DLM: Pollock, *Moody*, 68–70; William R. Moody, *Life of Moody*, 137–40; J. MacPherson, *Henry Moorhouse: The English Evangelist* (Glasgow, Scotland: John Ritchie, n. d.); and Findlay, *American Evangelist*, 126. The next chapter includes a section on Moody's doctrine of the love of God.
152. The next chapter will discuss the role of the Bible in Moody's life and ministry.
153. William R. Moody, *Life of Moody*, 140.
154. Findlay, *American Evangelist*, 251. Moody did not meet Darby during his visit to Britain in 1867; Darby was in the United States. However, the two would meet when Moody returned to the States in the late 1860s and later in England.

155. Paul Boyer, *When Time Shall Be No More: Prophecy Belief in Modern American Culture* (Cambridge, MA: The Belknap Press of Harvard University, 1992), 87. The centrality of Darby's role in the emergence of the Plymouth Brethren is demonstrated by the fact they were sometimes referred to as "Darbyites."

156. This sketch is drawn from "The Papers of John Nelson Darby," John Rylands University Library Archives, Manchester, England, http://archiveshub.jisc.ac.uk/data/gb133–jnd.

157. William Blair Neatby, *A History of the Plymouth Brethren*, 2nd ed. (London: Hodder and Stoughton, 1902), 13. Interestingly, Francis Newman, the brother of famous Roman convert John Henry Newman, spent much time with Darby. Darby would eventually bring Francis Newman into the Brethren movement.

158. Findlay, *American Evangelist*, 125–26. Findlay cites Henry A. Ironside, *A Historical Sketch of the Brethren Movement* (Grand Rapids, MI: Zondervan Publishing House, 1942).

159. John Nelson Darby, "Synopsis of the Books of the Bible: 2 Timothy," The Christian Classics Ethereal Library, http://www.ccel.org/d/darby/synopsis/2Timothy.html. Darby's fully developed position can be found in John Nelson Darby, "The Inspiration of the Scriptures," *Collected Writings of J. N. Darby* (London: Morrish, n.d.), 6:350–65. The next chapter will detail Moody's view of the Bible.

160. Quoted in Winston Terrance Sutherland, "John Nelson Darby: His Contributions to Contemporary Theological Higher Education" (PhD dissertation, North Texas State, 2007), 8. Darby also saw his conversion as being "brought by grace to feel he could entirely trust the word of God alone." This stands in sharp contrast to the alternative of trusting established religion as reified in the Anglican Church with its formal system connected to the state of England. Quoted in Sutherland, 10.

161. Ibid., 27.

162. For a detailed study on Darby's hermeneutical methodology, see F. S. Elmore, "A Critical Examination of the Doctrine of the Two Peoples of God in John Nelson Darby" (ThD dissertation, Dallas Theological Seminary, 1990), 124–200.

163. John Nelson Darby, *Letters of J. N. Darby*, reprint ed. (Sunbury, PA: Believers Bookshelf, 1971), 2:259.

164. Dorsett, *Passion*, 137.

165. Robert T. Grant, report to J. N. Darby, August 9, 1868, Sibthorpe Manuscripts, The John Rylands University Library, Manchester University, Manchester, England.

166. Quoted in Ernest Sandeen, *Roots of Fundamentalism* (Grand Rapids, MI: Baker Books, 1978), 166. "C. H. Mackintosh was born in October 1820, at Glenmalure Barricks, County Wicklow, Ireland, the son of the captain of a Highland regiment. Mackintosh was converted at the age of eighteen through the letters of a devout sister, and the reading of J. N. Darby's *Operations of the Spirit*." At twenty-four, he briefly opened a private school at Westport. However, shortly

after that, he felt compelled to enter the ministry and spent the rest of his life writing on or lecturing from the Bible. See "Charles Henry Mackintosh," Stem Publishing, http://www.stempublishing.com/authors/Biographies/chmackintosh.html.

167. Moody's emphasis on premillennialism was a distinctive of his relative to earlier revivalists like Finney. Gundry claims Moody was "the first noteworthy premillennial preacher of revival and evangelicalism in America." Gundry, *Love Them In*, 178. This will be further developed in the next chapter.

168. Robert Kieran Whalen, "Millenarianism and Millennialism in America: 1790–1880" (PhD dissertation, State U of New York at Stony Brook, 1971), 27–101. Whalen argues convincingly that premillennialism was picking up in potency before the Civil War. Moody would be one of the key figures in bringing it to a prominent position among evangelicals.

169. Timothy P. Weber, *Living in the Shadow of the Second Coming: American Premillennialism 1875–1982* (Grand Rapids, MI: Academie Books, 1983), 32–33.

170. For the case for Spurgeon's premillennialism, see Dennis M. Swanson, "Charles H. Spurgeon and Eschatology: Did He Have a Discernible Millennial Position?" (MDiv Thesis, Masters Seminary, n.d.).

171. Ibid. I am dependent on Swanson's work throughout this section.

172. Bebbington, *Britain: A History*, 62. Amillennialism was held by several influential theologians on both sides of the Atlantic.

173. This work has been reprinted several times, most recently by the Theonomist Dominion Press, and is looked to as a foundational work by theonomist authors. Kenneth A. Kantzer, "Our Future Hope: Eschatology and the Role of the Church," *Christianity Today* (February 1987), 5. An interview article with Gleason Archer, Jack Davis, Anthony Hoekema, Alan Johnson, and John Walvoord. Iain H. Murray, *The Puritan Hope: Revival and the Interpretation of Prophecy* (Carlisle, PA: Banner of Truth Trust, 1971). In this book, Murray presents an excellent historical theology of postmillennialism, centering on the Puritans, particularly the English Puritans.

174. Robert G. Clouse, "Views of the Millennium," in *Dictionary of Evangelical Theology*, ed. Walter A. Elwell (Grand Rapids, MI: Baker Book House, 1984), 2:715.

175. Ibid., 716.

176. Boyd Hilton, *The Age of Atonement: The Influence of Evangelicalism on Social and Economic Thought 1795–1865* (Oxford: Clarendon Press, 1988), 17.

177. Ralph Brown, "Evangelical Social Thought," in *Journal of Ecclesiastical History* 6, no. 1 (January 2009): 126–27.

178. Weber, *Shadow of the Second Coming*, 234.

179. Ibid.

180. The difference between British and American premillennialists is intriguing. It goes well beyond the scope of this book to try to explain the differences. However, it appears to be a worthy topic for additional research.

181. Both their comments are evaluations of the overall effect of American premillennialism through the 1980s.
182. See Marsden, *Fundamentalism*, 43–71.
183. Jonathan M. Butler, "Adventism and the American Experience," *The Rise of Adventism*, ed. Edwin Gaustad (New York: Harper, 1974), 174–206, cited in Weber, *Shadow of the Second Coming*, 235. The following paragraphs are drawn mainly from Weber's summary, 235–37.
184. Nathaniel West, ed. *Premillennial Essays* (Chicago: Fleming H. Revell, 1879), 270–312.
185. Weber, *Shadow of the Second Coming*, 235.
186. Ibid.
187. Ibid.
188. Ibid., 235–36.
189. Ibid.
190. Dorsett, *Passion*, 132; Bebbington, *Dominance*, 45.
191. D. L. Moody to C. H. Spurgeon, October 11, 1881, MBI Archives.
192. From an address Moody delivered at Metropolitan Tabernacle in 1884, see *C. H. Spurgeon's Autobiography, Compiled from His Diary, Letters, and Records* (London: Passmore and Alabaster, 1900), 4:247.
193. Findlay described the relationship between Moody and Spurgeon as "a bit strained" and claimed the "ties between the two men were never strong." However, Findlay was wrong given the quote above and the following several pages in the chapter. Findlay, *American Evangelist*, 145.
194. Pollock, *Moody*, 66.
195. Moody gives an extended account of this event and speaks of Spurgeon's influence on him.
196. *C. H. Spurgeon's Autobiography*, 4:247.
197. Ibid.
198. Quoted in Ernest W. Bacon, *Spurgeon: Heir of the Puritans* (London: George Allen & Unwin, 1967), 157.
199. *C. H. Spurgeon's Autobiography*, 4:169–70.
200. Ibid., 170.
201. Ibid., 247.
202. Dorsett, *Passion*, 396.
203. In the "Notes" section of *The Sword and the Trowel* from 1875, Spurgeon defends Moody's work every month from March until July. He repeated his defense of Moody in *The Sword and the Trowel* in 1882.
204. Robert Shindler, *The Life and Legacy of Charles Haddon Spurgeon: From the Usher's Desk to the Tabernacle Pulpit* (New York: A. C. Armstrong, 1892), 207. No date is given for the quote.
205. Dorsett, *Passion*, 396. Dorsett notes a series of seven letters from Spurgeon to Moody written in 1884 in an attempt to arrange a dinner at his home.

206. A similar account appears in *Record of Christian Work* (August 1929), which notes the following: "After the death of the great London preacher Charles H. Spurgeon Mrs. Spurgeon made a duplicate of the study Bible in which he noted in the margins the texts on which he had preached, and gave this to D. L. Moody."

207. William R. Moody, *Life of Moody*, 447.

208. Dorsett, *Passion*, 133. In the next chapter, I will discuss Moody's relationship to Calvinism. About Moody's willingness to criticize Spurgeon, Dorsett points out Moody was critical of Spurgeon's Sunday school and his ministry with children generally.

209. I am indebted to Thomas Breimaier's unpublished paper "Moody, Spurgeon, and the Historical Unity of Evangelicalism," May 2007, for the content of this brief biographical section.

210. Patricia Kruppa, *Charles Haddon Spurgeon: A Preacher's Progress* (New York: Garland Publishing, 1982), 19–20.

211. Ibid., 88.

212. Many contemporary figures who espouse Puritan theology see Spurgeon as a Victorian Puritan. See, for instance, D. Martyn Lloyd-Jones, *The Puritans: Their Origins and Successors* (Edinburgh: The Banner of Truth Trust, 1987), 258. He writes that Spurgeon's thought is "a perfect example of Puritan thinking."

213. Charles Spurgeon, "The Necessity of the Spirit's Work" (sermon on May 8, 1859), *The New Park Street Pulpit* 5 (Pasadena, TX: Pilgrim Publications, 1975), 251.

214. Charles Spurgeon, "The Superlative Excellence of the Holy Spirit," sermon on June 12, 1861, *The Metropolitan Tabernacle Pulpit* 10, 337.

215. Michael Haykin, "'Where the Spirit of God Is, There Is Power': An Introduction to Spurgeon's Teaching on the Holy Spirit," *Churchman* 106, no. 3 (1992).

216. Charles Spurgeon, "The Holy Spirit in Connection with our Ministry," in *Lectures to My Students* (London: Marshall, Morgan & Scott, 1954), 186–87.

217. David Nelson Duke, "Charles Haddon Spurgeon: Social Concern Exceeding an Individualist, Self-Help Ideology," *Baptist History and Heritage* 22, no. 4 (1987): 7–56. I am indebted to this source for much of the structure and content of this section.

218. For additional insights on Spurgeon's and the Tabernacle's activities, see Robert Shindler, *The Life and Legacy of Charles Haddon Spurgeon: From the Usher's Desk to the Tabernacle Pulpit* (New York: A. C. Armstrong, 1892), 269–70; Kathleen Heasman, *Evangelicals in Action: An Appraisal of Their Social Work in the Victorian Era* (London: Geoffrey Boles, 1962); and Albert Roger Meredith, "The Social and Political Views of Charles Haddon Spurgeon, 1834–1892" (PhD dissertation, Michigan State University 1973), 175–76.

219. Duke, "Charles Haddon Spurgeon," 47.

220. Charles Spurgeon, "The Present Crisis" (sermon on July 13, 1879), *The Metropolitan Tabernacle Pulpit* 25 (Pasadena, TX: Pilgrim Publications, 1972), 391.

221. Charles Spurgeon, "The Candle" (sermon on April 24, 1881), *The Metropolitan Tabernacle Pulpit* 27 (Pasadena, TX: Pilgrim Publications, 1972), 226.

222. Charles Spurgeon, "The Peacemaker" (sermon on December 8, 1861), *The Metropolitan Tabernacle Pulpit* 7 (Pasadena, TX: Pilgrim Publications, 1972), 593.

223. Duke, "Charles Haddon Spurgeon," 48. The Spurgeon quote is from Charles Spurgeon, "The Present Religion" (sermon, May 1858), *The New Park Street Pulpit* 4 (Pasadena, TX: Pilgrim Publications, 1975), 253–54.

224. Spurgeon, "The Candle," 222.

225. William R. Moody, *Life of Moody*, 241.

226. Duke, "Charles Haddon Spurgeon," 49.

227. Charles Spurgeon, "Preaching for the Poor" (sermon on January 25, 1857), *The New Park Street Pulpit* (Pasadena, TX: Pilgrim Publications, 1975), 3:63.

228. Quoted by R. J. Helmstadter, "Spurgeon in Outcast London," in *The View from the Pulpit: Victorian Ministers in Society*, ed. P. T. Phillips (Toronto: Macmillan, 1978), 161.

229. Meredith, "Spurgeon," 57–58.

230. This quote reflects Spurgeon's view: "I hope the Society will do something when it is started. I don't want you to wear a lot of peacock feathers and putty medals, nor to be always trying to convert the moderate drinkers, but go in for winning the real drunkards, and bring the poor enslaved creatures to the feet of Jesus, who can give them liberty." Susannah Spurgeon and Joseph Harrald, *C. H. Spurgeon's Autobiography*, 4:70.

231. Duke, "Charles Haddon Spurgeon," 50–51.

232. Charles Spurgeon, "John Ploughman's Letter on War," in *The Sword and the Trowel* (August 1870), 353–55. Both Moody and Spurgeon had firsthand experience with war. Moreover, both express disdain for war; note Moody's comments from earlier in the chapter.

233. Duke, "Charles Haddon Spurgeon," 51–54.

234. Quoted in Meredith, "Spurgeon," 175–76.

235. Charles Spurgeon, "The Prosperous Man's Reminder" (sermon on October 27, 1878), *The Metropolitan Tabernacle Pulpit* (Pasadena, TX: Pilgrim Publications, 1972), 24:606.

236. Charles Spurgeon, "Israel and Britain: A Note of Warning" (sermon on June 7, 1885), *The Metropolitan Tabernacle Pulpit* (Pasadena, TX: Pilgrim Publications, 1973), 31:322.

237. *C. H. Spurgeon's Autobiography*, 4:132.

238. Daniels, *Moody: His Words*, 475.

239. The sign outside Moody's church in Chicago read, "Ever welcome to this house of God are strangers and the poor." There is one striking difference between Moody's and Spurgeon's Sunday schools. See D. L. Moody to Farwell, March 12, 1867, Biographical Files, MBI Archives: "I was at Spurgeon's Sabbath School and it is not as good as the mission on the corner of Michigan and Dearborn streets. They had no paint on the rooms, dark and gloomy. They have no way to heat them, and I inquired if it were not cold. They said it was sometimes but they got it full of breath etc., and warmed up the people, no ventilation, only

windows . . . I then went to Newman Hall's church and Sabbath schoolrooms
. . . they had a partition up so the boys will not see the girls. The rooms are dirty many of the seats are of plain boards, no backs to them."

240. Findlay, *American Evangelist*, 364.

241. David Bebbington, "Transatlantic," 4–5.

242. Dorsett, 165. The woman Moody chose to spearhead the effort was Emma Dryer, who was also instrumental in forming what became known as Moody Bible Institute (see chapter 5).

243. As has been noted, Moody's first school was the Northfield Seminary for Women, founded in 1879.

244. William R. Moody, *Life of Moody*, 154.

245. Ibid., 145.

246. Quoted in Dorsett, *Passion*, 257.

247. Don Sweeting in George, *Mr. Moody*, 43.

248. For further description of the fire, see Miller, *City of the Century*, 142–71.

249. Pollock, *Moody*, 107.

250. Sweeting in George, *Mr. Moody*, 39–48. Although others have pointed out the Chicago Fire's role in Moody's life, I am particularly indebted to Sweeting's interpretation of this event.

251. William R. Moody, *Life of Moody*, 145.

252. Richard S. Rhodes, *Moody's Latest Sermons* (Chicago: Rhodes & McClure, 1998), 680–81.

253. A copy of this letter is in the archives of the Moody Bible Institute.

254. William R. Moody, *Life of Moody*, 149.

255. Ibid.

256. Whittle Diary, September 4, 1875, quoted in Findlay, *American Evangelist*, 194. This portion of the diary was once held in the MBI Archives and subsequently lost. Another portion of the diary is at the United States National Archives in Washington, DC.

257. "D. L. Moody on Anointing in 1875," D. L. Moody Papers, Yale Divinity School Library.

258. Sarah Cooke, *Wayside Sketches: or, The Handmaiden of the Lord* (Grand Rapids, MI: Shaw, 1895), 393.

259. This anecdote and all of the quotations are from William R. Moody, *The Life of Dwight L. Moody* (New York: Macmillan, 1930), 146. See also R. A. Torrey, *Why God Used D. L. Moody* (Chicago: Bible Institute Colportage Association, 1923), 45–46.

260. Cooke, *Wayside Sketches*, 393.

261. R. A. Torrey, *Why God Used D. L. Moody* (Chicago: Bible Institute Colportage Association, 1923), 45–46.

262. William R. Moody, *Life of Moody* (1930), 147.

263. Cooke, *Wayside Sketches*, 393.

264. D. L. Moody Papers, Yale Divinity School Library.

265. C. I. Scofield, *Plain Papers on the Doctrine of the Holy Spirit* (Chicago: Fleming H. Revell, 1899), 9.

266. Grant Wacker, "The Holy Spirit and the Spirit of the Age in American Protestantism, 1880–1910," *Journal of American History*, 72, no. 1 (June 1985), 45–62. Wacker argues convincingly that the intense interest in the Holy Spirit combined with a shared anxiety about the state of the church helps explain the continued cooperation of liberals and conservatives throughout the nineteenth century.

267. David Bundy, "Keswick and the Experience of Evangelical Piety," *Modern Christian Revivals*, eds. Edith Blumhofer and Randall Balmer (Chicago: University of Illinois Press, 1993); and J. C. Pollock, *The Keswick Story: The Authorized History of the Keswick Convention* (London: Hodder and Stoughton, 1964). The name *Keswick* is an English town where annual religious conferences have been held since 1875. The conference emphasized holy living without teaching perfectionism. Its origins were in the American Wesleyan Holiness movement; the work of Charles Finney, Phoebe Palmer, and Asa Mahan; the writings of Charles Boardman; and the Mildmay conferences.

268. Charles W. Nienkirchen, *A.B. Simpson and the Pentecostal Movement* (Peabody, MA.: Hendrickson, 1992). There are nuances between these two positions. For example, A. B. Simpson, the Christian and Missionary Alliance founder, explicitly denied perfectionism but embraced all the charismatic gifts. However, he denied any charismatic gifts were a necessary test of the Spirit's baptism.

269. Wacker, "Holy Spirit and the Spirit of the Age," 47–48. As we have seen, Moody was connected with the Mildmay conferences, which were one of the forerunners of the Keswick movement. In a future chapter, I will discuss Moody's interaction with Keswick.

3. Moody's Theology: A Survey of His Basic Commitments

1. "Moody Talks of Faith," *Journal* (New Bedford, MA), undated clipping, probably 1895, D. L. Moody Collection, MBI Archives.

2. E. J. Goodspeed, *A Full History of the Wonderful Career of Moody and Sankey in Great Britain and America* (Cleveland: C. C. Wick, 1876), 107–8.

3. *Signs of Our Times*, March 10, 1875, 149; cf. Shanks, ed., *College Students at Northfield* (1888), 217–18.

4. By practical, I mean Moody was more interested in the practical matters of converting sinners and discipling converts rather than theological speculation. So it falls within the sphere of revivalist concerns.

5. William R. Moody, *Life of Moody*, 107.

6. For a summary of various theories about Moody's attitude toward theology, see Gundry, *Love Them In*, 62–70.

7. "Addresses delivered by Mr. D. L. Moody, General Conference, Saturday Evening, August 12, 1899," typed manuscript, MBI Archives, 4.

8. D. L. Moody, *Wondrous Love* (London: J. E. Hawkins, 1875), 261–64; D. L. Moody, *Glad Tidings: Comprising Sermons and Prayer-Meeting Talks Delivered*

at the N. Y. Hippodrome (New York: E. B. Treat, 1876), 270–73.

9. Daniels, *Moody: His Words*, 262.

10. McDowell, *What D. L. Moody Means to Me*, 17.

11. Gundry's *Love Them In* is the definitive work on Moody's theology. As the title indicates, Gundry sees love as the central theme in Moody's preaching. See also Darrel B. Robertson, "The Chicago Revival, 1876: A Case Study in the Social Function of a Nineteenth-Century Revival" (PhD dissertation, The University of Iowa, 1982), 221.

12. D. L. Moody, *Secret Power: Or, The Secret of Success in Christian Life and Work* (Chicago: Fleming H. Revell, 1881), 10.

13. This belief is a recurring theme in Moody's preaching. See, for example, the sermons titled "How God Loves Men" and "God Hates Sin and Loves the Sinner." Both were preached regularly and can be found in Dwight Moody, *New Sermons, Addresses and Prayers by Dwight Lyman Moody* (Chicago: Thompson & Wakefield, 1877), 165–80.

14. D. L. Moody, *Heaven: Where It Is, Its Inhabitants, and How to Get There* (Chicago: Fleming H. Revell, 1884), 11.

15. Ibid., 99.

16. Findlay, *American Evangelist*, 237. He references Romans 5:5 as grounds for his belief. Dwight Moody, *Secret Power: Or, The Secret of Success in Christian Life and Work* (Chicago: Fleming H. Revell, 1881), 12.

17. D. L. Moody, *Secret Power*, 50.

18. Ibid., 11–12.

19. Ibid., 50.

20. Ibid.

21. William Moody, *Life of Moody*, 151.

22. D. L. Moody, *Secret Power*, 11–12.

23. William Moody, *Life of Moody*, 151.

24. D. L. Moody, *To The Work! To The Work!* (Chicago: Fleming H. Revell, 1884), 28.

25. D. L. Moody, *Secret Power*, 10–11.

26. D. L. Moody, *The Gospel Awakening* (Chicago: Fleming H. Revell, 1883), 379–80.

27. D. L. Moody, *Secret Power*, 10–11.

28. Ibid., 11.

29. Ibid.

30. D. L. Moody, *Secret Power*, 13.

31. Ibid., 50.

32. D. L. Moody, *New Sermons*, 19.

33. Ibid.

34. Gundry, *Love Them In*, 97–101. In this section, Gundry shows how Moody's approach differed from others, including at least one Scottish preacher who accused Moody of not believing in hell.

35. D. L. Moody, *Glad Tidings*, 242–51.

36. Quoted in Gundry, *Love Them In*, 99.

37. Daniels, *Moody: His Words*, 106. Also, in one of his published sermons, Moody said: "Mark you my friends, I believe in eternal damnation; I believe in the pit that burns, in the fire that's never quenched, in the worm that never dies, but I believe that the magnet that goes down to the bottom of the pit is the love of Jesus." D. L. Moody, *Great Joy: Comprising Sermons and Prayer-Meeting Talks, Delivered at the Chicago Tabernacle* (New York: E. B. Treat, 1877), 359.

38. John Page Hopps, *Mr. Moody's Late Sermon on Hell, Theological Tracts, 1770–1882*, British Library Archive, #4371 e34.

39. Quoted in Gundry, *Love Them In*, 218.

40. Ibid.

41. Quoted in Findlay, *American Evangelist*, 421.

42. "Third Annual Illinois State Christian Convention," *Advance* 2, no. 62 (November 5, 1868), 2.

43. Dorsett, *Passion*. He makes this point throughout his book.

44. Quoted in: Thomas E. Corts, "D. L. Moody: Payment on Account," *Mr. Moody and the Evangelical Tradition*, ed. Timothy George (London: T&T Clark, 2004), 69. Corts goes on to describe Moody as a "walking, talking iconoclast" (70).

45. D. L. Moody, *New Sermons*, 14.

46. Ibid.

47. D. L. Moody, *The Way to God and How to Find It*, chapter 4.

48. Josiah Strong, *Our Country: Its Possible Future and Its Present Crisis*, rev. ed. (New York: Baker and Taylor Company, 1891), 96.

49. William R. Moody, *Life of Moody*, 68ff.

50. August J. Fry, *D. L. Moody: The Formative Years, 1856–1873* (Chicago: University of Chicago, 1955), 2.

51. William R. Moody, *Life of Moody*, 284.

52. Dorsett, *Passion*, 238–40; 289–90. In addition to those cited above, Dorsett gives numerous other examples illustrating Moody's relationship to the Roman Church. Most notably, he tells how F. B. Meyer recalled that when Moody's mother died, the local Roman Catholic Church asked to supply a pallbearer. Timothy George makes a similar point. George, *Mr. Moody*, 6.

53. William R. Moody, *Life of Moody*, 215.

54. Pollock, *Moody*, 131.

55. Letter to Moody, March 17, 1875, D. L. Moody Collection, MBI Archives.

56. Dorsett, *Passion*, 239.

57. D. L. Moody, *Glad Tidings*, 331.

58. Dorsett, *Passion*, 239.

59. The organ is displayed at the Northfield Historical Society in Northfield, MA.

60. Paul Moody, *My Father*. John Pollock records similar events and reactions. He writes: "[Moody's] willingness to co-operate [with Roman Catholics] went far beyond the imagination of his friends, who were shocked that he subscribed

towards the building of St. Patrick's Roman Catholic church for Northfield's Irish colony, and horrified when he accepted an invitation from a friend who had turned Roman to meet Archbishop Corrigan of New York, to whom he said 'he wanted to see New York shaken for Christ and wouldn't it be a great thing if all the churches swung into a simultaneous effort.' . . . The Archbishop had the power to do it for the Roman Catholic churches, and the other churches would follow the lead." Pollock, *Moody Without Sankey*, 251.

61. F. B. Meyer, "D. L. Moody: A Prophet of God," *Northfield Echoes* 7, no. 1 (1900), 29.

62. D. L. Moody, letter to A. P. Fitt, January 2, 1899, D. L. Moody Papers, Yale Divinity School Library.

63. Gundry, *Love Them In*, 172. Gundry cites numerous sermons in Baltimore and Dublin to support his claim.

64. "Questions answered by Mr. Moody, at General Conference, Tuesday Afternoon, August 16, 1898," MBI Archives.

65. Meyer, "D. L. Moody," 29.

66. For example, W. Robertson Smith, the chair of Old Testament at Aberdeen Free Church College, was brought up on charges by the Free Church in Scotland. He was eventually stripped of his position in 1881. What is interesting is the role supporters of Moody played. Some, like Horatius and Andrew Bonar, were part of the prosecuting party, while others, like Alexander Whyte, George Adam Smith, and Henry Drummond, were among Smith's fiercest supporters.

67. Findlay notes and documents the continued esteem that Gladden, Abbott, and Harper held for Moody late in their lives. Findlay, *American Evangelist*, 411.

68. See, for example, Jacob Dorn, *Washington Gladden: Prophet of the Social Gospel* (Columbus: Ohio State University Press, 1967). Dorn also described Gladden's high regard for Moody on page 380.

69. Lyman Abbot, *Theology of An Evolutionist* (New York: Houghton Mifflin, 1897), 76.

70. Washington Gladden, "Clear-Headed, Broad-Minded, Great-Hearted," *The Congregationalist and Christian World* (November 12, 1914), 234.

71. Dorsett, *Passion*, 123.

72. Quoted in Pollock, *Moody*, 60.

73. Ibid., 60.

74. Dorsett, *Passion*, 289.

75. William R. Moody, *Life of Moody*, 203. Moody referred to the local church as "the best institution found under heaven." He goes on, "I have always been a member of the church. . . . Christ died in order to redeem the church, and everyone who is faithful to him, ought to support it." David M. Gustafson, *D. L. Moody and Swedes: Shaping Evangelical Identity Among Swedish Mission Friends 1867–1899* (Linköping, Sweden: Linköping University, 2008), 310.

76. *Cleveland Leader*, November 9, 1879.

77. D. L. Moody, "The Sinner's Excuses Swept Away" in *The New Sermons of Dwight Lyman Moody* (New York: Henry S. Goodspeed, 1890), 193.

78. Quoted in Marsden, *Fundamentalism*, 33. See also Lyman Abbott, "Snap-Shots of My Contemporaries, Dwight Lyman Moody—Evangelist," *The Outlook* (June 22, no year), 324–27, MBI Archives. Several times Abbott lauds Moody's "breadth of spirit" and "Catholicity."

79. Henry Drummond and George Adam Smith, *Dwight L. Moody*, MBI Archives, 1. This is five pages of typed-out material collected together in a file. It lists no date or publisher.

80. D. L. Moody, *Glad Tidings*, 452.

81. D. L. Moody, *Golden Counsels* (Boston: United Society of Christian Endeavor, 1899), 1.

82. *Moody Mass Meeting* (New York City, Carnegie Hall, October 27, 1937), 5–6, MBI Archives.

83. "Where Would Mr. Moody Stand?" *The Christian Century* (July 12, 1923), 870–72. By the term "moderate," I mean Paul acknowledges Moody was conservative. Still, he wanted to separate him from the militant, combative form of fundamentalism that emerged in the early twentieth century.

84. Paul D. Moody, "Moody Becoming a Veiled Figure," *Christian Century*, August 1923, 979.

85. Chapman, *Life and Work*, 396. Chapman identified the three as (1) belief in the authority of the Bible, (2) the premillennial second coming of Christ, and (3) the work of the Holy Spirit. See 396–413.

86. *Manual of the Illinois Street Independent Church* (Chicago: Guilbert & Clissold, 1867), 6, 15. Although this was a nondenominational church, it is clear the Congregationalists played a significant role. Notice, for example, the similarity between the article above and the corresponding article from the *Congregational Manual*: "Article 2. We believe that the Scriptures of the Old and New Testaments were given by inspiration of the Holy Ghost and are the only infallible rule of faith and practice." *Minutes of the General Assemblies of Illinois, at Their 23rd Annual Meeting, Ottawa, Illinois*, May 1868 (Quincy, IL: 1886), 51–52. See also Joseph E. Roy, *A Manual of Principles, Doctrines, and Usages of Congregational Churches* (Boston: Congregational Publishing Society, n. d.), 31. The similarity to Darby's position outlined in the previous chapter is striking as well.

87. *Manual of the Illinois Street Independent Church*, 10.

88. D. L. Moody, *To All People: Comprising Sermons, Bible Readings, Temperance Addresses, and Prayer-Meeting Talks, Delivered in the Boston Tabernacle* (New York: E. B. Treat, 1877), 298.

89. D. L. Moody to William Moody, October 20, 1888, D. L. Moody Papers, Yale Divinity School Library.

90. D. L. Moody, *The Gospel Awakening*, 429–30.

91. *Montreal Daily Star*, November 29, 1894. Quoted in Gundry, *Love Them In*, 203.

92. *Boston Traveler*, January 5, 1897. Quoted in Findlay, *American Evangelist*, 409.

93. Gundry, *Love Them In*, 212–27. Gundry carefully documents Moody's repudiation of higher critical methods.

94. Paul Moody, *My Father*, 191.

95. William R. Moody, *Life of Moody*, 496.

96. D. L. Moody, *To All People*, 67, 71, 275.

97. Chapman, *Life and Work*, 398.

98. See Chapman, *Life and Work*, 397: "But someone else asks, 'what am I going to do when I come to a thing that I cannot understand?' I answer, 'I thank God that there are heights in it that I have never scaled, and depths in it that I have never sounded, because if I could understand it all, I would know that a man not greater than myself had written it. When it is beyond me in places, I know that God must have written it. It is one of the strongest proofs that the Bible must have come from God that the wise men in all the ages have been digging down into it, and never yet have sounded its depths.'"

99. J. W. Hanson, *The Life and Works of the World's Greatest Evangelist Dwight L. Moody* (Chicago: W. B. Conkey, 1900), 165.

100. The Free Church Monthly Record of February 1874, 27. This is the Free Church in Scotland.

101. D. L. Moody, *Notes from My Bible: From Genesis to Revelation* (Chicago: Fleming H. Revell, 1895), 194.

102. Ibid., 176.

103. Ibid., 196.

104. D. L. Moody, *To All People*, 448.

105. D. L. Moody to George Moody, March 17, 1857, MBI Archives. While other early letters do not contain direct quotes from the Bible, they contain allusions to the text. See, for example, the earlier referenced letters: D. L. Moody to mother, September 25, 1856; D. L. Moody to brother, October 19, 1856; D. L. Moody to mother, September 24, 1860; D. L. Moody to mother, September 13, 1862. D. L. Moody Papers, Yale Divinity School Library.

106. D. L. Moody to Samuel Moody, January 13, 1862, MBI Archives.

107. D. L. Moody, *Pleasure and Profit in Bible Study*, 54.

108. D. L. Moody to Samuel Moody, 1862, MBI Archives.

109. Daniels, *Moody: His Words*, 174.

110. McDowell, *What D. L. Moody Means to Me*, 26.

111. D. L. Moody, *How to Study the Bible* (Chicago: Fleming H. Revell, 1876), 79.

112. William R. Moody, *Life of Moody*, 163.

113. Valerie M. Kedlec, "Dwight L. Moody in the British Isles," *Church Management* (1953), 79, MBI Archives.

114. D. L. Moody to William Moody, January 21, 1885, D. L. Moody Papers, Yale Divinity School Library.

115. D. L. Moody to William Moody, March 22, 1884, D. L. Moody Papers, Yale Divinity School Library.

116. D. L. Moody to William Moody, May 10, 1884, D. L. Moody Papers, Yale Divinity School Library.

117. D. L. Moody to William Moody, October 18, 1884, D. L. Moody Papers, Yale Divinity School Library.

118. D. L. Moody inscription in Bible to granddaughter Irene, Summer 1895, D. L. Moody Papers, Yale Divinity School Library.

119. George Adam Smith, *The Life of Henry Drummond* (New York: Doubleday & McClure, 1898), 57.

120. The Missionary Record of the United Presbyterian of February 1874, 76.

121. D. L. Moody, *To All People*, 67, 71.

122. McDowell, *What D. L. Moody Means to Me*, 12.

123. "Prospectus, Northfield Young Ladies Seminary, 1879," *Northfield Seminary Calendars, 1879-1889.*

124. Record of Christian Work (February 1886), 5.

125. D. L. Moody, *Notes from My Bible*, unnumbered page at the front. See also page 228.

126. D. L. Moody, *To All People*, 350.

127. Ibid., 349.

128. *The Christian*, December 2, 1875, 7.

129. D. L. Moody, *Heaven*, 9.

130. James S. Bell, editor, *The D. L. Moody Collection: The Highlights of His Writings, Sermons, Anecdotes, and Life Story* (Chicago: Moody Press, 1997), 288. Taken from *D. L. Moody's Pleasure and Profit in Bible Study* (Chicago: Fleming H. Revell, 1895).

131. Ibid., 288. This is an instance of implied perspicuity, i.e., the belief that the Bible is a plain book; thus, anyone can read it and get the gist of its teachings.

132. Ibid.

133. Ibid., 289.

134. Ibid.

135. D. L. Moody, *Notes from My Bible*, 233.

136. Robertson, "The Chicago Revival," 220. Another indication of his commitment to perspicuity is found in his work *How to Study the Bible*. He declares that truth is best seen through an unbiased study of the Bible. By that, he means without reference to creeds or doctrines.

137. James Brooks, *The Truth* 5 (1879), 314; repeated in *The Truth*, 23 (1897), 80-82.

138. One example is Princeton professor Francis L. Patton. During a lecture on homiletics, Patton comments on the practice. While acknowledging their profound knowledge of the English Bible, he cautions against thinking a sermon is merely, "with the help of Cruden's Concordance, chasing a word through the Bible, making a comment or two on the passages as you go along." Earlier, he says, "I suppose that the Bible-reading is a feature of the school of thought of which Mr. Moody is such a distinguished leader," *Presbyterian and Reformed Review* 1 (1890), 36-37.

139. For an extended discussion on this topic, see Ernest R. Sandeen, *The Roots of Fundamentalism: British and American Millenarianism 1800–1930* (Grand Rapids, MI: Baker Book House, 1970), 136–39.

140. In Moody's case, it helps explain one of his concerns with higher critical methods. To Moody, higher criticism made much of the Bible unattainable to laypeople. He believed higher criticism was "ruining revival work and emptying the churches." Moody thought no one would expend time and energy in practical Christian work unless they were confident of the message. As Moody saw it, higher criticism robbed laypeople of religious certainty. Quoted in Weber, *Shadow of the Second Coming*, 36.

141. *The Christian* (December 2, 1875), 7.

142. D. L. Moody, *To All People* (New York: E. B. Treat, 1877), 360.

143. E. J. Goodspeed, *D. L. Moody in Philadelphia* (Hammond, IN: Helton Publications, n.d.), 84. This is a reprint of an 1877 publication titled *The Wonderful Career of Moody and Sankey in Great Britain*.

144. D. L. Moody, *New Sermons, Addresses and Prayers* (St. Louis: N. D. Thompson, 1877), 190.

145. The following quote is just one example of his approach: "I think that every order that the Lord has given us, and ever commanded us to do, ought to be carried out literally. . . . If the Word of God doesn't teach it, my friends, don't you receive it; but let us be ready and willing to bow to Scripture, because we read that all Scripture is given by inspiration; that we are not to be one sided Christians and take up one truth and harp on that all the time; but to take up the whole Word of God." D. L. Moody, *To All People*, 499–500.

146. Daniels, *Moody: His Words*, 256.

147. Again, I am using Larsen's definition.

148. In *Love Them In*, Gundry traces these three themes throughout most of Moody's sermons. See also Marsden, *Fundamentalism*, 35. In addition, one of Moody's personal Bibles at the archives in Northfield Schools contains the following comment on the inner leaf: "This book teaches three things, Ruin, Redemption, Regeneration."

149. Daniels, *Moody: His Words*, 256.

150. D. L. Moody, *New Sermons*, 128.

151. D. L. Moody, *Twelve Select Sermons*, 21.

152. Ibid.

153. D. L. Moody, *Moody's Sermons, Addresses and Prayers* (St. Louis: N. D. Thompson, 1877), 259.

154. D. L. Moody, *Twelve Select Sermons*, 120.

155. Ibid., 26.

156. Ibid., 28.

157. Quoted by Gundry, *Love Them In*, 102.

158. D. L. Moody, *Twelve Select Sermons*, 120.

159. D. L. Moody, *Notes from My Bible*, 184.

160. See Findlay, *Moody*, 236.
161. Benjamin B. Warfield, "The Atonement," in *The New Schaff-Herzog Encyclopedia of Religious Knowledge*, vol. 1, ed. Samuel M. Jackson (Grand Rapids: Baker, 1951), 353.
162. D. L. Moody, *Glad Tidings*, 244–45.
163. D. L. Moody, *Moody's Sermons, Addresses and Prayers*, 154.
164. Jane MacKinnon, *Recollections of 1874*, 47, MBI Archives.
165. Daniels, *Moody: His Words*, 426.
166. D. L. Moody, *Heaven*, 94.
167. D. L. Moody, *Twelve Select Sermons*, 35.
168. D. L. Moody, *Anecdotes and Illustrations of D. L. Moody: Related by Him in His Revival Work* (Chicago: Rhodes and McClure, 1877), 183.
169. D. L. Moody, *Addresses and Lectures* of *D. L. Moody, with a Narrative of the Awakening* (New York: Randolph and Co., 1875), 96.
170. Dwight Moody, *The Gospel Awakening*, 261–62. He also makes this point in pages 99 and 250.
171. D. L. Moody, *Glad Tidings*, 80.
172. Ibid., 417.
173. Gundry, *Love Them In*, 111, 120. Gundry argued decisively that Moody held to substitutionary atonement contra Findlay's view. I am indebted to Tom Breimaier's "Moody, Spurgeon, and the Historical Unity of Evangelicalism" (unpublished paper, May 2007) for this structure. Breimaier agrees with Gundry, contra Findlay.
174. D. L. Moody, *To All People*, 199.
175. D. L. Moody, *The Way to God and How to Find It*, 23.
176. Ibid., 25–26.
177. Ibid., 27.
178. Ibid., 30.
179. Gundry, "Demythologizing Moody," in George, *Mr. Moody*, 17–20. In fact, Gundry argues elsewhere that Moody holds to election, but believed it was to be taught to believers, not unbelievers. Gundry, *Love Them In*, 141. For additional insight on the relationship between Christianity and democracy in America, see Nathan O. Hatch, *The Democratization of American Christianity* (New Haven, CT: Yale University Press, 1991).
180. Dorsett, *Passion*, 136–37, 243.
181. D. L. Moody, *Notes from My Bible*, 121; Bebbington, "Moody as Transatlantic Evangelical" (unpublished paper, November 2004, 9–10); Gundry, *Love Them In*, 138–43.
182. D. L. Moody, *Secret Power*, 7.
183. Asa Mahan, *The Baptism of the Holy Ghost* (London: Elliot Stock, 1876). This book also included a work from Charles Finney entitled *The Enduement of Power*. Moody's first pastor, Edward Kirk, was an early disciple of Finney.
184. Marsden, *Fundamentalism*, 38.

185. Dwight Moody, *Sowing and Reaping*, 83.

186. Moody was not a Pentecostal either. Although he emphasizes being baptized in the Spirit, there is no evidence he either spoke in tongues or encouraged speaking in tongues.

187. See Pollock, *The Keswick Story*, 66–67. Pollock quotes Daniel Whittle's account during the 1883 London campaign (but offers no citation for Whittle's statement).

188. Preaching in 1877, Moody said, "My friends, it is impossible to find a perfect Christian. They will not be perfect till they arrive in the kingdom of the Master and they are washed in the blood of the Lamb." D. L. Moody, *New Sermons*, 373.

189. D. L. Moody, *Glad Tidings*, 363–64. Also, in a sermon from Moody delivered in Liverpool in 1875, he reminded the audience to "remember that they would always have two natures, flesh as well as spirit, to the end of their pilgrimage on earth." Quoted in George, *Mr. Moody*, 85.

190. Chapman, *Life and Work*, 410.

191. Ibid., 410–11.

192. Daniels, *Moody: His Words*, 396.

193. D. L. Moody, "The Gift of Power," in *Short Talks*, 18.

194. D. L. Moody, *Secret Power*, 45. For an analysis see Derek Tidball, "Power— 'In' and 'Upon': a Moody Sermon," in George, *Mr. Moody*, 117–26.

195. Daniels, *Moody: His Words*, 396.

196. Chapman, *Life and Work*, 411.

197. William R. Moody, *Life of Moody*, 280.

198. When asked about lay evangelism he said, "Nothing can stop a man who is red hot and full of the Spirit of God. I believe that a man or a woman who is filled with the Spirit of God can gain access to the hearts of the people, and can have conversions anywhere and everywhere." Quoted in William R. Moody, *Life of Moody*, 450.

199. Chapman, *Life and Work*, 403. J. Wilber Chapman called this one of his three cardinal truths.

200. R. A. Torrey, *Why God Used D. L. Moody*, 56.

201. Ibid., 55. Further evidence of Moody's impact on Torrey is seen in Torrey's writings. See *The Baptism with the Holy Spirit* (New York: Fleming H. Revell, 1897) and *The Person and Work of the Holy Spirit as Revealed in the Scriptures and Personal Experience* (New York: Fleming H. Revell, 1910).

202. Marsden, *Fundamentalism*, 78.

203. D. L. Moody, *New Sermons*, 535.

204. Timothy Weber, *Living in the Shadow*. See also Ernest R. Sandeen, *The Roots of Fundamentalism*, 103–31. Timothy Weber makes this point and notes how it connects premillennialists to earlier strands of evangelicalism. For another look at millennialism in America, see Boyer, *When Time Shall Be No More*.

205. Chapman, *Life and Work*, 400–1.

206. Gundry, *Love them In*, 178.

207. Findlay, *Dwight L. Moody*, 253.
208. D. L. Moody, "When My Lord Jesus Comes," in *The Christian Herald*, February 23, 1910, 168–69.
209. Ibid.
210. D. L. Moody, "When Jesus Comes Again," in *The Christian Herald*, December 21, 1910, 1208–9. For context on this point, see Gundry, *Love Them In*, 190.
211. These include R. A. Torrey, J. Wilbur Chapman, James M. Gray, A. T. Pierson, and James H. Brookes, to name a few. See also Derek J. Tidball, *Who Are the Evangelicals?: Tracing the Roots of Today's Movements* (London: Marshall Pickering, 1994), 64, 143. Timothy Weber observes, "D. L. Moody, 'Mr. Evangelical' to nearly everyone at the end of the century, was an early premillennial convert, and nearly every major evangelist after him adopted his eschatology." Weber, *Living in the Shadow*, 32–33.
212. Ernest Sandeen makes this point. He wrote that the Northfield Conferences gave the premillennialists a "nationally prominent platform from which to teach and an extraordinary opportunity to establish themselves as prominent, reputable Protestant leaders." Sandeen, *Roots of Fundamentalism*, 175.
213. Daniels, *Moody: His Words*, 475.
214. D. L. Moody, *Notes from My Bible*, 185.
215. Daniels, *Moody: His Words*, 467.
216. Chapman, *Life and Work*, 402–3. Commenting on postmillennialism in another sermon he said, "Some people say, 'Christ will come in the other side of the millennium.' Where do you get it? I can't find it. The Word of God tells me nowhere to watch and wait for the coming of the millennium, but for the coming of the Lord. I don't find anyplace where God says the world is growing better and better, and that Christ is to have a spiritual reign of a thousand years. I find that the earth is to grow worse and worse." D. L. Moody, *New Sermons*, 534.
217. Daniels, *Moody: His Words*, 468.
218. D. L. Moody, *New Sermons*, 534.
219. Ibid., 534–35. His lieutenants repeated this theme. For example, J. Wilbur Chapman in reference to premillennialism said, it was "one of the never-failing inspirations in my ministry. It has constantly stirred me on to increased activity in connection with my evangelistic work, and but for this blessed hope, I think that many times I would have grown discouraged and felt like giving everything up." J. Wilbur Chapman, *A Reason for My Hope* (New York: "Our Hope" Publishing Office, 1916), 4.
220. Daniels, *Moody: His Words*, 468.
221. D. L. Moody, *New Sermons*, 535.
222. Ibid.
223. Quoted in Marsden, *Fundamentalism*, 38.
224. Ibid., 35.
225. D. L. Moody, *New Sermons*, 535.

4. Moody's Social Vision: His Theological Understanding of Social Ills

1. Quoted in Chartier, "Social Views of D. L. Moody," 31.
2. William R. Moody, *Life of Moody*, 171.
3. Daniels, *Moody: His Words*, 185–86.
4. *New York Times*, February 19, 1876, 8.
5. William R. Moody, *Life of Moody*, 170.
6. D. L. Moody, *To All People*, 136.
7. D. L. Moody, *To All People*, 198. Also see Daniels, *Moody: His Words*, 293: "I would like to have men explain the destruction of drunkards' appetite for liquor by natural causes. No. It is a miracle of grace, a miracle wrought by the divine Spirit, through faith in a divine Savior."
8. Fry, *D. L. Moody*, 42.
9. Quoted in Findlay, *American Evangelist*, 274–75.
10. D. L. Moody, *To All People*, 450.
11. Ibid., 499–551.
12. "Noon Prayer Meeting," *Advance* 1, no. 45 (July 9, 1869), 6.
13. "Noon Prayer Meeting," *Advance* 1, no. 24 (February 13, 1868), 6.
14. Ibid.
15. Fry, *D. L. Moody*, 42.
16. Dorsett, *Passion*, 379–80.
17. D. L. Moody, *To The Work! To The Work!* 109–10. Also see *New York Times*, November 8, 1875, where Moody connects love and work. He argues love "should be the spring of man's service to God. Men should work for God for love, not for duty."
18. D. L. Moody, *The New Sermons, Addresses and Prayers* (New York: J. W. Goodspeed, 1880), 604–5.
19. He cited Psalms 15 and Ecclesiastes 10:18. D. L. Moody, *The New Sermons, Addresses and Prayers*, 604–5.
20. D. L. Moody, *To All People*, 487.
21. William R. Moody, *Life of Moody* (1930 edition), 308–9.
22. D. L. Moody, *To All People*, 137.
23. Moody, *The New Sermons of Dwight Lyman Moody* (New York: 1880), 811. At a revival in Boston in 1877, Moody was asked, "Do you think it best that children sign a covenant that they will not lie, swear, drink etc?" He replied, "Well I did, but I got over it. I don't think much of covenants. I would not say anything against signing the pledge, but I think the only hope is in Christ." Moody, *To All People*, 180.
24. "Mr. Moody's Answers to Practical Questions," *The Christian: A Weekly Record of Christian Life, Christian Testimony, and Christian Work* (May 7, 1874) 5:6–7, 292–93. See also William R. Moody, *Life of Moody*, 449–50.
25. William R. Moody, *Life of Moody*, 433.

26. Hambrick-Stowe, 174. Elsewhere Finney is described as "forever chary of any diversion, no matter how worthy in itself, from the work of saving souls." Ibid., 111. In fact, because of his insistence that evangelism is the priority, abolitionists like the Tappans ultimately shunned Finney. Finney's experience with the Tappans foreshadowed Moody's relationship with the temperance movement in general and Frances Willard in particular. See also Marilyn J. Westerkamp, *Women and Religion in Early America, 1600–1850: The Puritan and Evangelical Traditions* (New York: Routledge, 1999), 164.

27. Frank S. Reader, *Moody and Sankey: An Authentic Account of Their Lives and Services* (New York: E. J. Hale and Sons, 1876), 227.

28. D. L. Moody, *New Sermons*, 128.

29. D. L. Moody, *Great Joy*, 520.

30. D. L. Moody, *The Way to God and How to Find It*, 30.

31. Quoted in McLoughlin, *Modern Revivalism*, 255.

32. Ibid.

33. Ibid.

34. Ibid., 256. Both this quote and the previous reinforce Moody's connection between conversion and work.

35. Ibid., 253.

36. Daniels, *Moody: His Words*, 431.

37. Quoted in Findlay, *Moody: American Evangelist*, 277.

38. Chartier, "Social Views of D. L. Moody," 28.

39. Quoted in Gundry, *Love Them In*, 151.

40. Quoted in Findlay, 361.

41. Quoted in Gundry, *Love Them In*, 151.

42. Samuel Fielden, *The Autobiographies of the Haymarket Martyrs*, ed. Philip Foner [1887] (New York, 1969), 149–50. As the title implies, Fielden was involved in the Haymarket Riot.

43. Ibid.

44. Miller, *City of the Century*, 233. For a more detailed discussion of the role of labor in Chicago, see Richard Schneirov, *Labor and Urban Politics: Class Conflict and the Origins of Modern Liberalism in Chicago, 1864–1897* (Urbana: University of Illinois Press, 1998).

45. Quoted in Findlay, *American Evangelist*, 327.

46. Miller, *City of the Century*, 468–482.

47. Quoted in Findlay, "Gapmen," 324. The quote raises the question of the effect of the Civil War on Moody. Given the link between socialism and revolution, one wonders how the specter of another bloodbath like the Civil War factored into Moody's anxiety over labor unrest.

48. Specifically, this event led to the development of the Moody Bible Institute. The following section will include that event of its origins.

49. Francis Murphy (1836–1907) was an American temperance evangelist born in Ireland who served in the Federal army during the Civil War. Beginning in

1870 at Portsmouth, New Hampshire, he started temperance reform clubs throughout that state and was their first president.
50. "Letters to A. P. Fitt," D. L. Moody Collection, MBI Archives.
51. For a more detailed discussion, see Chartier, "Social Views of D. L. Moody," 17–34.
52. D. L. Moody, *Bible Characters* (Chicago: Fleming H. Revell, 1888), 105.
53. Quoted in Gundry, *Love Them In*, 151.
54. *New York Times*, March 12, 1890, 9.
55. Chartier, "Social Views of D. L. Moody," 18.
56. Ibid., 18–19.
57. Quoted in Gundry, *Love Them In*, 151.
58. Quoted in Findlay, *American Evangelist*, 264–65.
59. D. L. Moody, "The Gospel Awakening," 390.

5. Moody's Social Action: The Triumphs

1. Daniels, *Moody: His Words*, 332.
2. D. L. Moody, *To the Work! To the Work!*, 130–31.
3. C. L. Thompson, "The Workingman's Sabbath," *Chicago Pulpit* 2, no. 48 (November 1872), 26–27.
4. Daniels, *Moody: His Words*, 531.
5. John Wolffe, *The Expansion of Evangelicalism* (Downers Grove, IL: InterVarsity, 2007), 181–83.
6. Ibid., 182.
7. To see the actual document, see "The Lost Museum Temperance Archive," http://www.lostmuseum.cuny.edu/archives/pledgenewwindow1.html.
8. For additional reading on the temperance movement, see Rebecca Smith, *The Temperance Movement and Class Struggle in Victorian England* (Chicago: Loyola University Press, 1993); Ann-Marie E. Szymanski, *Pathways to Prohibition: Radicals, Moderates, and Social Movement Outcomes* (Durham: Duke University Press, 2003); Donald Barr Chidsey, *On and Off the Wagon: A Sober Analysis of the Temperance Movement from the Pilgrims Through Prohibition* (Ann Arbor: University of Michigan, 1969); and Joseph R. Gusfield, *Symbolic Crusade: Status Politics and the American Temperance Movement* (Chicago: University of Illinois Press, 1986).
9. Hambrick-Stowe, 174; and Tom Calarco, *The Underground Railroad in the Adirondack Region* (New York: McFarland, 2004), 28.
10. William R. Moody, *Life of Moody*, 30. As a schoolchild prank, Moody posted a notice on the schoolhouse door of an upcoming lecture from an out-of-town temperance speaker. Of course, the lecturer never appeared, but the meeting drew a large crowd. In addition, the *Northfield Gazette* and *Greenfield Courier* contained regular coverage of numerous temperance meetings during the 1840s and 1850s.

11. William R. Moody, *Life of Moody*, 449.

12. See James B. Dunn, ed., *Moody's Talks on Temperance, with Anecdotes and Incidents in Connection with the Tabernacle Temperance Work in Boston* (New York: National Temperance Society and Publication House, 1877); and Daniels, *Moody: His Words*.

13. Miller, *City of the Century*, 191, 446–47.

14. Frances Willard, *Glimpses of Fifty Years* (Chicago: H. G. Smith, 1899), 358.

15. Dorsett, *Passion*, 252–54; and Findlay, *American Evangelist*, 282.

16. *Springfield* (Massachusetts) *Republican*, February 16, 1879. Cited in Findlay, *American Evangelist*, 283.

17. William R. Moody, *Life of Moody*, 563.

18. McDowell, *What D. L. Moody Means to Me*, 9.

19. Henry Drummond, *Dwight L. Moody: Impressions and Facts* (New York: McClure, Phillips, 1900), 83.

20. William R. Moody, *Life of Moody*, 194. Moody often lamented his lack of education. "He himself had the scantiest equipment for his life-work, and he daily lamented—though perhaps no one else ever did—his deficiency." Drummond, *Moody: Impressions and Facts*, 85.

21. William Fred Campbell, "Dwight L. Moody and Religious Education" (MA Thesis, Yale Divinity School, 1949), 44–45. A copy is available in the MBI Archives.

22. Findlay, *American Evangelist*, 312–14; James Findlay, "Education and Church Controversy: The Later Career of Dwight L. Moody," *New England Quarterly* 39, no. 2 (June 1966), 210–32.

23. William R. Moody, *Life of Moody*, 319.

24. Campbell, "Moody and Religious Education," 49.

25. *Hand-book of the Northfield Seminary and the Mt. Hermon School* (Chicago: Fleming F. Revell, 1899), 14.

26. Both Durant and Marshall would serve as trustees at Northfield. Findlay, *American Evangelist*, 309.

27. Burnham Carter, *So Much to Learn: The History of the Northfield Mount Hermon School in Commemoration of the 100th Anniversary 1980* (Northfield, MA: Northfield Mount Hermon School, 1976), 17. This history notes Howard's role in the formation of the Northfield school.

28. Findlay, *American Evangelist*, 309.

29. The early settlers in New England—especially the Puritans—referred to America as a wilderness, partly because they sought the spiritual growth associated with coming through the wilderness in the Bible. From their viewpoint, the moral life was one of hard work and determination, and they approached the task of building a new world in the wilderness as an opportunity to prove their moral worth. What resulted was a land preoccupied with toil. This becomes part of the culture of New England. It is still a widely held belief about New England culture and natives. For a detailed analysis, see D. T. Rodgers, *The Work Ethic in Industrial America, 1850–1920* (Chicago: The University of Chicago Press, 1978).

30. William R. Moody, *Life of Moody*, 320.

31. William R. Moody, *Life of Moody* (1930), 308.

32. The Bible study portion of the curriculum was extensive and reflected Moody's views on perspicuity and literal interpretation.

33. *Hand-book of the Northfield Seminary*, 10–11.

34. Ibid., 70, 71.

35. Dorsett, *Passion*, 174.

36. William R. Moody, *Life of Moody*, 322–24.

37. *Hand-book of the Northfield Seminary*, 9–10.

38. William R. Moody, *Life of Moody* (1930), 309.

39. Some of this emphasis is probably traceable to O. O. Howard.

40. *The Christian*, October 7, 1880, 11.

41. *Hand-book of the Northfield Seminary*, 195.

42. Dorsett, *Passion*, 287–88. Dorsett points out that these early classes included Asians as well. He notes Booker T. Washington was invited to speak at the school, and some early graduates returned to the American South to form orphanages for black children.

43. *Hand-book of the Northfield Seminary*, 19.

44. Drummond, *Moody: Impressions and Facts*, 100.

45. Ibid., 103.

46. William R. Moody, *Life of Moody*, 521.

47. The students are described as "orphans of much promise and no means, and promising boys belonging to the mission Sunday schools of cities. There are many sons of clergymen, of missionaries, of Christian widows, and other Christian parents of very limited means but earnest piety, who have from the first devoted their children to the service of God, and brought them up with that in view. But they can scarcely afford to give the needed schooling to their sons. There are many young men who have been thrown early upon their own re-sources, who have supported themselves in various trades and clerkships, whose school-life is early broken off." *Hand-book of the Northfield Seminary*, 93–94.

48. In 1897, the following denominational affiliations were reported by the students: Congregationalists—82; Baptists—38; Methodists—35; Presbyterians—34; Episcopal—11; Independent—5; Roman Catholic—4; Reformed—3; Chris-tian—2; Swedish Lutheran—1; United Church of Christ—1; Disciples—1; United Presbyterian—1; Friends—1; and 8 claimed no church affiliation. *The Hermonite*, June 15, 1897. Dorsett points out the school's racial diversity. Dorsett, *Passion*, 287–88.

49. The class of 1889 included students from thirty-two nations, with one of the class officers being an ex-slave from Virginia. Carter, 49.

50. Carter, 27.

51. William R. Moody, *Life of Moody* (1930), 314.

52. *Hand-book of the Northfield Seminary*, 114.

53. William R. Moody, *Life of Moody* (1930), 315.

54. *Hand-book of the Northfield Seminary*, 114–17.

55. Ibid., 106–7.

56. Carter, 84.

57. "History of Moody Bible Institute," https://www.moody.edu/about/our-bold-legacy/history-of-moody-bible-institute/.

58. For a full treatment see Nina K. Bissett, *Woman of Nobility: The Story of Sophronia Emeline Cobb Dryer* (Portland, OR: Wipf and Stock, 2016).

59. Findlay, *American Evangelist*, 323.

60. Ibid.

61. *Record of Christian Work* (January 1886), 1.

62. Chicago Department of Health, *Report 1881 and 1882*, 52, 70–71.

63. Ibid., 122–23, 191. Jane Addams gave a similar description. She wrote, "Little idea can be given of the filthy and rotten tenements, the foul stables and dilapidated outhouses, the piles of garbage fairly alive with diseased odors, and the numbers of children filling every nook, working and playing in every room, eating and sleeping on every window-sill, pouring in and out of every door, seeming literally to pave every scrap of yard." James Weber Linn, *Jane Addams: A Biography* (Chicago: University of Illinois Press, 2000), 98–99.

64. D. L. Moody, letter sent out by the Chicago Evangelistic Society, June 1887. He also points out that arrests for disorderly conduct and crime were over 40,000 in 1886, thus filling the jails to overflowing.

65. Olenik, *The Social Philosophy of D. L. Moody*, 34.

66. Gene Getz, *MBI: The Story of Moody Bible Institute* (Chicago: Moody Press, 1969), 36. Taken from the address at Farwell Hall, Chicago, January 2, 1886. See also Findlay, "Gapmen." These schools were to be trendsetters, among the first of their type. By 1920, thirty-nine similar institutions existed in the U. S. and Canada. For an excellent survey of this movement, see Virginia Brereton, *Training God's Army: The American Bible School 1880–1940* (Bloomington: Indiana University Press, 1990).

67. The college still exists in Glasgow, although it is now known as the International Christian College.

68. George Eyre-Todd, *Who's Who in Glasgow in 1909: A Biographical Dictionary of Nearly Five Hundred Living Glasgow Citizens and of Notable Citizens Who Have Died Since January 1, 1907* (no publisher and no date).

69. Bebbington, "Moody as Transatlantic Evangelical" in George, *Mr. Moody*, 89.

70. Ibid., 82. For additional reading see F. V. Waddleton, "The Bible Training Institute, Glasgow" (unpublished manuscript, 1979).

71. Dorsett, *Passion*, 252–54.

72. Frances Willard to Emma Moody, quoted in Frances E. Willard, *Happy Half Century* (London: Ward, Lock and Bowden, 1894), 261–68.

73. Dorsett, *Passion*, 303–5. In fact, Moody never spelled out his position on women's ordination.

74. Mark James Toone, "Evangelicalism in Transition: A Comparative Analysis of the Work and Theology of D. L. Moody and His Protégés, Henry Drummond and R. A. Torrey" (PhD Diss., 1988, University of St. Andrew's), 94.

75. Clipping from a newspaper dated September 13, 1898, History File, Northfield Bible Training School, Northfield Archives.

76. D. L. Moody, *Men of the Bible*, 67.

77. Dorsett, *Passion*, 292–97. Dorsett presents a sampling of stories drawn from students at Moody's school that demonstrate Moody's generosity toward the students.

78. William R. Moody, *Life of Moody*, 514.

79. D. L. Moody, *The Gospel Awakening*, 389–90.

80. Chapman, *Life and Work*, 183; and Chartier, "Social Views of D. L. Moody," 41.

81. The YMCA joined with the Chicago Theological Seminary and Hahnemann Medical College in response to the 1866 cholera epidemic. Together they "nursed the sick, offered prayers, performed last rites, and helped bury the dead." Dorsett, *Passion*, 125–26.

82. Daniels, *Moody: His Words*, 37.

83. Dorsett, *Passion*, 122.

84. Ibid., 124.

85. D. L. Moody, *Heaven*, 124.

86. Ibid.

87. G. W. Coleman to D. L. Moody, January 24, 1899, MBI Archives. This letter contains details of the association's work in this regard. It includes a report on the current inventory of books and Bibles, the numbers of volumes sent to various prisons, and plans to seek donations to increase the number of books available to be sent out. It also notes plans to translate texts into Spanish for distribution. The letter ends with an account of the impact on the prisoners in one prison.

88. Bebbington, *Dominance*, 48; and Andrew Aird, *Glimpses of Old Glasgow* (Glasgow: Aird & Coghill, 1894), 200. Bebbington also states, "A group of men associated with the Glasgow campaign threw themselves into politics to achieve Christian objectives." David Bebbington, "Moody" in George, 87.

89. Chartier, "Social Views of D. L. Moody," 58.

90. William Reid, *Authentic Records of Revival Now in Progress in the United Kingdom* (London: James Nisbet, 1860), 452.

91. Carubbers Christian Centre, "History," https://www.carrubbers.org/about/us.php#history.

92. Chartier, "Social Views of D. L. Moody," 59.

93. Ibid., 59–60.

6. Moody's Social Action: Learning from His Failures

1. John R. Mott, "Moody's Power with College Men" in *Dwight L. Moody: The Discoverer of Men and Maker of Movements*, ed. John MacDowell (New York: Fleming H. Revell, 1915), 54.

2. H. B. Hartzler, *Moody in Chicago, Or the World's Fair Gospel Campaign* (Chicago: Fleming H. Revell, 1894), 33–34. It is noteworthy that while Moody's meetings in the North were integrated, there is at least one occasion where in deference to Southern whites, African Americans were not invited to YMCA meetings held in Northfield. See Alfreda M. Duster, ed., *Crusade for Justice: The Autobiography of Ida B. Wells* (Chicago: University of Chicago Press, 1970), 132.

3. Mrs. Robert Peddie, ed., *A Consecutive Narrative of the Remarkable Awakening in Edinburgh, Under the Labours of Messrs Moody and Sankey* (London: S. W. Partridge, 1874), 45–46. Also see the account in Gustavus D. Pike, *The Singing Campaign for Ten Thousand Pounds; Or, The Jubilee Singers in Great Britain* (New York: American Missionary Association, 1875), 145–58.

4. Joe M. Richardson, *A History of Fisk University, 1865–1946* (Tuscaloosa: University of Alabama Press, 1980), 36. For a full analysis of Moody's relationship to the Fisk singers, see David W. Stowe, "'An Inestimable Blessing': The American Gospel Invasion of 1873," *American Theosophical Quarterly* (September 2002): 189–212; Toni P. Anderson, *Tell Them We Are Singing for Jesus: The Original Fisk Jubilee Singers and Christian Reconstruction, 1871–1878* (Macon, GA: Mercer University Press, 2010).

5. In 1909, the Fisk Jubilee Singers performed a week of concerts at the Moody Church in Chicago. See "The Moody Church Jubilee Month," *Chicago Tribune*, November 6, 1909.

6. William Hoyt Coleman, quoted in William R. Moody, *Life of Moody*, 277.

7. "Sunbeams" (news item), *New York Sun*, May 14, 1876, 4.

8. "Our Augusta Letter," *Atlanta Constitution*, May 4, 1876, 1.

9. Whittle Diary, April 28, 1876, cited in Findlay, 279. At the time of Findlay's research in the mid-1960s, the diary was in the Moody Bible Institute Archives, but was subsequently lost. Whittle served on General Sherman's staff during the Civil War and was wounded at Vicksburg, where he met Moody. Whittle's daughter later married Moody's oldest son, William.

10. This analysis is based on more than seventy-five contemporary news accounts for Chattanooga (Jan. 25–31), Knoxville (Jan. 28–31), Nashville (Feb. 2–4), and Memphis, Tennessee (Feb. 5–8); New Orleans, Louisiana (Feb. 9–19); Galveston (Feb. 21–28), San Antonio (Feb. 28–March 2), and Dallas, Texas (March 4–7); Mobile (March 10–13) and Selma, Alabama (March 14–18); Charleston (March 23–28) and Columbia, South Carolina (March 31–April 1); Atlanta, Georgia (April 2–12); and Norfolk, Virginia (April 13–21).

11. Based on local news accounts for Louisville, Kentucky (Jan. 1–Feb. 12, 1888), and Richmond, Virginia (March 26–April 12, 1894).

12. Findlay, *American Evangelist*, 281. Some have accused Moody of tolerating segregated meetings to keep white audiences.

13. Dwight Moody, *New Sermons, Addresses and Prayers by Dwight Lyman Moody* (New York: Henry S. Goodspeed and Co., 1877), 485.

14. "A Plea for Tolerance: Mr. Moody's Scathing Denunciation of Uncharitable Protestants, *New York Times*, July 5, 1890, 1. Quotes a Moody address at the summer conference in Northfield.

15. "Race Prejudice—Is It Waning?," *American Missionary* 49, no. 7 (July 1895): 220; "Mr. Moody in Texas," 221. See also Blum, 144: "It was a marvelous turn of events. The most noteworthy evangelical of the late nineteenth century took a clear stand against racial segregation. Tragically, it was too late. Moody no longer wielded the public power he once had, and this action garnered almost no attention from the press. By this time his influence had waned considerably."

16. For example, see his 1896 visit to Nashville: "Four Special Sermons," *Nashville American*, February 10, 1896, 5.

17. Findlay, *American Evangelist*, 280.

18. Alfreda M. Duster, ed., *Crusade for Justice: The Autobiography of Ida B. Wells* (Chicago: University of Chicago Press, 1970), 111–12, 151.

19. Miriam Decosta-Willis, ed., *The Memphis Diary of Ida B. Wells: An Intimate Portrait of the Activist as a Young Woman* (Boston: Beacon Press, 1995), 41–42.

20. "Oration of Frederick Douglass," *American Missionary* 39, no. 6 (June 1885): 164. Later summarized in "Crossing the Color Line: A Brief Historical Survey of Race Relations in American Evangelical Christianity" in Robert J. Prieas and Alvaro L. Nieves, eds. *This Side of Heaven* (New York: Oxford University Press), 114.

21. *Works of Francis Grimké*, vol. 3, ed. Carter G. Woodson (Washington, DC: The Associated Publishers, 1942), 420.

22. See "Moody and Sankey: Closing of the Great Revival Meeting in Jacksonville," *Savannah Morning News*, March 23, 1886, 5. Meetings were held in the Park Opera House, with assigned times "for colored people only."

23. "Mr. Moody's Wise Course," *Savannah Morning News*, March 7, 1886, 5.

24. Ibid.

25. Ibid.

26. Francis J. Grimké, "Mr. Moody and the Color Question in the South," *The Independent*, July 22, 1886, 7.

27. Ibid.

28. Ibid.

29. "Without Gloves, D. L. Moody Denounced by Colored Clergymen," *Standard Union of Brooklyn*, Friday 10, 1887, 1.

30. Ibid.

31. "The New York Annual Conference," *Christian Record*, July 8, 1887, 1.

32. "They Say," *Washington Bee*, March 10, 1894, 1.

33. "The Negro His Own Enemy," *Washington Bee*, April 28, 1894, 2. For other critiques of Moody from black-owned newspapers, see *Western Appeal* (Saint Paul, Minnesota), June 13, 1885, and August 6, 1887; *Iowa State Bystander* (Des Moines, Iowa), June 22, 1894, and May 1, 1896; and *Richmond Planet* (Richmond, Virginia), April 7, 1894.

34. Booker T. Washington, "The Tuskegee Normal and Industrial Training School" (transcription of address on August 13, 1895), *Northfield Echoes*, vol. 2 (1895): 501–5.
35. Booker T. Washington, "The Atlanta Exposition Address," Atlanta Cotton States and International Exposition, September 18, 1895; see transcription at https://www.nps.gov/bowa/learn/historyculture/atlanta1-1.htm. Critics dubbed his address as "The Atlanta Compromise."
36. Booker T. Washington to Emma Revell Moody, December 23, 1899.
37. L. H. Smith to Dwight Moody, March 19, 1896, D. L. Moody Collection, Moody Bible Institute Archives.
38. See "Lynchings: By State and Race, 1882–1968," UMKC School of Law (statistics provided by the Archives at Tuskegee Institute), http://law2.umkc.edu/faculty/projects/ftrials/shipp/lynchingsstate.html.
39. Francis J. Grimké, "The Anglo-American and Southern Outrages," *The Independent*, June 22, 1893, 4.
40. Ibid.
41. Ibid., 95–96. Francis Willard is the founder of the Woman's Christian Temperance Union. She worked briefly as director of women's meetings for Moody.
42. Ibid., 96.
43. D. L. Moody, "Revivals," address delivered on August 2, 1899, East Northfield, Massachusetts. Transcribed in *Moody's Latest Sermons* (Chicago: Fleming H. Revell, 1900), 177. I am not aware of any earlier statements by Moody on lynching.
44. Francis J. Grimké, "The Anglo-American and Southern Outrages," *The Independent*, June 22, 1893, 4.
45. Edward J. Blum, *Reforging the White Republic: Race, Religion, and American Nationalism*, 1865–1898 (Baton Rouge: Louisiana State University, 2005), 144–45.
46. The brief section draws on four influential works about religion in the Civil War: Mark A. Noll, *The Civil War as a Theological Crisis* (Chapel Hill: University of North Carolina, 2006); Harry S. Stout, *Upon the Altar of the Nation; A Moral History of the Civil War* (New York: Penguin Books, 2006); George C. Rable, *God's Almost Chosen People: A Religious History of the American Civil War* (Chapel Hill: University of North Carolina, 2010); and James P. Byrd, *A Holy Baptism of Fire and Blood: The Bible and the American Civil War* (New York, NY: Oxford University Press, 2021).
47. James M. McPherson, *For Cause and Comrades: Why Men Fought in the Civil War* (New York: Oxford University Press, 1997). See especially "Religion Is What Makes Brave Soldiers," 63–76.
48. Mark A. Noll, *The Civil War as a Theological Crisis* (Chapel Hill: University of North Carolina Press, 2006), 11.
49. Ibid.
50. Noll, *The Civil War as a Theological Crisis*, 11. "The nation's formal religious life was dominated by Protestant institutions, with over 83 percent of the value of

church property, over 92 percent of the seating accommodations in houses of worship, and over 95 percent of the churches themselves (about 50,000 of them)."

51. Richard J. Carwardine, *Evangelicals, and Politics in Antebellum America* (New Haven, CT: Yale University Press, 1993), 44.

52. Thomas Cary Johnson, *The Life and Letters of Robert Louis Dabney*, (Richmond, VA: The Presbyterian Committee of Publication, 1903), 129.

53. Ibid., 44.

54. Lincoln's Second Inaugural Address, National Park Service, https://www.nps .gov/linc/learn/historyculture/lincoln-second-inaugural.htm. Frederick Douglass later commented that Lincoln's address sounded "more like a sermon than a state paper." See *The Life and Times of Frederick Douglass: From 1817–1882* (London: Christian Age Office, 1882), 318.

55. Mark Noll, *The Civil War as a Theological Crisis*, 314–15.

56. Dwight L. Moody, *To the Work! To the Work! Exhortations to Christians* (Chicago: Fleming H. Revell, 1880), 118.

57. "Short Sermons," *The Appeal*, December 2, 1899, 3.

58. See the accounts in H. B. Hartzler, *Moody in Chicago or The World's Fair Gospel Campaign* (New York: Revell, 1894), 96–101, 120–25; A. W. Williams, *Life and Work of Dwight L. Moody, the Great Evangelist of the Nineteenth Century* (Chicago: P. W. Ziegler, 1900), 280–83; and William R. Moody, *The Life of D. L Moody*, 416–18.

59. "Miss Dr. Stoecker," *Chicago Tribune*, September 4, 1893, 6.

60. "He Comes to Preach," *Chicago Tribune*, September 5, 1893, 9. The article subhead reads, "Dr. Stoecker Not to Discuss The Jew Problem in Chicago. The German Evangelist Says His Mission to America Has Nothing to Do with an Anti-Semitic Crusade."

61. H. B. Hartzler, *Moody in Chicago*, 101.

62. "Big Throng Hears Parson Stoecker," *Chicago Tribune*, September 11, 1893, 2.

63. See, for example, a letter signed by J. R. to the editor of the *American Israelite* (December 10, 1875) discussing Moody's revival meetings in Philadelphia.

64. Yaakov Ariel, "An American Evangelist and the Jews: Dwight L. Moody and His Attitudes Toward the Jewish People," 22/23 (1989), *Immanuel*, 41. Also see Yaakov Ariel, *An Unusual Relationship: Evangelical Christians and Jews* (New York: New York University Press, 2013).

65. As noted in chapter 2, the slavery question divided the Presbyterians in 1838, the Methodists in 1844, and the Baptists in 1845.

66. For examples of Moody's conflict avoidance, see Lyle Dorsett, *A Passion for Souls*, 370, 402–3, 404–5.

67. Washington Gladden, "Clear-Headed, Broad-Minded, Great-Hearted," *The Congregationalist and Christian World* (November 12, 1914): 234.

68. Dorsett, *A Passion for Souls*, 370.

69. Ibid., 402.

70. D. L. Moody, letter to mother, March 4, 1862, Special Collections, D. L. Moody Papers, Yale Divinity School Library.

7. Conclusion: Lessons from Moody's Work

1. William R. Moody, *The Life of D. L. Moody*, 238.
2. Gamaliel Bradford, *D. L. Moody—A Worker in Souls* (New York: Doran, 1927), 104.
3. Charles Goss, *Echoes from the Platform and Pulpit* (Hartford, CT: A. O. Worthington, 1900), 96.
4. Ibid, 96–97.
5. Timothy George, ed., *Mr. Moody and the Evangelical Tradition* (New York: T&T Clark, 2004), 4–5.
6. Goss, *Echoes from the Pulpit*, 97.
7. Daniels, *Moody: His Words*, 36–37.
8. Attributed to D. L. Moody; source unknown.
9. D. L. Moody, *The Overcoming Life and Other Sermons* (Chicago: Fleming H. Revell, 1894), 42.
10. Ibid.
11. Ibid., 43.
12. D. L. Moody, *Glad Tidings: Comprising Sermons and Prayer-Meeting Talks Delivered at the New York Hippodrome* (New York: E. B. Treat, 1875), 47.
13. D. L. Moody, *Men of the Bible* (Chicago: Bible Institute Colportage Association, 1898), 67.
14. William R. Moody, *The Life of D. L. Moody*, 134. This quote was repeated in several Moody biographies after his death. The account given here by his son seems to be the first.
15. Ibid.

BIBLIOGRAPHY

Alhstrom, Sydney E. *A Religious History of the American People*. New Haven, Connecticut: Yale University Press, 1974.

Bebbington, David. *Evangelicalism in Modern Britain: A History from the 1730s to the 1980s*. London: Unwin Hyman, 1989.

———. *The Dominance of Evangelicalism: The Age of Spurgeon and Moody*. Downers Grove, IL: InterVarsity Press, 2005.

Belmonte, Kevin. *D. L. Moody—A Life: Innovator, Evangelist, World-Changer*. Chicago: Moody Publishers, 2014.

Byrd, James P. *A Holy Baptism of Fire and Blood: The Bible and the American Civil War*. New York, NY: Oxford University Press, 2021.

Chapman, J. Wilbur. *The Life and Work of D. L. Moody*. Philadelphia: American Bible House, 1900.

Chartier, Myron. "The Social Views of Dwight L. Moody and Their Relation to the Workman of 1860–1900," *Fort Hayes Studies*, History Series No. 6 (August 1969).

Curtis, Richard K. *They Called Him Mr. Moody*. New York: Doubleday, 1962.

Daniels, William H. *Moody: His Words, Work, and Workers*. New York: Nelson & Phillips, 1877.

Davidoff, Leonore, and Catherine Hall. *Family Fortunes: Men and Women of the English Middle Class, 1780–1850*. Chicago: University of Chicago Press, 1987.

Day, Richard E. *Bush Aglow: The Life Story of Dwight Lyman Moody, Commoner of Northfield*. Philadelphia: Judson Press, 1936.

Decosta-Willis, Miriam ed., *The Memphis Diary of Ida B. Wells: An Intimate Portrait of the Activist as a Young Woman*. Boston: Beacon Press, 1995.

Dedmon, Emmett. *Great Enterprises: 100 Years of the YMCA of Metropolitan Chicago*. Chicago: Rand McNally, 1957.

Dorsett, Lyle. *A Passion for Souls: The Life of D. L. Moody*. Chicago: Moody Publishers, 2003.

Evensen, Bruce J. *God's Man for the Gilded Age: D. L. Moody and the Rise of Modern Mass Evangelism*. New York: Oxford University Press, 2003.

Everett, Edward Franklin. *Descendants of Richard Everett of Dedham, Massachusetts*. Boston: Privately Printed, 1902.

Findlay, James F. Jr. *Dwight L. Moody: American Evangelist 1837–1899*. Chicago: University of Chicago Press, 1969.

Fitt, A. P. *A Shorter Life of D. L. Moody*. Chicago: Bible Institute Colportage Association, 1900.

Fry, August F. Jr., *D. L. Moody: The Formative Years 1856–1873*. Unpublished BD thesis, Chicago Theological Seminary, 1955.

George, Timothy, ed. *Mr. Moody and the Evangelical Tradition*. London: Clark, 2004.

Getz, Gene. *MBI: The Story of Moody Bible Institute*. Chicago: Moody Press, 1969.

Goss, Charles F. *Echoes from the Pulpit and Platform*. Hartford: A. D. Worthington, 1900.

Gundry, Stanley. *Love Them In: The Life and Theology of Dwight Moody*. Grand Rapids, MI: Baker Books, 1976.

Houghton, Will H., and Chas. T. Cook. *Tell Me About Moody*. London: Marshall, Morgan & Scott, 1936.

Levy, George. *To Die in Chicago: Confederate Prisoners at Camp Douglas 1862–65* (Gretna, LA: Pelican Publishing, 1999).

Long, Kathryn T. *The Revival of 1857–1858*. New York: Oxford University Press, 1998.

Marsden, George. *Fundamentalism and American Culture*. New York: Oxford University Press, 1980.

Moberg, David. *The Great Reversal*. New York: J. B. Lippincott, 1972.

Moody, Dwight L. *Bible Characters*. Chicago: Fleming H. Revell, 1888.

———. *Glad Tidings: Comprising Sermons and Prayer-Meeting Talks Delivered at the New York Hippodrome*. New York: E. B. Treat, 1876.

———. *Golden Counsels.* Boston: United Society of Christian Endeavor, 1899.

———. *The Gospel Awakening: Comprising the Sermons and Addresses, Prayer-Meeting Talks and Bible Readings of the Great Revival Meetings Conducted by Moody and Sankey.* Chicago: Fleming H. Revell, 1883.

———. *Great Joy: Comprising Sermons and Prayer-Meeting Talks, Delivered at the Chicago Tabernacle.* New York: E. B. Treat, 1877.

———. *Heaven: Where It Is, Its Inhabitants, and How to Get There.* Chicago: Fleming H. Revell, 1884.

———. *How to Study the Bible.* Chicago: Fleming H. Revell, 1876.

———. *Moody's Sermons, Addresses and Prayers.* St. Louis: N. D. Thompson, 1877.

———. *New Sermons, Addresses and Prayers.* St. Louis: N. D. Thompson, 1877.

———. *The New Sermons, Addresses and Prayers.* New York: J. W. Goodspeed Publishers, 1880.

———. *The New Sermons of Dwight Lyman Moody.* New York: 1880.

———. *Pleasure and Profit in Bible Study.* Chicago: Fleming H. Revell, 1895.

———. *Secret Power: Or, The Secret of Success in Christian Life and Work.* Chicago: Fleming H. Revell, 1881.

———. *Short Talks.* Chicago: Bible Institute Colportage Association, 1900.

———. *Sowing and Reaping.* Chicago: Fleming H. Revell, 1898.

———. *Ten Select Sermons.* Chicago: Fleming H. Revell, 1881.

———. *To All People: Comprising Sermons, Bible Readings, Temperance Addresses, and Prayer-Meeting Talks, Delivered in the Boston Tabernacle by Dwight Moody.* New York: E. B. Treat, 1877.

———. *To The Work! To The Work! Exhortations to Christians.* Chicago: Fleming H. Revell, 1884.

———. *Twelve Select Sermons.* Chicago: Fleming H. Revell, 1881.

———. *The Way to God and How to Find It.* Chicago: Fleming H. Revell, 1884.

Moody, William R. *The Life of D. L. Moody* (Official Authorized Edition). New York: Fleming H. Revell, 1900.

Moody, Paul D. *My Father.* Boston: Little, Brown, 1938.

Müller, George. *The Life of Trust, Being a Narrative of the Lord's Dealings with George Müller.* Boston: Gould and Lincoln, 1873.

Noll, Mark. *The Civil War as a Theological Crisis.* Chapel Hill: University of North Carolina, 2006.

———. *The Rise of Evangelicalism: The Age of Edwards, Whitefield and the Wesleys.* Downers Grove: InterVarsity Press, 2003.

Olenik, Dennis. *The Social Philosophy of D. L. Moody.* DeKalb: Northern Illinois University, 1964.

Orr, J. Edwin. *The Fervent Prayer, The Worldwide Impact of the Great Awakening of 1858.* Chicago: Moody Press, 1974.

Pollock, J. C. *Moody: the Biography.* Chicago: Moody Press, 1963.

Smith, Timothy L. *Revivalism and Social Reform in Mid-Nineteenth-Century America.* New York: Abingdon Press, 1957.

Smith, Wilbur. *An Annotated Bibliography of D. L. Moody.* Chicago: Moody Press, 1948.

Spurgeon, Charles H. *The Autobiography of Charles H. Spurgeon*, vol. 4. Edited by Susannah Spurgeon and W. J. Harrald. Chicago: Curts & Jennings, 1900.

Stout, Harry S. *Upon the Altar of the Nation: A Moral History of the Civil War.* New York: Penguin, 2006.

Wolffe, John. *The Expansion of Evangelicalism: The Age of Wilberforce, More, Chalmers and Finney.* Downers Grove: Intervarsity Press, 2007.

Lyle Dorsett reveals the heart of this great evangelist, his strengths, weaknesses, and motivations to find a man after God's own heart.

MOODY Publishers®

From the Word to Life®

Dwight Lyman Moody was the greatest evangelist of the nineteenth century. His greatest riches were found in the love of his Lord and the souls that were changed. In these pages, today's believers will find a model of biblical passion, vision, and commitment.

Also available as an eBook

INNOVATOR, EVANGELIST, WORLD-CHANGER

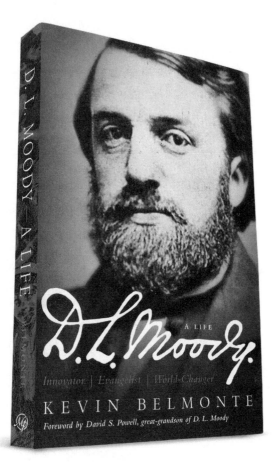

MOODY Publishers

From the Word to Life

Who was this man? A visionary educator and fundraiser, D. L. Moody was also a renowned evangelist in the nineteenth century. Drawing on the best, most recent scholarship, *D. L. Moody—A Life* chronicles the incredible journey of one of the great souls of history.

Also available as an eBook